Pets Welcome!
California

As "cover girl," officer manager of Bon Vivant Press

and owner of authors, Robert and Kathleen Fish,

I would like to share the joys of our vacations and working

trips to produce our *Cooking Secrets* series. Special thanks

to my bon vivant canine pal, Danny.

— ***Dreamer Dawg***

CALIFORNIA EDITION

Pets Welcome

A Guide to Hotels, Inns, and Resorts That Welcome You and Your Pet

KATHLEEN AND ROBERT FISH

SECOND EDITION

BON VIVANT

Library of Congress Cataloging-in-Publication Data

Pets Welcome™ California—Second Edition
A Guide to Hotels, Inns and Resorts That Welcome You and Your Pet

Fish, Kathleen DeVanna
99-76728
ISBN 1-883214-35-1
$15.95 softcover
Includes indexes

Copyright ©2000 by Kathleen DeVanna Fish

Cover photography by Robert N. Fish
Editorial direction by Judie Marks
Production management by Nadine Guarrera
Cover design by Smith Bowen Advertising, Inc.
Illustrations by Gopa Design; and Gerrica Connolly, Design Studio
Interior by Cimarron Design

Published by Bon Vivant Press
a division of The Millennium Publishing Group
P.O. Box 1994
Monterey, CA 93942

Printed in Canada by Friesens

Contents

Introduction

Traveling with people we love and whose company we enjoy can be one of life's great pleasures. Our pets can be counted among those who enrich our lives. So it is little wonder that over 40 million of us choose to take our pets along with us when we travel.

Whether embarking on a wine-tasting adventure in Northern California's Napa Valley or Sonoma regions, exploring the breathtaking Central Coast's natural bounty that has awed and inspired artists and romantics for decades or setting out on a sightseeing safari to the San Diego Zoo or other Southern California attractions, we offer you recommendations for unforgettable places to stay.

The wonderful thing is that hundreds of hotels, inns, guest ranches and bed and breakfasts throughout California welcome pets with open arms.

Of course, just as they each offer different amenities and accommodations, they also have a wide range of pet policies.

That's why Pets Welcome™ will be a handy resource for you, to help you discover and select some of the best places to stay when traveling with your four-legged companions. We have researched and ranked a broad spectrum of places, from romantic hideaways to inns that have made a trademark name for themselves in the hospitality industry.

For example, when planning a day in Napa Valley exploring and sampling the vineyards' best, you might want to start at Calistoga, famous for its hot springs and local charm, too. There you will find the enchanting cottages of the Washington Street Lodging within walking distance of downtown Calistoga. When venturing into quaint Carmel-by-the-Sea, local inns such as the Cypress Inn offer you a touch of history, an abundance of style and unparalleled scenic splendor in one of California's most pet-friendly environments. A single visit to Carmel Beach reveals the lofty place dogs hold in the community.

Of course, some find comfort in name recognition and industry names such as Residence Inn by Marriott tell travelers they are ensured of home-style accommodations. And it wouldn't seem like home without your pet, now would it?

Each hotel or inn was chosen because of its ambiance, special charm, guest amenities and, of course, its pet friendliness. We have bestowed each with our three-, four- or five-paw designation.

In addition, original pen-and-ink artists' renderings share a glimpse of each place's awaiting character and charm.

We have included lodging that should meet all types of travel needs and budgets, from luxurious and romantic to high-tech and convenient, from secluded and quirky or to warm and rustic.

In addition to the accommodation summaries, this guide book provides maps and details on points of interest throughout California, including parks, beaches and wineries.

Whether you and your pet are travel veterans or setting out on a trip together for the first time, you'll no doubt learn a valuable lesson or two from the travel tips provided by the Humane Society of the United States. These helpful hints offer insight into traveling by car, plane and other modes of transportation, offering specialized guidance on crating animals, documentation and basic care and courtesy information. Being an informed pet owner will make your trip more enjoyable and comfortable for both you and your animal.

It is our hope that as you travel throughout California, you will return time and time again to this book as you would to your favorite—finding comfort in knowing that the places found within welcome both you and your pet, that details are both useful and intriguing and that it can open doors to new and exciting adventures. In fact, we hope you use it so much that it becomes, well, dog-eared.

❖

Abbreviations Used in this Book

AAA	American Automobile Association
ABA	American Breeders Association
AKC	American Kennel Club
AARP	American Association of Retired Persons

Top Ten Travel Tips

1 Bring your pet's own food, dishes, litter and litter box, leash, collar with ID tags, a first aid kit and a bottle of water from home. This will make your pet more comfortable, prepare you for emergencies and decrease the chances of an upset stomach from a strange brand of food. Maintain the normal feeding and walking schedule as much as possible. Be sure to bring old bath towels or paper towels in case of an accident and plastic bags to dispose of your pet's waste. It is a good idea to bring a picture of your pet for identification purposes in case you and your pet become separated.

2 Bring your pet's vaccination records with you when traveling in state, and a health certificate when traveling out of state. If you plan on boarding him at anytime during your vacation, call the boarding kennel to reserve his space, see what they require you to bring and if they require a health certificate.

3 Bring your pet's favorite toys, leash, grooming supplies, medications and bedding. It is a good idea to bring an old sheet or blanket from home to place over the hotel's bedding, just in case your pet gets on the bed. It will also come in handy to protect your car seats from hair and dirty paws.

4 Tape the address of where you are staying on the back of your pet's ID tag or add a laminated card or new ID tag to your pet's collar, or add a second collar with a friend or family members phone number. This information is also good to have on your pet's collar in case of a natural disaster so that someone out of your area can be contacted if you and your pet become separated.

5 Do not leave your pets unattended in a hotel room. The surroundings are new and unfamiliar to your animal and may cause him to become upset and destroy property he normally would not or bark excessively and disturb your neighbors. You also run the risk of his escaping. If a maid should open the door to clean your room, the pet may see this as a chance to find you and escape, or worse, he may attack the maid out of fear.

6 Train your pet to use a crate. This will come in handy if you ever need to travel by plane. Make sure the crate has enough room for your pet to stand up comfortably and turn around inside. Be sure to trim your pet's nails so that they don't get caught in the crate door or ventilation holes. Crates come in handy in hotel rooms, too. If your pet is already used to being in a crate, he will not object if you leave him in one long enough for you to go out to breakfast. Never take your pet with you if you will have to leave him in the car. If it is 85 degrees outside, within minutes the inside of the car can reach over 160 degrees, even with the windows cracked, causing heat stroke and possible death. According to The Humane Society of the United States, the signs of heat stress are: heavy panting, glazed eyes, a rapid pulse, unsteadiness, a staggering gait, vomiting, or a deep red or purple tongue. If heat stroke does occur, the pet must be cooled by dousing him with water and applying ice packs to his head and neck. He should then be taken to a veterinarian immediately.

7 When your pet is confined to a crate, the best way to provide water for your pet is to freeze water in the cup that hooks onto the door of your pet's crate. This way they will get needed moisture without the water splashing all over the crate. Freezing water in your pet's regular water bowl also works well for car trips.

8 Be sure to put your pet's favorite toys and bedding in the crate. Label the crate with "LIVE ANIMAL" and "THIS END UP," plus the address and phone number of your destination, as well as your home address and phone number and the number of someone to contact in case of an emergency.

9 When traveling by plane, be sure to book the most direct flights possible. The less your pet has to be transferred from plane to plane, the less chance of your being separated. This is also important when traveling in hot or cold weather. You don't want your pet to have to wait in the cargo hold of a plane or be exposed to bad weather for any longer than necessary. Check with airlines for the type of crate they require and any additional requirements. They are very strict about the size and type of crate you may carry on board.

 Do not feed your pet before traveling. This reduces the risk of an upset stomach or an accident in his crate or your car. When traveling by car, remember that your pet needs rest stops as often as you do. It is a good idea for everyone to stretch their legs from time to time. If your pet is unfamiliar with car travel, then get him use to the car gradually. Start a few weeks before your trip with short trips around town and extend the trips a little each time. Then he will become accustomed to the car before your trip and it will be more pleasant for all involved.

Traveling With Your Pet

Courtesy of The Humane Society of the United States (HSUS)
2100 "L" Street, N.W.
Washington, D.C. 20037
© 1995 HSUS. All rights reserved.

 f you are planning a trip and you share your life with a pet, you have a few decisions to make before you set off. The following are tips to help you plan a safer and smoother trip for both you and your pet.

SHOULD YOU TRAVEL WITH YOUR PET?

Some pets are not suited for travel because of temperament, illness or physical impairment. If you have any doubts about whether it is appropriate for your pet to travel, talk to your veterinarian.

If you decide that your pet should not travel with you, consider the alternatives: Have a responsible friend or relative look after your pet, board your pet at a kennel or hire a sitter to visit, feed and exercise your pet.

If a friend or relative is going to take care of your pet, ask if that person can take your pet into his or her home. Animals can get lonely when left at home alone. Be sure your pet is comfortable with his or her temporary caretaker and any pets that person has.

If you choose to board your pet, get references and inspect the kennel. Your veterinarian or local shelter can help you select a facility. If you are hiring a sitter, interview the candidates and check their references. (A pet sitter may be preferable if your pet is timid or elderly and needs the comfort of familiar surroundings during your absence.)

Whatever option you choose, there are a few things to remember. Your pet should be up-to-date on all vaccinations and in sound health. Whoever is caring for your pet should know the telephone number at which you can be reached, the name and telephone number of your veterinarian and your pet's medical or dietary needs. Be sure your pet is comfortable with the person you have chosen to take care of him or her.

If You Plan to Travel with Your Pet

THE PRE-TRIP VETERINARY EXAMINATION

Before any trip, have your veterinarian examine your pet to ensure that he or she is in good health. A veterinary examination is a requisite for obtaining legal documents required for many forms of travel.

In addition to the examination, your veterinarian should provide necessary vaccinations such as rabies, distemper, infectious hepatitis and leptospirosis. If your pet is already up-to-date on these, obtain written proof.

Your veterinarian may prescribe a tranquilizer for the pet who is a nervous traveler; however, such drugs should be considered only after discussion with your veterinarian. He or she may recommend a trial run in which your pet is given the prescribed dosage so you can observe the effects. Do not give your pet any drug not prescribed or given to you by your veterinarian.

LEGAL REQUIREMENTS

When traveling with your pet, it is always advisable to keep a health certificate (a document from your veterinarian certifying that your pet is in good health) and medical records close at hand. If you and your pet will be traveling across state lines, you must obtain from your veterinarian a certificate of rabies vaccination.

Although pets may travel freely throughout the United States as long as they have proper documentation, Hawaii requires a 120-day quarantine for all dogs and cats. Hawaii's quarantine regulations vary by species, so check prior to travel.

If you and your pet are traveling from the United States to Canada, you must carry a certificate issued by a veterinarian that clearly identifies the animal and certifies that the dog or cat has been vaccinated against rabies during the preceding 36-month period. Different Canadian provinces may have different requirements. Be sure to contact the government of the province you plan to visit.

If you and your pet are traveling to Mexico, you must carry a health certificate prepared by your veterinarian within two weeks of the day you cross the border. The certificate must include a description of your pet, the lot number of the rabies vaccine used, indication of distemper vaccination and a veterinarian's statement that the animal is free from infectious or contagious disease. This certificate must be stamped by an office of the U.S. Department of Agriculture (USDA). The fee for the stamp is $4.

Get Ready to Hit the Road

TRAVEL CARRIERS

Travel carriers are useful when your pet is traveling by car; they are mandatory when your pet is traveling by air. Your pet's carrier should be durable and smooth-edged with opaque sides, a grille door and several ventilation holes on each of the four sides. Choose a carrier with a secure door and latch. If you are traveling by air, the carrier should have food and water dishes. Pet carriers may be purchased from pet-supply stores or bought directly from domestic airlines. Select a carrier that has enough room to permit your animal to sit and lie down but is not large enough to allow your pet to be tossed about during travel. You can make the carrier more comfortable by lining the interior with shredded newspaper or a towel. (For air-travel requirements, see the "Traveling by Air" section.)

It is wise to acclimate your pet to the carrier in the months or weeks preceding your trip. Permit your pet to explore the carrier. Place your pet's food dish inside the carrier and confine him or her to the carrier for brief periods.

To introduce your pet to car travel in the carrier, confine him or her in the carrier and take short drives around the neighborhood. If properly introduced to car travel, most dogs and cats will quickly adjust to and even enjoy car trips.

CAREFUL PREPARATION IS KEY

When packing, don't forget your pet's food, food and water dishes, bedding, litter and litter box, leash, collar and tags, grooming supplies and a first aid kit and any necessary medications. Always have a container of drinking water with you.

Your pet should wear a sturdy collar with ID tags throughout the trip. The tags should have both your permanent address and telephone number and an address and telephone number where you or a contact can be reached during your travels. Companies such as 1-800-Help-4-Pets offer a 24-hour Nationwide Lost and Found hotline, in addition to emergency vet referrals and rescue assistance.

Traveling can be upsetting to your pet's stomach. Take along ice cubes, which are easier on your pet than large amounts of water. You should keep feeding to a minimum during travel. (Provide a light meal for your pet two or three hours before you leave if you are traveling by car and four to six hours before departure if you are traveling by airplane.) Allow small amounts of water periodically in the hours before the trip.

On Your Way

TRAVELING BY CAR

Dogs who enjoy car travel need not be confined to a carrier if your car has a restraining harness (available at pet-supply stores) or if you are accompanied by a passenger who can restrain the dog. Because most cats are not as comfortable traveling in cars, for their own safety as well as yours, it is best to keep them in a carrier.

Dogs and cats should always be kept safely inside the car. Pets who are allowed to stick their heads out the window can be injured by particles of debris or become ill from having cold air forced into their lungs. Never transport a pet in the back of an open pickup truck.

Stop frequently to allow your pet to exercise and eliminate. Never permit your pet to leave the car without a collar, ID tag and leash.

Never leave your pet unattended in a parked car. On warm days, the temperature in your car can rise to 160 degrees in a matter of minutes, even with the windows opened slightly. Furthermore, an animal left alone in a car is an invitation to pet thieves.

TRAVELING BY AIR

Although thousands of pets fly every year without experiencing problems, there are still risks involved. The Humane Society recommends that you do not transport your pet by air unless absolutely necessary.

If you must transport your companion animal by air, call the airline to check health and immunization requirements for your pet.

If your pet is a cat or a small dog, take him or her on board with you. Be sure to contact airlines to find out the specific requirements for this option. If you pursue this option, you have two choices: Airlines will accept either hard-sided carriers or soft-sided carriers, which may be more comfortable for your pet. Only certain brands of soft sided carriers are acceptable to certain airlines, so call your airline to find out what carrier to use.

If your pet must travel in the cargo hole, you can increase the chances of a safe flight for your pet by following these tips:

• Use direct flights. You will avoid the mistakes that occur during airline transfers and possible delays in getting your pet off of the plane.

• Always travel on the same flight as your pet. Ask the airline if you can watch your pet being loaded and unloaded into the cargo hold.

• When you board the plane, notify the captain and at least one flight attendant that your pet is traveling in the cargo hold. If the captain knows that pets are on board, he or she may take special precautions.

- Do not ship pug-nosed dogs and cats such as Pekinese, Chow Chows and Persians in the cargo hold. These breeds have short nasal passages that leave them vulnerable to oxygen deprivation and heat stroke in cargo holds.

- If traveling during the summer or winter months, choose flights that will accommodate temperature extremes. Early morning or late evening flights are better in the summer; afternoon flights are better in the winter.

- Fit your pet with two pieces of identification—a permanent ID tag with your name and home address and telephone number and a temporary travel ID with the address and telephone number where you or a contact person can be reached.

- Affix a travel label to the carrier, stating your name, permanent address and telephone number and final destination. The label should clearly state where you or a contact person may be reached as soon as the flight arrives.

- Make sure your pet's nails have been clipped to protect against their hooking in the carrier's door, holes and other crevices.

- Give your pet at least a month before your flight to become familiar with the travel carrier. This will minimize his or her stress during travel.

- Your pet should not be given tranquilizers unless they are prescribed by your veterinarian. Make sure your veterinarian understands that this prescription is for air travel.

- Do not feed your pet for four to six hours prior to air travel. Small amounts of water can be given before the trip. If possible, put ice cubes in the water tray attached to the inside of your pet's kennel. A full water bowl will only spill and cause discomfort.

- Try not to fly with your pet during busy travel times such as holidays and summer. Your pet is more likely to undergo rough handling during hectic travel periods.

- Carry a current photo of your pet with you. If your pet is lost during the trip, a photograph will make it easier for airline employees to search effectively.

- When you arrive at your destination, open the carrier as soon as you are in a safe place and examine your pet. If anything seems wrong, take your pet to a veterinarian immediately. Get the results of the examination in writing, including the date and time.

Do not hesitate to complain if you witness the mishandling of an animal—either yours or someone else's—at any airport.

If you have a bad experience when shipping your animal by air, contact The HSUS, the U.S. Department of Agriculture (USDA) and the airline involved. To

HUMANE SOCIETY OF THE UNITED STATES

contact the USDA write to: USDA, Animal, Plant and Health Inspection Service (APHIS), Washington, D.C. 20250.

TRAVELING BY SHIP

With the exception of assistance dogs, only a few cruise lines accept pets—normally only on ocean crossings and frequently confined to kennels. Some lines permit pets in private cabins. Contact cruise lines in advance to find out their policies and which of their ships have kennel facilities. If you must use the ship's kennel, make sure it is protected from the elements.

Follow the general guidelines suggested for other modes of travel when planning a ship voyage.

TRAVELING BY TRAIN

Amtrak currently does not accept pets for transport unless they are assistance dogs. (There may be smaller U.S. railroad companies that permit animals on board their trains.) Many trains in European countries allow pets. Generally, it is the passengers' responsibility to feed and exercise their pets at station stops.

HOTEL ACCOMMODATIONS

There are approximately 8,000 hotel, motels and inns across the United States that accept guests with pets. Most hotels set their own policies, so it is important to call ahead and ask if pets are permitted and if there is a size limit.

IF YOUR PET IS LOST

Whenever you travel with your pet, there is a chance that you and your pet will become separated. It only takes a moment for an animal to stray and become lost. If your pet is missing, immediately canvas the area. Should your pet not be located within a few hours, take the following action:

• Contact the animal control departments and humane societies within a 60-mile radius of where your pet strayed. Check with them each day.

• Post signs at intersections and in store fronts throughout the area.

• Provide a description and a photograph of your missing pet to the police, letter carriers or delivery people.

• Advertise in newspapers and with radio stations. Be certain to list your hotel telephone number on all lost-pet advertisements.

A lost pet may become confused and wary of strangers. Therefore, it may be days, or even weeks, before the animal is retrieved by a Good Samaritan. If you must continue on your trip or return home, arrange for a hotel clerk or shelter employee to contact you if your pet is located.

16

DO YOUR PART TO MAKE PETS WELCOME GUESTS

Many hotels, restaurants and individuals will give your pet special consideration during your travels. It is important for you to do your part to ensure that dogs and cats will continue to be welcomed as traveling companions. Obey local animal-control ordinances, keep your animal under restraint and be thoughtful and courteous to other travelers.

If you have more specific questions or are traveling with a companion animal other than a dog or cat, contact the Companion Animals section of the HSUS.

HELPFUL HINTS

- To transport birds out of the United States, record the leg-band or tattoo number on the USDA certificate and get required permits from the U.S Fish and Wildlife Service.

- Carry a current photograph of your pet with you. If your pet is lost during a trip, a photograph will make it easier for others (airline employees, the police, shelter workers, etc.) to help find your pet.

- While thousands of pets fly without problems every year, there are risks involved. The HSUS recommends that you do not transport your pet by air unless absolutely necessary.

- Whenever you travel with your pet, there is a chance that you and your pet will be separated. If your pet is lost, immediately canvas the area and take appropriate action.

101
5
97
★Trinity
Center   ★Mount
          Shasta
★Eureka   ★O'Brien
★Fortuna ★Redding
                    395
          5
          ★Chico   ★Blairsden
Westport   ★Graeagle
          ★Willows Sierra City★ ★Truckee
Mendocino   ★Tahoe Vista
101   ★Elk   ★ ★South
★Yorkville   ★Georgetown   Lake Tahoe
★Geyserville   ★Coloma
          Sacramento★ ★Cameron Park   50
Calistoga   80 ★Rancho Cordova
St. Helena★ ★Yountville
Inverness★ ★Vallejo   95   NEVADA
Point Reyes Station★ ★Antioch ★Jamestown ★Bridgeport
San Francisco★ ★Concord   Sonora★   395   6
Millbrae★ ★Walnut Creek Groveland★ ★Yosemite
Half Moon Bay★ ★San Ramon El Portal★ ★Fish ★Mammoth
Redwood City★ ★Fremont   Camp   Lakes
Santa Clara★ ★San Jose   ★Merced   95
          ★San Mateo
Santa Cruz★ ★Aptos   ★Madera   395
Monterey★   ★Salinas   ★Fresno
Pacific Grove★ ★Carmel ★Reedley   15
Carmel★ ★Valley
          ★Coalinga
          101   ★Ridgecrest
                                            95
San Luis Obispo★ ★Bakersfield
Pismo Beach★ ★Tehachapi   15   40
          ★Santa Maria   ★Needles
Lompoc★   ★Ojai   West   West
          Santa Barbara Hollywood Covina San ★Lake Arrowhead
          ★Ventura ★Arcadia Bernardino★ ★Big Bear Lake
                    Beverly★ Pomona★ ★Ontario ★Joshua Tree
          Santa Monica★ ★Los Angeles ★La Mirada
          Manhattan Beach★ ★Anaheim ★Palm Springs
          Torrance★ ★Costa Mesa
          Downey★ ★Laguna Beach   10
          Newport Beach★
                    ★Lake San Marcos ★Vista ★Escondido
                    La Jolla★
          Coronado★ ★San Diego
          Chula Vista★   8
                              95
                         MEXICO

Northern California

Ramada Inn

Ramada Inn
2436 Mahogany Way
Antioch, CA 94509
800-900-9100 ▪ 925-754-6600

Room Rates:	$79–$99, including continental breakfast. AAA and AARP discounts.
Pet Charges or Deposits:	$25 per stay.
Rated: 3 Paws 🐾🐾🐾	117 rooms and suites with refrigerators, some microwaves, in-room safes, laundry and dry cleaning service and conference facilities.

T he heart of the scenic "California Delta" is home to the Ramada Inn. The inn offers numerous amenities, spacious rooms and suites and easy access to the wine country, the Sacramento River and the San Joaquin River.

The delta area has abundant natural beauty, winding waterways, parks and aquatic playgrounds. Here you can enjoy boating, fishing or participate in various water sports. If you prefer, relax by the outdoor heated pool and soak up some sun. The spacious grounds of the inn and nearby park are scenic places for you and your dog to get some exercise. Or, pack a picnic lunch and head down to the waterfront for the day.

Feather River Park Resort

Feather River Park Resort
Blairsden, CA 96103
530-836-2328

Cabin Rates:	$82–$182. No credit cards accepted.
Pet Charges or Deposits:	Manager's prior approval required.
Rated: 3 Paws 🐾🐾🐾	Housekeeping cabins with private bath, kitchen, fireplace, barbecue, laundry facilities, pools, recreational facility, playground, golf and tennis.

F eather River Park Resort is situated on 160 acres of the Mohawk Valley in Plumas County in the heart of the High Sierras' "Lake Country." This old-fashioned haven offers guests and their families, including their pets, meadows, vast canyons, crystal-clear streams and lakes, with lots of country-side to explore.

Your log cabin, built in the early 1900s, offers such creature comforts as a fully equipped kitchen, private bath, fireplace and barbecue. Everything is supplied for you, even your linens and bedding.

Activities include swimming, bicycling, volleyball, ping pong, golf, tennis and a playground for the kids. For real outdoor adventures, there are hiking trails, horseback riding and the best trout fishing you could ask for within minutes of the resort.

Pink Mansion

1415 Foothill Boulevard
Calistoga, CA 94515
800-238-7465 ▪ 707-942-0558
Web Site: www.pinkmansion.com ▪ Email: pink@napanet.net

Room Rates:	$135-$225, including breakfast.
Pet Charges or Deposits:	$15 per day. Manager's prior approval required.
Rated: 3 Paws 🐾🐾🐾	6 intimate rooms and suites, each with a private bath, some with fireplaces; valley or forest views, indoor heated pool, large Victorian parlor, common drawing room, dining room and breakfast area, lavish breakfast and afternoon wine tasting, within walking distance to town and near many wineries.

°Combining turn-of-the-century elegance with modern amenities, the Pink Mansion is a restored 1875 home in keeping with the spirit of its last resident, Aunt Alma Simic. Under her care in the 1930s, the house was repainted pink and christened the Pink Mansion. Now it's a landmark in Calistoga.

Choose the large, Victorian-style Rose Suite with a sunken sitting room and raised hearth fireplace, or the Garden Room with its light airiness and panoramic view of Mount St. Helena and the Palisades. The Angel Room is set in the corner of the mansion and features pieces from Aunt Alma's personal collection of angels. The Wine Suite is a secluded haven featuring wine collections, a custom made "Napa Bed" and a fireplace. The Forest Room is a wonderful retreat with antique furnishings and a view of the forest. The Oriental Room, decorated in mauve tones and Asian antiques, has a small sun deck with views of the forest.

You and your pet will enjoy the large garden areas and landscaped grounds.

Triple-S-Ranch

Triple-S-Ranch
4600 Mt. Home Ranch Road
Calistoga, CA 94515
707-942-6730
Website: www.triplesranch.com

Cabin Rates:	$50–$70.
Pet Charges or Deposits:	None.
Rated: 3 Paws 🐾🐾🐾	9 cabins with bathrooms, linens, swimming pool, horseshoes, bocci ball, restaurant and cocktails. Open April 1 to Dec. 31.

I f you are looking for charming, rustic cabins when visiting the Calistoga area, the Triple-S-Ranch is a popular getaway. Located only three miles from town in the Sonoma Mountains, the ranch offers guests a chance to step back in time. There are no telephones, televisions or cooking facilities, except for the barbecue areas.

For your recreational pleasure there are horseshoes, bocci ball and a heated pool. If you enjoy wine tasting, visit some of the tasting rooms and local wineries in the area. Your dog will appreciate all the open space surrounding the ranch, offering plenty of room for a hike and an opportunity to explore the outdoors in the heart of the Sonoma Mountains.

At mealtime, find your way to the legendary Triple-S-Ranch Restaurant and Bar, known for its onion rings and serving up everything from steak and lobster to hamburgers. The dress is casual and the portions are large.

Washington Street Lodging

Washington Street Lodging
1605 Washington Street
Calistoga, CA 94515
707-942-6968
Website: www.napalinks.com/wsl/

Cottage Rates: $90–$125, including continental breakfast.
Pet Charges or Deposits: $15 per stay Manager's prior approval required.
Rated: 3 Paws 🐾🐾🐾 5 cottages with full or partial kitchen, some with decks, television.

W hen looking for a secluded, riverside setting, try one of the private cottages at Washington Street Lodging. Here you will enjoy cozy, country decor with many extra touches to make you feel right at home. Each of the five cottages offers guests a private bath and a full or partial kitchen. Enjoy a continental breakfast served in your room before heading off for a day of wine tasting or sightseeing in nearby downtown Calistoga.

Located within walking distance of the Napa River, you and your pet can hike along the riverbank or pack a picnic lunch and spend the afternoon enjoying nature.

Cameron Park Inn – Best Western

Cameron Park Inn – Best Western
3361 Coach Lane
Cameron Park, CA 95682
800-601-1234 ▪ 916-677-2203
Website: www.bestwestern.com

Room Rates:	$60–$75, including continental breakfast. AAA and AARP discounts.
Pet Charges or Deposits:	Small pets only. Manager's prior approval required.
Rated: 3 Paws 🐾🐾🐾	63 spacious rooms, some with kitchens; heated swimming pool and laundry facilities.

L ocated in the historic Gold Country between Sacramento and Placerville is the Cameron Park Inn – Best Western. Here guests may choose to relax by the heated swimming pool, head out for a day of wine tasting at one of the local wineries or explore the Gold Country and historic towns, where you can spend the day trying to strike it rich by panning for gold.

For truly adventurous vacationers, there is white-water rafting on the South Fork of the American River. Or at near by Folsom Lake, spend the day fishing or boating. If golf is your game, hit the links at the nearby course. Eldorado National Forest offers you and your pet plenty of room to roam and explore the great outdoors.

Holiday Inn

Holiday Inn
685 Manzanita Court
Chico, CA 95926
800-310-2491 (CA only) ▪ 800-465-4329 ▪ 530-345-2491
Email: chisls1@winshipway.com

Room Rates:	$75-$95. AAA and AARP discounts.
Pet Charges or Deposits:	$25 per stay.
Rated: 3 Paws 🐾🐾🐾	172 guest rooms and suites, outdoor pool, whirlpool, complimentary airport shuttle, banquet and conference facilities, complimentary morning coffee, restaurant and cocktail lounge with live entertainment and complimentary buffet.

The Holiday Inn is within two miles of California State University at Chico and Bidwell Mansion and State Historic Park. Chico's only full-service hotel is affordable and centrally located, near both commercial and rural areas for antique shopping, touring breweries or hiking the wilds.

Molly Gunn's Restaurant serves up a varied menu, while Molly Gunn's Bar was voted the area's "Best Happy Hour," offering a 25-foot-long complimentary buffet, nightly drink specials and dancing.

If you are looking for a nearby picnic spot or a place to spend the day with your pooch, the Bidwell Mansion and State Historic Park has more than 2,000 acres to explore.

Golden Lotus Bed and Breakfast Inn

Golden Lotus Bed and Breakfast Inn
1006 Lotus Road
Coloma, CA 95613
530-621-4562

Room Rates:	$85–$125, including breakfast.
Pet Charges or Deposits:	$20 per day.
Rated: 3 Paws 🐾🐾🐾	2 cottages with separate baths and 6 inn rooms with private baths, full library, sitting areas, veranda, flower and herb gardens, restaurant.

An old Indian campground on the American River is the site of the enchanting Golden Lotus Bed and Breakfast Inn. The main inn consists of six charming rooms. The Westward Ho room reflects the Old West. The Orient Express takes you to China, with an Asian flavor. The Secret Garden is a secluded room with cheery wicker furniture. Wish Upon takes you away to greet the magic genie. Pirates' Cove whisks you away on Persian rugs. Tranquillity boasts a relaxing, English-cottage motif with soft colors. The two cottages that allow pets are The Honeysuckle, with two rooms separated by a bath, with a mini kitchen and a floral and wicker decor; and The Hideaway, which consists of three small rooms and a full bath in a Southwestern decor.

For your dining pleasure, the historic Adam's Red Brick Restaurant is next to the inn and offers a varied menu, plus desserts.

Sheraton Concord Hotel

Sheraton Concord Hotel
45 John Glenn Drive
Concord, CA 94520
800-325-3535 ▪ 925-825-7700
Website: www.sheraton.com

Room Rates:	$105–$765. AAA, AARP, AKC and ABA discounts.
Pet Charges or Deposits:	$10 per day. Small pets only.
Rated: 4 Paws 🐾🐾🐾🐾	324 guest rooms and suites, some with refrigerators, valet laundry, Executive Club floor, indoor pool, spa, putting green, golf course, exercise room, restaurant and lounge with nightly entertainment, close to area attractions.

T he Sheraton Concord Hotel sports a fashionable exterior as well as convenient touches inside. Guest rooms and suites feature remote-control television, in-room coffeemaker, two telephones, data port hookup and, for the business traveler, an oversized work station. Guests may enjoy the indoor pool, spa, exercise room or the putting green in the enclosed tropical garden atrium, with its flowing streams and koi ponds. For die-hard golfers, the Buchanan Field Golf Course is adjacent to the hotel.

The Executive Club floor caters to the business traveler with upgraded services and amenities, an exclusive club-like atmosphere, a complimentary continental breakfast and hors d'oeuvres served in the evening.

Greenwood Pier Inn

Greenwood Pier Inn
5928 South Highway 1
P.O. Box 336
Elk, CA 95432
707-877-9997
Website: www.greenwoodpierinn.com ▪ Email: gwpier@mcn.org

Room Rates:	$120–$250, including continental breakfast.
Pet Charges or Deposits:	$15 per day. Manager's prior approval required.
Rated: 3 Paws 🐾🐾🐾	Rooms, cabins and cottages, many with panoramic views, fireplaces, spas, restaurant and room service.

Perched atop an ocean bluff with myriad rock formations and panoramic views in the old lumber town of Elk, the Greenwood Pier Inn dubs itself a "garden-by-the-edge-of-the-sea that grows flowers for your room."

Though your choice of accommodations is varied in this quirky complex of fairy-tale cottages, no matter which you choose, it will include a private bath, fireplace and handmade quilts on a comfortable bed. Guests can relax on the deck with a glass of wine and scan the sea for an occasional whale spouting, watch the sea gulls soar through the sky and the seals sun themselves on the rocks below as the fog gently rolls in.

The Café is open daily, offering creative dinners of local seafood, accompanied by fresh veggies from the inn's garden. The flower-bordered paths and seaside gardens are the perfect setting for celebrations or simply for a stroll.

Eureka Inn

Eureka Inn
518 Seventh Street
Eureka, CA 95501
800-862-4906 ▪ 707-442-6441
Website: www.eurekainn.com ▪ Email: innplacetobe@eurekainn.com

Room Rates:	$99–$279. AAA, AARP and AKC discounts.
Pet Charges or Deposits:	Small pets only. Manager's prior approval required.
Rated: 4 Paws 🐾🐾🐾🐾	105 rooms and luxury suites, fireplaces, wet bars, kitchens, formal dining areas, valet laundry, Jacuzzi tub, sauna, heated pool, restaurants and lounges.

T he Eureka Inn is set like a gem in one of California's most magnificent natural environments. Forests of towering redwoods, miles of wave-washed shore and cascading mountain streams offer endless allure.

Since 1922, the inn has enchanted guests with its elegance, sophistication, European flair and Tudor styling. You can almost hear the footsteps of history on the polished hardwood floors. Registered as a National Historic Place, the inn's lofty ceilings, redwood beams and baronial half-timbering exude classic English manor house richness.

Relax in the deep leather settees by the inviting fire in the Grand Lobby before enjoying the inn's tradition of fine dining in a variety of restaurants and lounges, which range from the intimately elegant to the eclectic. Venturing out can mean exploring a fern-shrouded canyon, standing beneath the world's tallest tree or greeting fishing boats as they return to harbor.

Country Inn – Best Western

Country Inn – Best Western
2025 Riverwalk Drive
Fortuna, CA 95540
800-679-7511 ▪ 707-725-6822
Website: www.bestwestern.com

Room Rates:	$58-$115. AAA, AARP and AKC discounts.
Pet Charges or Deposits:	$20 per stay. Small pets only. Manager's prior approval required.
Rated: 3 Paws 🐾🐾🐾	66 rooms, indoor-outdoor pool, indoor whirlpool, laundry facilities, microwaves and refrigerators.

T his country resort inn was voted USA Today Readers' Choice Award for the "Best Weekend Getaway." The 66-unit inn is set in the heart of the Redwood Empire near North Coast attractions, including the Eel and Van Duzen rivers, which lure anglers for a bit of salmon and steelhead fishing.

Guests can relax in the indoor whirlpool or take a swim in the 83-degree swimming pool in a setting that affords picture-window views to the lush, landscaped grounds.

For other leisure pursuits, the inn is within minutes of Victorian Ferndale, the Scotia Sawmill Tour, and the Avenue of the Giants, as well as ocean beaches, parks and restaurants.

Residence Inn by Marriott

Residence Inn by Marriott
5400 Farwell Place
Fremont, CA 94536
800-331-3131 ▪ 510-794-5900
Website: www.residenceinn.com

Suite Rates:	$159–$179, including continental breakfast buffet. Call for discounts.
Pet Charges or Deposits:	$10 per night. $75 cleaning fee.
Rated: 3 Paws 🐾🐾🐾	80 suites, all with living rooms and separate sleeping areas, full kitchens, some with fireplaces; meeting facilities, 2 heated pools, whirlpool, sports court, cable television, VCR and movie library, complimentary evening beverages, laundry facilities, airport transportation and pet exercise area.

T ravelers will appreciate the comforts and conveniences offered at the Residence Inn by Marriott. The accommodations are spacious, with separate sleeping and living areas and wood-burning fireplaces. Amenities include fully equipped kitchens, daily maid service, laundry facilities and room service from any of the local restaurants. A hosted continental breakfast buffet and informal hospitality happy hour are included.

The Residence Inn by Marriott offers a heated swimming pool, two whirlpools, three barbecue areas, a sports court where you can play a game of basketball, volleyball or tennis and landscaped grounds for a stroll with your dog.

American River Inn

American River Inn
Main at Orleans Street
P.O. Box 43
Georgetown, CA 95634
800-245-6566 ▪ 530-333-4499
Website: www.pcweb.net/ari ▪ Email: ari@pcweb.net

Room Rates:	$85–$115, including full breakfast and evening hors d'oeuvres with local wines.
Pet Charges or Deposits:	Manager's prior approval required. Sorry, no cats.
Rated: 3 Paws 🐾🐾🐾	18 guest rooms and 7 suites, some with fireplaces and private balconies; Jacuzzi.

Y ou will find tranquillity at this historic inn in the heart of the Gold Country off Highway 49. The grounds include a beautiful Victorian garden, surrounding a mountain pool and inviting Jacuzzi. English holly trees and 80-foot redwoods provide a serene setting amongst fruit trees and vines.

The gardens yield a delicious bounty for breakfast, served in the dining room or on the porch in warmer weather. The grounds also provide a number of recreational activities such as badminton, croquet court, a horseshoe pit, table tennis and a putting green.

Guest rooms are decorated in country Victoriana, with armoires, down comforters and featherbeds. No phones or television to disturb the serenity here. Each evening, guests are invited to enjoy hors d'oeuvres and local wines, while they relax to the sounds of Liberace or Roger Williams on the player piano in the Inn's parlor. In winter, you'll be warmed by the parlor's fireplace.

Isis Oasis Lodge

Isis Oasis Lodge
20889 Geyserville Avenue
Geyserville, CA 95441
800-679-PETS ▪ 707-857-3524
Website: www.isisoasis.org ▪ Email: isis@saber.net

Room Rates:	$65–$250, including full breakfast.
Pet Charges or Deposits:	None.
Rated: 3 Paws 🐾 🐾 🐾	Lodge with 12 private rooms and shared baths; retreat house that sleeps up to 15; a four-bedroom house with two baths, full kitchen and fireplaces; and 2 cottages, one with full kitchen and private hot tub.

I f you are looking for a magical retreat for the mind and body when visiting the wine country, try the Isis Oasis Lodge. The Lodge has 12 private rooms with Egyptian motif and shared baths. The Retreat House is a three-bedroom, three-bath house that sleeps up to 15. The Tower is a small cottage with a view and private half-bath and shower. The Vineyard House has four bedrooms, two fireplaces, a full kitchen and scenic views. The Isis Suite is a Victorian bedroom and sitting room with private bath. The Wine Barrel Room, Tipi and Pyramid are alternative style rooms with a bathhouse.

The lodge is located on ancient Pomo Indian ceremonial grounds. It has been a gathering place for groups and individuals seeking an extraordinary experience for years. Guests may spend the day hiking, swimming in the heated pool, relaxing in one of the patio areas, taking wine-tasting tours or visiting the many resident animals. Located near the river, there is plenty of open space for you and your dog to explore.

Gray Eagle Lodge

Gray Eagle Lodge
5000 Gold Lake Road
Graeagle, CA 96103
800-635-8778 ▪ 530-836-2511
Website: www.grayeaglelodge.com

Cabin Rates:	$155–$200, including breakfast, dinner and daily maid service.
Pet Charges or Deposits:	$10 per day. Sorry, no cats.
Rated: 3 Paws 🐾🐾🐾	18 cabins with full baths (showers only) and refrigerators; many outdoor activities, game room, restaurant, bar and gift shop.

Merely step out of the door and the adventure begins at Gray Eagle Lodge, where miles of trails lead to meadows and ponds, ridges and peaks and alpine lakes galore. And should you anglers come back with a "big one"—a fish or a fish tale—the inn keeps champagne on ice to reward the best fish stories.

Established in 1923, the family-owned-and-operated lodge offers guests their choice of 18 rustic cabins with full baths. There are no cooking facilities, but the room rate includes breakfast and dinner. The dinner menu offers daily selections ranging from pan-seared rainbow trout, medallions of pork tenderloin to slow-roasted Long Island duckling. For a small fee, the chef will gladly prepare a picnic lunch or even cook up your catch of the day.

This "dog friendly" lodge is set among 1 million acres of Plumas National Forest, which includes the Feather River, several lakes, recreation areas and plenty of room to roam. Gray Eagle Creek is next to the lodge and affords fishing

and rafting fun. Gray Eagle Falls spills into a pond, creating an inviting swimming hole. Add mountain biking, hiking, two golf courses and horse stables nearby, and what more could you ask for? How about no phones or televisions as distractions.

Sorensen's Resort

Sorensen's Resort
14255 Highway 88
Hope Valley, CA 96120
800-423-9949 ▪ 530-694-2203
Website: www.sorensensresort.com

Room Rates:	$95–$350.
Pet Charges or Deposits:	Room rate as deposit. Two-pet limit. Designated cabins.
Rated: 3 Paws 🐾🐾🐾	3 bed-and-breakfast rooms and 27 cottages and cabins with fireplaces or wood-burning stoves, sitting areas, full kitchens and sleeping accommodations for up to 6.

C lose to more than 100 lakes, streams and some of the best skiing in the Sierras, you'll discover Sorensen's Resort. Here you'll find a romantic hideaway or a hostel for your ski trip with friends and family. The amenities, activities and down-home hospitality make guests feel right at home. The cozy Country Café is perfect for a warm brew or a cozy meal. There are plenty of activities to keep you busy, including the classes and guide service from the Horse Feathers Fly-Fishing School, river-rafting tours and ski instruction from the Hope Valley Cross-Country Ski Center.

The Ark

The Ark
180 Highland Way
P.O. Box 273
Inverness, CA 94937
800-808-9338 ▪ 415-663-9338
Website: www.rosemarybb.com ▪ Email: rosemarybb@aol.com

Cottage Rates:	$180, including breakfast.
Pet Charges or Deposits:	$25 per stay. Manager's prior approval required.
Rated: 4 Paws 🐾🐾🐾🐾	Cottage for 2 to 6 guests, with full kitchen.

T ucked away in the forest a mile up the ridge from the village of Inverness, The Ark is a romantic, private hideaway an hour north of the Golden Gate Bridge, next to the magnificent Point Reyes National Seashore.

Built and named in 1971 by a class of UC-Berkeley architecture students, The Ark offers seclusion in the form of a charming, two-room cottage with a spacious main room with a wood-burning stove, overlooking the forest. The cozy, comfortable furnishings include original works by local artists.

Recreational options include whale-watching, horseback riding or taking a leisurely walk on the beach with your dog. Just down the road are the marshy headwaters of Tomales Bay, a noted place for bird watching. If you're feeling especially adventurous, try Papermill Creek for rafting and kayaking.

Dancing Coyote Beach

Dancing Coyote Beach
12794 Sir Francis Drake Boulevard
P.O. Box 98
Inverness, CA 94937
415-669-7200

Cottage Rates: $100–$175, including breakfast supplies placed in cottage kitchens. AAA, AARP, AKC and American Airlines discounts.

Pet Charges or Deposits: Small pets only. Designated cottage only.

Rated: 4 Paws 🐾🐾🐾🐾 4 cottages with galley kitchens, skylights, fireplaces and bay views.

Dancing Coyote Beach delivers privacy and bed-and-breakfast charm, only 80 minutes from the cultural energy of San Francisco. Situated in the midst of Point Reyes National Seashore, Dancing Coyote Beach offers a convenient home base for bicycling, hiking, whale watching, bird watching and beachcombing.

Each of the four cottages has a galley kitchen, skylights, fireplace and views of the bay. For dining, enjoy breakfast on your own private deck in the morning sun or a romantic fireside dinner at night or wander into sleepy Inverness to sample the menus of several fine restaurants.

This place is a quiet retreat, free of the noise of electronics and bustle. Guests are encouraged to stroll along the sandy beach following the graceful curve of the shoreline or to heed the call of sheltering pines and cedars and warm, sunny spots.

Rosemary Cottage

Rosemary Cottage
75 Balboa Avenue
P.O. Box 273
Inverness, CA 94937
800-808-9338 ▪ 415-663-9338
Website: www.rosemarybb.com ▪ Email: rosemarybb@aol.com

Cottage Rates:	$152–$256, including kitchen stocked with full breakfast fixings.
Pet Charges or Deposits:	$25 per stay. Manager's prior approval required.
Rated: 5 Paws 🐾🐾🐾🐾🐾	Cottage for two to four guests, views of Point Reyes National Seashore.

L ocated on Inverness Ridge, Rosemary Cottage is a romantic French-country "pied-a-terre." A wall of windows provides a dramatic forest view of Point Reyes National Seashore. A large deck under an aging oak overlooks the herb garden in this secluded hideaway.

Guests will appreciate the many hand-crafted details, large bedroom, high ceilings and wood-burning stove.

Only minutes from the beach, travelers can enjoy fishing, boating, whale watching, horseback riding or a walk on the beach with the dog. Miles of hiking trails at Point Reyes National Seashore are only 10 minutes from the cottage. Just down the road are the marshy headwaters of Tomales Bay, a great place for bird watching. For rafting or kayaking, try Papermill Creek. If you would prefer to just relax, stay at the cottage and soak in the garden hot tub.

National Hotel

National Hotel
18183 Main Street
P.O. Box 502
Jamestown, CA 95327
800-894-3446 ▪ 209-984-3446
Website: www.national-hotel.com ▪ Email: info@national-hotel.com

Room Rates:	$80–$120, including buffet breakfast.
Pet Charges or Deposits:	$10 per day. Manager's prior approval required.
Rated: 3 Paws 🐾🐾🐾	9 guest rooms. Original saloon, restaurant patio dining. Soaking tub.

T he historic National Hotel, located in the heart of Jamestown, is filled with reminders of California's Gold Rush era. No self-respecting gold miner would stay in any hotel that didn't offer a saloon in which to relax and spend their hard-earned gold dust. Sit at the 19th century redwood bar and order your favorite beverage. Patio dining on the vine-covered terrace will make your lunch or dinner a memorable experience.

Each of the award-winning, renovated hotel rooms features brass beds, patchwork quilts, lace curtains and a friendly ghost. Among the newer amenities are modern plumbing, great mattresses and private baths. A separate soaking room with an antique, claw-footed tub will take you back in time and can be shared by two.

The Stanford Inn by the Sea

the Stanford Inn by the Sea
Coast Highway 1 and Comptche Ukiah Road
P.O. Box 487
Mendocino, CA 95460
800-331-8884 ▪ 707-937-5615
Website: www.stanfordinn.com ▪ Email: info@stanfordinn.com

Room Rates: $215–$625, including gourmet breakfast.
Pet Charges or Deposits: $25 per stay for 1st pet; $12.50 for each additional pet.
Rated: 5 Paws 🐾🐾🐾🐾🐾 23 guest rooms and 10 suites, furnished with antiques; "welcome" gifts for pets at check-in.

S et in historic gardens between the coastal forest and the Pacific Ocean is The Stanford Inn by the Sea. On a small, certified organic working garden and farm, the inn embodies the best of the rugged Mendocino Coast. The inn offers a buffet champagne breakfast and organic meals, along with amenities found in fine hotels, while maintaining a cozy, homey feeling.

Rooms paneled with pine or redwood and decorated with antiques, plants and art from local artists make you want to linger by the fire just a little longer before heading out.

One of the greenhouses encloses the pool, spa and sauna as well as a variety of orchids, bougainvillea, hibiscus and other lush tropicals.

Westin San Francisco Airport

Westin San Francisco Airport
1 Old Bayshore Highway
Millbrae, CA 94030
800-228-3000 ▪ 650-692-3500
Website: www.westin.com ▪ Email: sfoap@westin.com

Room Rates:	$89–$475.
Pet Charges or Deposits:	Pets under 25 pounds. Manager's prior approval required.
Rated: 3 Paws 🐾🐾🐾	393 rooms including 3 suites, many with bay views, landscaped grounds, in-room refreshment center, business center, conference facilities, heated indoor pool, saunas, whirlpool, fitness center, 24-hour room service, restaurant and lounge, coffee and gift shop, across from Bayfront Park.

San Francisco's waterfront is home to the Westin San Francisco Airport. Located just two minutes from the airport and 15 minutes from downtown, business travelers and vacationers alike appreciate the convenience of this resort-like hotel. Amenities include 393 luxury rooms, many with bay views.

The fitness-minded should check out the hotel's fully equipped fitness center or grab the leash and take your dog for a run on the six-mile jogging trail at the Bayfront Park across the street from the hotel.

Hungry for Mediterranean food? The Alfiere Restaurant is a bistro featuring exotic cuisine in a relaxing setting. The Lobby Lounge and The Bar are perfect for a casual business meeting or get-together with friends.

Mount Shasta Cabins

Mount Shasta Cabins
500 South Mount Shasta Boulevard
Mount Shasta, CA 96067
800-565-9422 ▪ 530-926-5396
Website: www.mtshastacabins.com ▪ Email: frontdesk@mtshastacabins.com

Cabin Rates:	$65–$170.
Pet Charges or Deposits:	Manager's prior approval required.
Rated: 3 Paws 🐾🐾🐾	20 guest cabins.

Mount Shasta Cabins offers vacation rentals in and around the Mount Shasta area at affordable rates. Each of the units has a fully equipped kitchen, linens, telephone, cable TV, barbecue, wood stove with wood provided, and, of course, privacy.

Some of the cabins are more remote, others are closer to town, with fenced-in yards for your pets. The best way to view the wide assortment of cabins is to check out their web site.

Tree House Motor Inn – Best Western

Tree House Motor Inn – Best Western
111 Morgan Way
Mount Shasta, CA 96067
800-545-7164 ▪ 530-928-3101
Website: www.bestwestern.com

Room Rates:	$74–$160. AAA and AARP discounts.
Pet Charges or Deposits:	$10 per day. Small pets only.
Rated: 3 Paws 🐾 🐾 🐾	95 rooms and deluxe suites, landscaped grounds, heated indoor pool, some refrigerators, views of Mount Shasta, banquet and convention facilities, fully equipped business center, restaurant and cocktail lounge.

Perched in the shadow of Mount Shasta is the Tree House Motor Inn – Best Western, where hospitality complements the rustic elegance of the inn. The warm glow of the natural wood paneling in the rooms, gourmet dining, the cozy warmth of the fireplace in the cocktail lounge, the view overlooking the majestic mountain and the serene atmosphere of the inn all add up to a relaxing stay.

The indoor heated pool is perfect for a dip any time of the year. Enjoy skiing and snow sports in the winter. When the weather warms up, there's plenty of fishing areas and water sports to keep you busy.

Holiday Harbor

Holiday Harbor
20061 Shasta Caverns Road
O'Brien, CA 96070
800-776-2628 ▪ 530-238-2383
Website: www.lakeshasta.com ▪ Email: holidayharbor@lakeshasta.com

Houseboat Rates:	$330 and up. Call for week rates.
Pet Charges or Deposits:	None.
Rated: 3 Paws 🐾🐾🐾	7 houseboats, all-weather cabin, railed walkways, range and oven, refrigerator, ice chest, cabin heater, 12-volt light system, shower, bunk beds, gas grill, RV park and campground.

J ust imagine cruising around scenic Shasta Lake with the whole family, including your pet, enjoying all the comforts of home aboard your own houseboat.

Much of what you need is provided—just bring your food, linens, games, grilling utensils and bathing suits. The staff will instruct you on the operating procedures of your houseboat. The Toy Box Rental Center has everything you need to rent, from fishing boats to Jet Skis.

The campground has 27 tree-studded sites with full hook-ups, by the water. There are laundry facilities, showers, restrooms, private docking for boats and a swimming area. Advanced reservations are required for tent camping.

The Tree House Bed and Breakfast

The Tree House Bed and Breakfast
73 Drake Summit
P.O. Box 1075
Point Reyes Station, CA 94956
800-495-8720 ▪ 415-663-8720
Website: www.treehousebnb.com

Room Rates: $110–$145, including continental breakfast.
Pet Charges or Deposits: None. All pets are welcome.
Rated: 5 Paws 🐾🐾🐾🐾🐾   3 private rooms, with separate entry and private bath.

Located one hour from either Santa Rosa or San Francisco, The Tree House Bed and Breakfast at Inverness on Point Reyes is a secluded destination for a weekend retreat or a relaxing vacation. Select from three private rooms. The Princess Room is furnished in antiques and a brass bed. The Queen's Quarters, attached to the main house with its own private entry, comes with a wet bar, private bathroom, queen-sized bed, fireplace and views of the valley. The King's Room, complete with private bath and king-sized bed, offers a private balcony and an expansive mountain view. All accommodations include a continental breakfast.

Once you are settled in your room, take your dog and head out for a day of hiking and bird watching at nearby Point Reyes National Seashore or Golden Gate Recreation Area.

Heritage Inn – Best Western

Heritage Inn – Best Western
11269 Point East Drive
Rancho Cordova, CA 95742
800-641-1076 ▪ 916-635-4040
Website: www.bestwestern.com

Room Rates:	$59–$79, including buffet breakfast. AAA, AARP and AKC discounts.
Pet Charges or Deposits:	$15 per stay.
Rated: 3 Paws 🐾🐾🐾	124 rooms and deluxe king suites, pool, sauna, fitness center.

Whether looking for outlet shopping, wine sipping or outdoor adventures, travelers will find that the Heritage Inn—Best Western offers an array of amenities and recreational opportunities. All rooms include coffee-makers, hair dryers and refrigerators. The deluxe king leisure suites have spacious living and bar areas. A complimentary breakfast buffet and manager's reception are offered daily.

You and your dog can strike out for a bit of exploring trails along the American River, Folsom Lake and Lake Natoma. Pet sitters are available if you wish to take in some of the local history or venture to area factory outlets or wineries.

Oxford Suites

Oxford suites
1967 Hilltop Drive
Redding, CA 96002
800-762-0133 ▪ 530-221-0100
Website: www.oxfordsuites.com

Suite Rates:	$69–$89, including full breakfast buffet, evening reception and hors d'oeuvres. AAA, AARP, Government/Military and Business Travel discounts available.
Pet Charges or Deposits:	$15 per stay. Sorry, no cats. Small pets only.
Rated: 3 Paws 🐾🐾🐾	139 suites with microwave ovens and refrigerators. Pool and spa.

Conveniently located just off Interstate 5 and only minutes west of downtown Redding, the Oxford Suites offer guest amenities that include a full breakfast buffet each morning and an evening reception with beverages and light hors d'oeuvres.

Guest suites are tastefully appointed and designed to provide comfort and convenience with work tables, sofas, microwaves, refrigerators, and remote-control TV and video player. Non-smoking and special assistance suites are available.

Hotel services also include guest laundry, valet service, 24-hour fax/copying services, and a convenience shop with food, beverage, gifts and video movie rentals.

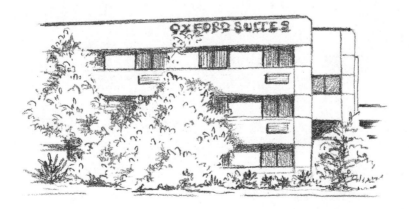

Hotel Sofitel San Francisco Bay

Hotel Sofitel San Francisco Bay
223 Twin Dolphin Drive
Redwood City, CA 94065
650-598-9000
Website: www.sofitel.com

Room Rates:	$89–$419. AAA discount.
Pet Charges or Deposits:	$20 per day.
Rated: 3 Paws 🐾🐾🐾	421 guest rooms and 42 suites. Health club, outdoor heated pool, minibars, 2 restaurants and lounge. Complimentary airport transportation.

Just minutes from the San Francisco International Airport, the Sofitel is located at a strategic junction leading to Silicon Valley, Stanford University, the surrounding Bay Area communities and the city itself.

This waterfront hotel has been recently renovated, offering guests minibars, in-room movies, full-service concierge, a full-service European spa, as well as two French restaurants with a genuine French bakery.

For recreation you will enjoy the outdoor heated pool, sauna and health club, plus a scenic jogging course. Nearby are excellent tennis and golf facilities.

Red Lion Inn

Red Lion Inn
1401 Arden Way
Sacramento, CA 95815
800-733-5466 ▪ 916-922-8041

Room Rates:	$79–$114. AAA and AARP discounts.
Pet Charges or Deposits:	$75 deposit of which $25 is non-refundable. Manager's prior approval required.
Rated: 3 Paws ❀ ❀ ❀	376 large rooms and 8 luxury suites, some with patios or balconies and refrigerators, conference facilities, putting green, 3 pools, wading pool, exercise room, guest laundry service, gift shop, room service, restaurants and cocktail lounge.

L ocated only minutes from the center of the city, the Red Lion Inn offers guests easy access to downtown, the state Capitol, and the entire Sacramento area. Here guests will enjoy spacious accommodations, complete with air conditioning, large work areas and meeting facilities for the business traveler, laundry and valet services and other luxuries.

After a day of sightseeing or business meetings, relax by one of the three pools, go for a stroll around the spacious grounds with your dog or enjoy a workout in the fully equipped exercise room.

For casual dining, have your meal poolside at the covered barbecue and bar, opt for the relaxing ambiance of the Coffee Garden or grab a quick bite at the lobby's Espresso Bar and Deli. After dinner, unwind with some hot jazz at Savanna's Lounge.

Campton Place Hotel

Campton Place Hotel
340 Stockton Street
San Francisco, CA 94108
800-235-4300 ▪ 415-781-5555
Website: www.camptonplace.com ▪ Email: reserve@camptonplace.com

Room Rates:	$275 and up. AAA discount.
Pet Charges or Deposits:	$35 per day.
Rated: 5 Paws 🐾🐾🐾🐾🐾	119 rooms and suites, concierge, acclaimed restaurant, five-star amenities, convenient to shopping, business, dining and entertainment.

J ust steps from San Francisco's Union Square and a step up from most hotels is one of the truly luxurious hotels in the world—Campton Place.

The accommodations at the Campton Place Hotel frequent the list of the "Readers' Choice Awards" of Condé Nast Travel magazine, which has ranked it "One of the top 25 U.S. hotels." The small niceties of a European inn combine with the polished precision of a grand hotel—concierge, newspaper delivery, thick robes, valet parking.

The elegant five-star restaurant at Campton Place continues to earn extraordinary acclaim. Diners enjoy award-winning cuisine, fine French and American wines and an ambiance graced by Wedgewood crystal and fresh flowers. The adjoining bar provides a cozy setting for afternoon tea or one of the hotel's famous dry martinis.

Clift Hotel

Clift Hotel
495 Geary Street
San Francisco, CA 94102
800-65-CLIFT ▪ 415-929-2300
Website: www.clifthotel.com ▪ Email: res@clifthotel.com

Room Rates:	$225 and up. AAA, AARP, AKC and ABA discounts.
Pet Charges or Deposits:	$40 per night.
Rated: 5 Paws 🐾🐾🐾🐾🐾	326 rooms and suites, business center, fitness center, 24-hour room service, overnight laundry and dry cleaning services, Guest Recognition Program and full-service concierge.

I n 1915, Fredrick C. Clift opened a hotel that rose out of the rubble of old San Francisco amid the futuristic fanfare of the Panama-Pacific Exposition, promising the grand tradition of days gone by while embracing America's growing world influence. The Clift Hotel has kept that promise. This 80-year-old "Grande Dame" has been impeccably maintained and continues to exude luxurious comfort.

Amid chandeliers and elegant decor, guests enjoy high-ranking service and amenities. Each room is decorated with fine linens and furnishings, and with an attention to detail. With the staff at your service 24 hours a day, virtually everything is available to you with just one phone call—even chocolate cake and milk at midnight.

For award-winning California French cuisine, look no further than the gracious, romantic environment of The French Room. The Redwood Room is an Art Deco lounge and piano bar built from a 2,000-year-old giant redwood tree

from Northern California. The redwood walls, 22-foot fluted columns and mural bar make this one of the most beautiful places in the world for cocktails.

The Mansions Hotel and Restaurant

The Mansions Hotel and Restaurant
2220 Sacramento Street
San Francisco, CA 94115
800-826-9398 ▪ 415-929-9444
Website: www.themansions.com

Room Rates:	$139–$350, including full breakfast and nightly magic performance.
Pet Charges or Deposits:	None.
Rated: 3 Paws 🐾🐾🐾	21 rooms and suites, billiard/game room, historic museum, magic parlor, sculpture gardens and views of the Golden Gate Bridge. Restaurant.

T here's magic in the air in more ways than one at The Mansions Hotel and Restaurant in the heart of San Francisco. When you step into the grand foyer with its crystal chandeliers, the creaking of the gumwood walls and Bach's music playing in the parlor, you are whisked back in time. Surrounded by tapestries, paintings and historic memorabilia, every room is different. Some have a terrace with a view of the Golden Gate Bridge, but all guest rooms include a private bath, fresh flowers, California apples and a special arrival gift.

The Mansions restaurant and dinner theater is one of San Francisco's top 10 dinner spots, offering an assorted menu from a light buffet to a lavish banquet. Make your reservations early for an evening of entertainment. There are haunting nightly performances in the Victorian Cabaret by America's most acclaimed illusionists. Listen closely—can you hear the whispers of the resident ghost, Claudia?

Marriott Fisherman's Wharf

Marriott Fisherman's Wharf
1250 Columbus Avenue
San Francisco, CA 94133
800-MARRIOTT ▪ 415-775-7555
Website: www.marriotthotels.com

Room Rates:	$150–$240. AAA discount.
Pet Charges or Deposits:	$5 per day. $50 per stay.
Rated: 3 Paws 🐾🐾🐾	300 rooms and suites with honor bars, some with refrigerators, meeting facilities, sauna, health club, valet service, restaurant and cocktail lounge.

S et in the heart of San Francisco's Northern Waterfront District is the renowned Marriott Fisherman's Wharf. From the moment you enter the hotel, you will be greeted by friendly staff and an inviting atmosphere, and the guest rooms are packed with amenities.

With such a central location, you may want to venture out for a day of sightseeing on the wharf, take a ride on a cable car or a boat tour of the bay. Then wind down with a workout in the hotel's health club or relax in the spa before dining at the hotel's restaurant, Spada, featuring an intimate atmosphere and casual California cuisine. Top off your dinner with a nightcap at the quiet, sophisticated Lobby Lounge.

The hotel boasts an exercise area for your pet to stretch his legs. Or stop by the desk for directions to a nearby local park if you feel like exploring the city with your pooch.

Marriott Hotel

Marriott Hotel
55 Fourth Street
San Francisco, CA 94103
800-MARRIOTT ▪ 415-896-1600
Website: www.marriotthotels.com

Room Rates:	$139 and up. AAA, AARP, AKC and ABA discounts.
Pet Charges or Deposits:	Small pets only.
Rated: 4 Paws 🐾🐾🐾🐾	1,498 rooms and suites with honor bars, heated indoor pool, whirlpool, sauna, steam room, exercise room, massage by appointment, business center, conference facilities, secretarial services, laundry, valet parking, airport limousine service, car rental desk, activities desk, room service, coffee shop, restaurants and lounges.

I n the midst of historic San Francisco is the elegant Marriott Hotel. This modern hotel offers all the amenities travelers expect in a four-star hotel. Guests will find richly decorated rooms and luxury suites, with such conveniences as individual climate controls, fire and personal safety systems and in-room mini bars.

Keep fit with an invigorating workout in the state-of-the-art health club, followed by a refreshing splash in the indoor pool or a relaxing soak in the whirlpool.

Sample the Garden Terrace's California cuisine and lavish buffets in a casual, family atmosphere. Kinoko features teppanyaki-style specialties prepared at your table. The Fourth Street Deli is a popular sports bar and offers light fare. The Atrium Lounge, located in the five-story atrium, serves cocktails and refreshments. Stop by the View Lounge for refreshments, cocktails and a spectacular view of the city.

Pan Pacific Hotel

Pan Pacific Hotel
500 Post Street
San Francisco, CA 94102
800-327-8585 ▪ 415-771-8600
Website: www.panpac.com ▪ Email: guest@sfo.pan-pacific.com

Room Rates:	$300 and up.
Pet Charges or Deposits:	$75 per stay. Small pets only.
Rated: 4 Paws ❀ ❀ ❀ ❀	330 rooms and 19 suites, personal valet, chauffeur-driven Rolls Royce, business center, conference facilities, exercise room, 24-hour room service, restaurant and cocktail lounge.

S an Francisco's Pan Pacific Hotel is synonymous with luxury and sophistication. Accommodations are augmented by sumptuous bathrooms with deep soaking tubs, soft terry cloth robes and a personal valet to attend to your every need, including a chauffeur-driven Rolls Royce at your disposal.

The Pan Pacific Bar offers a compelling diversion from the bustling city below. The Pacific Restaurant has become a destination in itself, with its relaxing environment, soft piano music, the splash of the fountain and the crackle of an inviting fire.

Westin St. Francis

Westin St. Francis
335 Powell Street – Union Square
San Francisco, CA 94102
800-WESTIN-1 ▪ 415-397-7000
Website: www.westin.com ▪ Email: stfra@westin.com

Room Rates:	$159 and up.
Pet Charges or Deposits:	Small dogs only. Manager's prior approval required.
Rated: 5 Paws 🐾🐾🐾🐾🐾	1,200 rooms and suites, in-room bars, business center, conference facilities, secretarial services, valet parking, exercise room, 2 dining rooms, coffee shop, cocktail lounge.

S ince 1904, the award-winning Westin St. Francis has been known for its rich heritage. Located in the heart of San Francisco, the 1,200 impeccably appointed guest rooms and luxurious suites offer an array of amenities. Whether hosting a gala for kings or an intimate gathering, you will appreciate the meticulous attention to detail. The grandfather clock in the lobby is the perfect place to rendezvous before dining at one of the five renowned restaurants.

Experience high tea and jazz in the opulent Compass Rose. Or to taste-test some of the more than 50 beers from around the world, stop by Dewey's Pub. The St. Francis Café has a bistro-style menu and serves breakfast and dinner.

Villa Hotel

Villa Hotel
4000 South El Camino Real
San Mateo, CA 94403
800-341-2345 ▪ 650-341-0966
Website: www.villahotel.com ▪ Email: villa@villahotel.com

Room Rates:	$109–$149. AAA and AARP discounts.
Pet Charges or Deposits:	$100 refundable deposit.
Rated: 3 Paws 🐾🐾🐾	272 rooms and 14 suites, business center, conference and banquet facilities, heated pool, exercise room, restaurant, coffee shop, cocktail lounge with live entertainment, gift shop, beauty and barber shops and massage therapist.

Whether vacationing in the Bay Area or attending a convention or seminar, the Villa Hotel offers comfort and convenience. Located 20 minutes from San Francisco and Silicon Valley, the possibilities for adventure, recreation and relaxation for you and your pet abound.

A full slate of recreational and business services are available for the asking. For dining and beverages, choose the gourmet menu of the hotel restaurant, the causal atmosphere of the Villa Coffee House or an evening of entertainment in the cocktail lounge.

Residence Inn by Marriott

Residence Inn by Marriott
1071 Market Street
San Ramon, CA 94583
800-331-3131 ▪ 925-277-9292
Website: www.residenceinn.com

Suite Rates:	$99–$199, including breakfast buffet. AAA and AARP discounts.
Pet Charges or Deposits:	$5 per day. $75 per stay.
Rated: 3 Paws 🐾🐾🐾	106 suites, all with living rooms and separate sleeping areas, full kitchens, some with fireplaces, meeting facilities, cable television, VCR and movie library, 2 heated pools, whirlpool, sports court, complimentary evening beverages, laundry facilities, airport transportation and pet exercise area.

When it comes to comfortable and affordable lodging, Residence Inn by Marriott – San Ramon often garners top honors. Voted the "Gold Hotel" award and "1994 Hotel of the Year," the inn offers inviting touches such as wood-burning fireplaces, separate sleeping and living areas, breakfast buffet and complimentary hospitality hours.

Start your day with the breakfast buffet served at the Gatehouse, followed by a day of sightseeing, and a visit to some of the major attractions. Or stay where you are and relax by the pool, swim a few laps or venture to the sports court for a game of tennis, volleyball or basketball. You and your dog can take a walk around the landscaped grounds and exercise area. There are even dog runs available, and a park is just across the street.

Herrington's Sierra Pines Resort

Herrington's Sierra Pines Resort
101 Main Street
P.O. Box 23J
Sierra City, CA 96125
800-682-9848 ▪ 530-862-1151
Website: www.qpg.com/h/herrington/

Room Rates:	$49–$90. AAA discount.
Pet Charges or Deposits:	None.
Rated: 3 Paws 🐾🐾🐾	19 guest rooms and 2 suites with balconies and decks. Trout pond, game room, restaurant and lounge.

Nestled at the base of the Sierra Buttes, with rocky peaks towering to 8,600 feet, the Yuba River meanders for a third of a mile through the Sierra Pines Resort, located in historic Sierra City. Founded in 1850 and once a booming mining town, Sierra City has become a popular tourist area.

Guest accommodations are attractively wood-paneled and feature comfortable beds and covered decks overlooking the river. A rainbow trout pond is well stocked for your viewing or fishing enjoyment.

Within a radius of nine miles, there are more than twenty mountain lakes, providing a spectacular setting for summer fishing, boating, hiking and sightseeing. During the winter, cross-country skiing and snowmobiling are just minutes away. Tahoe's North Shore is within an hour's drive, and two 18-hole golf courses are less than a half hour away.

Gold Lodge

Gold Lodge
480 West Stockton Avenue
Sonora, CA 95370
800-363-2154 ▪ 209-532-3952
Website: www.goldlodge.com ▪ Email: motel@goldlodge.com

Room Rates:	$39–$69, including continental breakfast. AAA and AARP discounts.
Pet Charges or Deposits:	$10 per stay. Manager's prior approval required.
Rated: 3 Paws 🐾🐾🐾	42 guest rooms and 2 guest suites. Pool, sun deck and hot tub. Exercise room and sauna. Picnic and barbecue areas.

I n 1848, miners from Sonora, Mexico, found gold here and established a camp. Sonora became known as the "Queen of the Southern Mines" and was the biggest town in the Mother Lode. Horse races and fights between bulls and bears were common. Miners and gold, hard work and saloons, gamblers and schemes, fire and drought—that was the town of Sonora.

After the Gold Rush, Sonora's central location kept it going. Today it is a busy county seat and the shopping area for Tuolumne County. It is the "nearest biggest little town" this side of Yosemite National Park. Tuolumne County's economy includes lumbering, tourism, cattle ranches, turkey and Christmas tree farms, apple and pear orchards and even a dolomite mine. A large number of movies and television shows are produced in the county.

The Gold Lodge in Historic Sonora is a great home base, offering convenience and comforts at affordable rates. Located across from the Mother Lode Fairgrounds, an excellent location for shows and competitions, it is surrounded by large lawn areas, with convenient parking at your door. Guest rooms are well appointed, with king- and queen-sized beds, in-room air conditioners, refrigerators and microwaves.

Inn at Heavenly Bed and Breakfast Lodge

Inn at Heavenly Bed and Breakfast Lodge
1261 Ski Run Boulevard
South Lake Tahoe, CA 96150
800-MY-CABIN ▪ 530-544-4244
Website: www.inn-at-heavenly.com ▪ Email: mycabin@sierra.net

Room Rates:	$125–$165. Call for discounts.
Pet Charges or Deposits:	$20 per day. $100 deposit. Sorry, no cats.
Rated: 4 Paws 🐾🐾🐾🐾	15-room bed and breakfast, some with kitchenettes, refrigerators and microwaves, private spa room, hot tub, sauna, steam room, separate cabins for parties of up to 16, lodge and park available for groups and weddings. Full-service wedding arrangements. Petsitters available upon request.

Set on 1½ acres of woods in South Lake Tahoe, the Inn at Heavenly Bed and Breakfast Lodge is a log-cabin-style lodge with a knotty-pine interior and exterior, with custom log furniture throughout.

Accommodations vary in size, some housing natural stone fireplaces, separate sitting areas, refrigerators and microwaves, but all offering large, homey rooms with patchwork quilts and views of the park. There is a private hot tub room, sauna and steam room available by reservation.

You and your canine pal will enjoy the park-like setting offering barbecues and picnic areas with log swings.

Spruce Grove Cabins

Spruce Grove Cabins
P.O. Box 16390
South Lake Tahoe, CA 96151
800-777-0914 ▪ 530-544-0549
Website: www.sprucegrovetahoe.com ▪ Email: info@sprucegrovetahoe.com

Cabin Rates:	$135–$225, including continental breakfast.
Pet Charges or Deposits:	$10 per day. $100 refundable deposit. Manager's prior approval required. Sorry, no cats.
Rated: 3 Paws 🐾🐾🐾	7 cabins with fully equipped kitchens, river-rock fireplaces and views. Fenced yard for pets.

Spruce Grove puts you amidst a private, quiet, secluded mountain resort off Ski Run Boulevard, at the foot of Heavenly Ski Area and within walking distance of Lake Tahoe, at the New Marina Village. You are close to shopping, restaurants, skiing, ski shuttles, beach, entertainment and casinos.

Spruce Grove offers private, knotty pine cabins and a hospitality room with shady grounds for relaxing or barbecues.

Tahoe Keys Resort

Tahoe Keys Resort
599 Tahoe Keys Boulevard
P.O. Box 20088
South Lake Tahoe, CA 96151
800-MY-TAHOE ▪ 530-544-5397
Website: www.tahoevacationguide.com ▪ Email: info@tahoevacationguide.com

Room Rates:	$100 and up per night. AAA and AARP discounts.
Pet Charges or Deposits:	$25 per stay. Manager's prior approval required.
Rated: 5 Paws 🐾🐾🐾🐾🐾	A private resort with waterfront condos, homes and villas. Front desk and concierge services, indoor and outdoor pool, spa, health club, lighted tennis courts, private beach; meeting, wedding and party facilities.

T ahoe Keys Resort is a 750-acre private resort at famed Lake Tahoe. This year-round resort offers waterfront vacation rentals of premier three- to six-bedroom homes, studios, condominiums and a VIP villa, all with views of the water or the surrounding mountains. All accommodations come with complete kitchens and fireplaces.

Tahoe Keys Resort is a complete destination resort at Lake Tahoe, featuring a waterfront restaurant, an indoor/outdoor swimming pool, spa and health club. Guests may spend their day bicycling, playing volleyball, basketball or tennis, boating, hiking with the dog, gaming at the casinos, relaxing on the private beach or participating in favorite water sports when the weather permits. In the winter, you are just minutes away from several prime cross-country and downhill ski areas.

Harvest Inn

Harvest Inn
1 Main Street
St. Helena, CA 94574
800-950-8466 ▪ 707-963-9463
Website: www.harvestinn.com ▪ Email: reservations@harvestinn.com

Room Rates:	$149–$650, including wine country continental breakfast. AAA discount.
Pet Charges or Deposits:	$75 per pet for up to 3 days. Manager's prior approval required. Small pets only.
Rated: 4 Paws 🐾🐾🐾🐾	54 rooms and suites with wet bars and refrigerators, many with fireplaces, antique furnishings, English Tudor style, surrounded by gardens and vineyards, 2 swimming pools and whirlpool.

N estled in the heart of Napa Valley are the charming, turn-of-the-century, English Tudor guest cottages of the Harvest Inn. The elegant but inviting guest rooms are reminiscent of the country gentry style of a bygone era. Many accommodations feature brick fireplaces, wet bars and refrigerators and are adorned with period antiques.

Reflecting the abundance of each season, colorful flowers and fruit-bearing trees grace lush lawns surrounding the inn's 14-acre working vineyard. Guests often stroll to the many neighboring wineries for tasting and guided tours. Forests and stately vineyards provide walking and/or jogging paths as part of the many extras. Bicycle some of the most exciting routes in the Bay Area or hike the scenic hillsides and meadows of Bothe-Napa State Park. The renowned shops and restaurants of St. Helena are only a few minutes away.

Holiday House

Holiday House
7276 North Lake Boulevard
P.O. Box 229
Tahoe Vista, CA 96148
800-294-6378 (CA and NV only) ▪ 530-546-2369

Room Rates:	$95–$185. Call for week rates.
Pet Charges or Deposits:	$25 per stay. Manager's prior approval required. $40 nonrefundable deposit.
Rated: 3 Paws 🐾🐾🐾	7 lakefront suites with kitchenettes, living rooms, separate bedrooms, cable TV, barbecues and hot tub.

L ocated on the picturesque North Shore of Lake Tahoe, the Holiday House is set among tall pine trees. Here guests will find comfortable accommodations with extras like decks and kitchenettes.

In the summer, take advantage of the waterfront locale by swimming, fishing, windsurfing, water skiing or rafting before heading into Tahoe for the nightlife. Winter promises just as much fun since it's only minutes from Northstar, Alpine Meadows, Squaw Valley and other ski resorts.

Cedar Stock Resort

Cedar Stock Resort
45810 State Highway 3
Trinity Center, CA 96091
800-982-2279 ▪ 916-286-2225
Website: www.cedarstock.com ▪ Email: info@cedarstock.com

Cabin Rates:	$50 and up. Call for week rates.
Houseboat Rates:	$85 and up. Call for week rates.
Pet Charges or Deposits:	$7 per day.
Rated: 3 Paws 🐾🐾🐾	Cabins and houseboats, recreational and fishing boat rentals, boat marina with berth rentals, grocery store, restaurant and cocktail lounge.

L ocated on Trinity Lake, Cedar Stock Resort offers a choice of cabins or houseboats. The cabins have a private bath, fully equipped kitchen and barbecue. You bring the rest. When you don't feel like cooking, try the Cedar Stock Restaurant, a popular dinner house for the entire county. Top off the evening at The Lodge bar and lounge, where the whole family can relax with a cocktail or a soda. There is even a grocery store for supplies. Guests may rent horses, fishing and recreational boats, water skis and Jet Skis.

A great way to relax and explore Trinity Lake is by houseboat. Cedar Stock Resort rents five types of houseboats, by the day or by the week. They come well-equipped. All you need to bring are linens, soaps, food, games and fishing gear. The rest you can buy at the resort's store.

Whichever accommodation you choose, with 500,000 acres of national parks surrounding the lake, your entire family, including your pets, are bound to have a great adventure.

Inn at Truckee

Inn at Truckee
11506 Deerfield Drive
Truckee, CA 96161
888-773-6888 ▪ 530-587-8888
Website: www.innattruckee.com ▪ Email: info@innattruckee.com

Room Rates:	$65–$145. AAA and AARP discounts.
Pet Charges or Deposits:	$11 per day.
Rated: 3 Paws 🐾🐾🐾	43 guest rooms. Hot tub and sauna.

T his alpine mountain inn offers convenience, comfort and value. World-class skiing and snowboarding are just minutes from the Inn's doorstep, as are many other winter activities.

During the summer months you are not far from stream and lake fishing, challenging golf courses, beautiful beaches and great hiking and bike-riding areas.

Guest rooms are comfortable and well appointed. Each morning, a complimentary pastry bar is available for guests in the spacious lobby, warmed by a river-rock fireplace. You are within walking distance of a shopping center with traditional and fast-foods restaurants.

Holiday Inn — Marine World Africa USA

Holiday Inn — Marine World Africa USA
1000 Fairgrounds Drive
Vallejo, CA 94589
800-HOLIDAY ▪ 707-644-1200
Website: www.holiday-inn.com ▪ Email: hldyinnvjo@aol.com

Room Rates:	$64–$125. AAA and AARP discounts.
Pet Charges or Deposits:	$25 per stay.
Rated: 3 Paws 🐾🐾🐾	164 rooms, located opposite the theme park; refrigerators, microwaves, courtyard pool and recreation area, game room, dry sauna, whirlpool, laundry facilities, meeting and banquet facilities, ballroom, restaurant and cocktail lounge, shuttle to San Francisco Airport.

Directly across the street from the Marine World Africa USA theme park and only 30 minutes from the San Francisco Bay Area is the Holiday Inn — Marine World Africa USA. Designed with comfort in mind, rooms are spacious and include refrigerators and microwaves, comfortable beds and tables and chairs perfect for finishing up that business report or enjoying your morning coffee.

Enjoy the moderate climate while basking in the sun, refreshing in the pool or working out at the health club that is minutes from the hotel. Of course, don't forget the thrills and adventures that await across the street at Marine World Africa USA.

Embassy Suites Hotel

Embassy Suites Hotel
1345 Treat Boulevard
Walnut Creek, CA 94596
800-EMBASSY • 925-934-2500
Website: www.embassy-suites.com • Email: sales@embassywc.com

Suite Rates:	$125-$169. AAA and AARP discounts.
Pet Charges or Deposits:	$10 per day. $75 nonrefundable deposit.
Rated: 4 Paws 🐾🐾🐾🐾	249 suites, each with kitchen and living room, dining/work area, mini-bar, refrigerator, microwave; atrium, meeting rooms, heated indoor pool, sauna, whirlpool, exercise room, library, game room, gift shop, restaurant and cocktail lounge.

I n 1989, Walnut Creek, with its specialty shops, department stores, theaters, restaurants and the Regional Art Center was voted "Most livable small city in the nation" by the Conference of Mayors. The Embassy Suites Hotel is located within two miles of the charming downtown area.

Accommodations feature a large private bedroom, living room with a sofa bed, galley kitchen, mini-bar, refrigerator, microwave and a well-lighted dining/work area. Relax in the garden atrium or on the outdoor sun deck with your complimentary morning paper, swim a few laps in the indoor pool or work out in the fitness center before heading out for a day of meetings or sightseeing. There is a shuttle service to anywhere within a five-mile radius, plus a nearby park allows for a quick romp with the dog.

When it comes to dining, the Taos Bar and Grill serves up Southwest cuisine with indoor or outdoor seating, or for a quick meal, stop by the Taos Deli, which offers more traditional American delicatessen fare.

Howard Creek Ranch

Howard Creek Ranch
40501 North Highway 1
P.O. Box 121
Westport, CA 95488
707-964-6725
Website: www.howardcreekranch.com

Room Rates:	$75–$160, including full breakfast. Off-season discounts available.
Pet Charges or Deposits:	$10 per day. Manager's prior approval required. Designated rooms or cabins. Sorry, no cats.
Rated: 3 Paws 🐾🐾🐾	7 rooms and suites, 3 cottages with handmade quilts, private decks or balconies, skylights, fireplaces or wood stoves, hot tub, sauna, microwave, refrigerator, gardens, horseback riding.

Woward Creek Ranch thrives in the rural splendor of sweeping mountain and ocean views on 40 acres near the "Lost Coast," a 60-mile-long wilderness area. Nestled on an oceanfront farm along the Mendocino Coast, the historic ranch was built in 1871. The New England-style farmhouse is bordered by miles of beach, mountains and open wilderness, making this the perfect place to take your pet.

Accommodations include cabins, suites and rooms furnished with antiques, large comfortable beds and handmade quilts, topped off with views of the ocean, mountains, creek or gardens.

Guests may relax in the hot tub, stroll the award-winning gardens, explore the 75-foot-long swinging footbridge over Howard Creek, spend the day horse-back riding or combing the beach. The ranch is listed on the National Historic Register.

Golden Pheasant Inn – Best Western

Golden Pheasant Inn – Best Western
249 North Humboldt Avenue
Willows, CA 95988
800-338-1387 ▪ 530-934-4603
Website: www.bestwestern.com

Room Rates:	$56–$150. AAA and AARP discounts.
Pet Charges or Deposits:	$10 per day.
Rated: 3 Paws 🐾🐾🐾	104 garden guest rooms and suites, some with fireplaces and Jacuzzis; landscaped grounds, 2 pools, laundry facilities, restaurant and tavern.

S urrounded by seven acres of landscaped gardens and lawns, the Golden Pheasant Inn – Best Western is a full-service inn offering guests accommodations normally found in big-city hotels, yet set in a quiet, relaxing country environment at an affordable price.

At this oasis just off Interstate 5, weary travelers can enjoy the pool or spa or explore the local scenery and nearby wildlife refuge.

The inn's restaurant and tavern offer American and Mexican cuisine in a newly renovated setting.

Sheep Dung Estates

Sheep Dung Estates
P.O. Box 49
Yorkville, CA 95494
707-894-5322
Website: www.sheepdung.com

Cottage Rates:	$100–$225, including kitchen stocked with breakfast fixings. Credit cards not accepted.
Pet Charges or Deposits:	None for two dogs; each additional dog is $20 per night.
Rated: 4 Paws ❀❀❀❀	5 cottages, with mini-kitchens, wood-burning fireplaces, private baths, set on several secluded acres.

Don't let the name fool you. Sheep Dung Estates is a unique country hideaway with grand views and meticulous attention to detail. Nestled on 160 acres of the picturesque Anderson Valley Hills, this retreat offers three secluded, comfortably furnished modern cottages, with queen-sized beds, mini-kitchens and wood-burning fireplaces. The Pond Cottage, Sunset Hill and Terra Cottage are each set on 15-40 acres with views of the rolling hills.

Mini-kitchens come fully stocked with breakfast fixings. After a day of sightseeing and a trip to the vineyards or wandering the rambling roads, you can prepare your evening feast and sit on your own private deck and toast the sun with a glass of local wine as it sets beyond the hills.

Vintage Inn

Vintage Inn
6541 Washington Street
Yountville, CA 94599
800-351-1133 ▪ 707-944-1112
Website: www.vintageinn.com ▪ Email: reservations@vintageinn.com

Room Rates:	$180–$325. AAA and AARP discounts.
Pet Charges or Deposits:	$25 per stay.
Rated: 4 Paws 🐾🐾🐾🐾	80 rooms with balcony or patio, views of the vineyard, mountain or town, fireplaces, refrigerators and whirlpool, nightly turndown, champagne breakfast, concierge, massage, air conditioning, conference facilities, landscaped grounds, heated lap pool, whirlpool spa, tennis courts, room service.

Nestled among the vineyards of the Napa Valley on lush, estate-like grounds is the country villa called the Vintage Inn. The Old World charm and contemporary amenities make this a popular choice for vacationers and business professionals.

After settling into your room with its custom furnishings, cozy fireplace and complimentary bottle of wine, stroll through the landscaped grounds and admire the pools, fountains and courtyards with your pet. For recreation, guests may play tennis, do a few laps in the heated pool, relax in the spa, treat themselves to a massage or visit the adjacent Vintage 1870, a restored winery with unique shops, restaurants and galleries.

Northern California

Leashes are required unless otherwise stated.

ARCATA

Arcata Community Forest and Redwood Park is off Samoa Boulevard at Union Street. Turn right onto 14th Street and continue through the forest to the parking area. Here you'll find 575 acres of lush forest. For more information, call (707) 822-7091.

Clam Beach County Park is 7 miles north of Arcata. Take the Clam Beach Park exit and head west for approximately 2 miles. Here your dog can run leash-free on the beach or play in the surf. For more information, call (707) 445-7652.

If you're looking for private, leash-free beaches, try Mad River County Park. It's a great place to bring a picnic and spend the day. Take the Guintoli Lane exit, turn right onto Heindon Road and follow the signs to the small parking lot at the end of the road. For more information, call (707) 445-7651.

BODEGA BAY

Doran Beach Regional Park, off Highway 1 on Doran Park Road, requires leashes but is a great place to take a brisk hike or a refreshing swim. For more information, call (707) 875-3540.

CHICO

Bidwell Park is a 2,250-acre city park stretching from the downtown area to the foothills of the Sierra Nevada. Here you have your choice of hiking and bicycling trails, a playground for the kids, ball fields, swimming, golf or horseshoes. For more information, call (530) 891-5556.

EUREKA

Samoa Dunes Recreation Area has 300 acres of leash-free coastal dunes. If you and your pet love the water, this is a great place to hike or take a dip in the ocean. Take Highway 255 to the Samoa Peninsula, turn left on New Navy Base Road for about 5 miles. There is a main lot for parking. For more information, call (707) 825-2300.

FREMONT

Ardenwood Historic Farm is on Ardenwood Boulevard, 25 miles north of Highway 84. The farm is a living history project showing farm life from the 1870s to the 1920s. The grounds of the George Washington Patterson's Victorian mansion are covered in beautiful gardens. Here you may purchase fresh picked vegetables, visit the period shops, picnic or visit resident farm animals. There is an entrance fee and a separate fee for tours of the mansion. For more information, call (510) 769-0663.

Coyote Hills Regional Park is west on Highway 84 then exit at Thornton Avenue-Paseo Padre Parkway. Head north 1 mile and the park is at 8000 Patterson Ranch Road. Here you will find a 976-acre wildlife refuge for white-tailed kites and red-tailed hawks. There are 2,400-year-old Indian shell mounds, a reconstructed Indian village, a freshwater marsh, picnic facilities and more than 40 miles of hiking, bicycling and jogging trails. While you are there, stop by the visitors center and the museum. There is a day-use fee and a fee for your dog. For more information, call (510) 795-9385.

Fremont Central Park is a waterfowl refuge and lake with jogging and bicycling trails plus a variety of boats for rent. The scenery is beautiful, on or off the water, and it is a wonderful place for a picnic or day on the lake. There is no entrance fee, but there is a swimming fee. The park is on Paseo Padre Parkway and Stevenson Boulevard. For more information, call (510) 791-4340.

Mission Peak Regional Preserve is 3,000 acres of spacious grasslands. There are plenty of trails to explore and wonderful views stretching from Mount Tamalpais to Mount Hamilton. Heading east, take Mission Boulevard to Stanford Avenue, turn right and head about one mile to the entrance. For more information, call (510) 635-0135.

Sunol Regional Wilderness offers hours of geological wonders and lots of scenic trails. Make sure to visit the whirlpools and waterfalls at Alameda Creek. To reach the park, go north on Interstate 680 and exit on Calaveras Road in Sunol. Turn right on Calaveras to Geary Road, then left into the park. For more information, call (510) 635-0135.

GLEN ELLEN

Jack London State Historic Park, 1 mile west on Jack London Ranch Road, offers visitors and leashed dogs 800 acres for picnicking, hiking, biking or horseback riding. Home and resting place of the famed author, his ranch house contains his personal papers, belongings and mementos. The park is open daily with guided tours offered on weekends. For more information, call (707) 938-5216.

GRAEAGLE – BLAIRSDEN

Plumas National Forest is 1,162,863 acres of wilderness straddling the Sierra Nevada and the Cascades Mountains. Here you will find forest lands and wonderful scenery where you can go camping, hiking, boating, fishing, swimming or rent horses and bicycles. The Feather River has carved several canyons and ravines full of white water and cascades. There is a 15,000-acre scenic area with the 640-foot Feather Falls above Lake Oroville. You can hike and camp along the river, but due to the rugged terrain and rapids, be sure to stick to the recreational zones for water sports. There are several entrances into the park. Contact Plumas National Forest for directions and further information at (916) 283-2050.

INVERNESS

Kehoe Beach is a half-mile hike from the road through wildflower fields. Here the whitecapped waves crash against the limestone cliffs forming tide pools. Leashes are required, but there is plenty of beach to comb. You'll enjoy watching the harbor seals and snowy plovers that have made this area their home. For more information, call (415) 663-1092.

Rocky cliffs rise from the sea at Point Reyes National Seashore. Here you and your dog can roam the beaches, but leashes are required. Take Bear Valley Road off of Highway 1. For more information, call (415) 663-1092.

Tomales Point, with its bluffs and moors, can be a temperamental place. The 4.7 miles of one-way hiking above the ocean is a favorite of many hikers. The mist and vapors from the sea will keep you cool as you hike the trail. Leashes are required, but it's a fine trail.

MENDOCINO

Jackson Demonstration State Forest has 50,000 acres of trees, trails and logging roads for you and your pooch to explore. It is 9 miles west of Willits, off Highway 20, east of Mendocino and Fort Bragg. For more information, call (707) 964-5674.

Mendocino Headlands State Park/Big River Beach requires leashes, but it's worth it to experience the spectacular scenery. Located off Highway 1 south; exit at the Mendocino Headlands State Park/Big River Beach sign. For more information, call (707) 964-5474.

Mendocino National Forest is 886,048 acres in the North Coast Mountain Range north of San Francisco. In addition to numerous scenic points, the park offers camping, picnicking, hiking, hang gliding, motorcycling areas, boating, boat rentals, fishing and swimming. The forest supervisor is at 420 E. Laurel Street, Willows, CA 95988. For more information, call (916) 934-2350.

MOUNT SHASTA

The Ellen Rupp Nature Study Area, situated in a pine forest, is the perfect place for you and your dog to study native plants along the half-mile trail before dipping your paws into a crystal clear stream. For more information, call (530) 926-4865.

Glass Mountain, off Highway 89 on Forest Service Road 43N99 on the southern edge of the mountain, is an intriguing place for geological hobbyists. An actual glass mountain caused by a volcanic vent, this rare geological phenomenon has a glass flow that spans 4,210 acres. For more information, call (530) 964-2184.

Medicine Lake Loop Trail is off Highway 89, near Bartle. Take Forest Service Road 49 to Medicine Lake Road. Once the center of an active volcano, the clear lake is stocked with 30,000 brook trout each year, offering visitors a chance to do some shore fishing. There are also ice caves for you and your dog to explore before heading to the smaller lakes in the area. For more information, call (530) 964-2184.

NORTH SHORE LAKE TAHOE

North Shore Tahoe Regional Park is in Tahoe Vista, at Donner Road and National Avenue off Highway 28. Leashes are required, but the 108 acres and 4 miles of hiking trails eventually run into the Tahoe National Forest, which is leash-free. For more information, call (530) 546-7248.

Tahoe National Forest has 797,205 acres that are part of the Lake Tahoe Basin. Leashes are required, but there are plenty of hiking trails and room to roam as well as activities galore from which to choose, including camping, boating, horseback riding, fishing and swimming. For more information, call (530) 265-4531.

RANCHO CORDOVA

Folsom Lake State Recreation Area is off Highway 50. Exit at Folsom and continue north to Folsom Auburn Road. Here you'll find plenty of wildlife, scenery and 80 miles of hiking trails. There is a day-use fee for the park and a small fee for the dog. For more information, call (800) 444-7275.

ROHNERT PARK

Crane Creek Regional Park is east of town on Pressley Road, off Roberts Road, then 2 miles east of Petaluma Hill Road. Here you will find oak and maple trees beside picturesque creekside trails, plus 128 acres to explore. For more information, call (707) 527-2041.

SACRAMENTO

American River Parkway, off Interstate 5 at Richards Boulevard; exit to Jibboom Street. Trails lead you along the American River, stretching from Discovery Park in Sacramento to Folsom. With no leash laws, you and your pet can take full advantage of the bike and equestrian trails. For more information, call (916) 366-2061.

Loch Leven Lake, a leash-free haven off Interstate 80 at the Big Bend exit, has everything from alpine meadows, grassy valleys, granite cliffs, towering woodlands and three beautiful lakes. The paths take you over the railroad tracks, across a creek and through the forest. You'll want to spend an entire day in this splendid place. For more information, call (916) 265-4531.

SAN FRANCISCO

Golden Gate Park requires leashes, but with 1,000 acres to explore, it won't slow you and your dog down. The park is bordered by Fulton, Lincoln and Stanyan streets and the Great Highway. There are leash-free areas within the park. You'll both enjoy the miles of bridle and foot paths that make this the perfect place to go hiking, play catch or have a picnic with your favorite canine.

Golden Gate National Recreation Area encompasses both rolling coastal hills and diverse urban park lands. Wrapping around San Francisco's northern and western edges and extending to San Mateo County, this national recreation area offers a leashless adventure for you and your dog. From the windswept sands of Ocean Beach to the Victorian Gardens of Sutro Heights and Lands End, the coastal trails thread through to China and Baker beaches.

The Golden Gate Promenade extends 3.5 miles along San Francisco Bay and connects Fort Point with Crissy Field and Fort Mason. The park is at the south end of the Golden Gate Bridge. Exit at Marina Boulevard and go southwest toward Fisherman's Wharf. The area from Marina Green to the west gate of Crissy Field is leash-free, making this a tail-wagging experience. The information center is at the Fort Mason headquarters. For more information, call (415) 556-0560.

SAN MATEO

Laurelwood Park, at Glendora and Cedarwood drives, is a tree-laden paradise for your dog. Here you can spend the day hiking along the stream and enjoy the great outdoors together.

SAN RAMON

Bishop Ranch Regional Open Space is a wonderfully serene park that is a haven for red-tailed hawks, turkey vultures and deer. The park is off Bolinger Canyon Road and San Ramon Valley Boulevard on Morgan Drive. For more information, call (925) 562-7275.

ST. HELENA

Bothe-Napa Valley State Park consists of 1,916 acres of meadows full of wildflowers in the spring and plenty of trails for hiking and biking, plus lots of wilderness to explore. It is located 3 miles northwest on State Route 29, near Bale Grist Mill State Historic Park, a restored flour mill. There are hiking trails that lead across the mill pond to Bothe-Napa Valley State Park. You may rent horses for a trail ride, go camping, picnicking, swimming or take a nature tour of the area. There is a small gate fee. Stop by the visitors' center for information on the park.

TRINITY CENTER

Trinity Lake is east of Highway 3. Here you can rent a boat and spend the day sailing, fishing or pack a picnic lunch and spend the day lazing on the shore with your dog. For more information, call (530) 623-6101.

WALNUT CREEK

Las Trampas Regional Wilderness Park is 3,600 acres of predominantly leash-free paradise for you and your dog. With acre after acre of wooded canyons, scenic wilderness, abundant hiking trails and spectacular views, you will want to spend the entire day exploring this untamed world off Highway 24. Take the Pleasant Hill exit south and turn right on Olympic Boulevard; then head for the Olympic Staging Area. For more information, call (925) 635-0135.

Mount Diablo State Park is a 3,849-foot summit overlooking 35 counties, 17 miles southeast on Diablo Road. This 18,000-acre park offers horse rentals, camping, picnicking, hiking and bicycle trails and a visitors' center with nature study programs. For more information, call (925) 635-0135.

WESTPORT

Westport Union Landing State Beach is on Highway 1. This isolated beach is great for a relaxing picnic. For more information, call (707) 937-5804.

WILLOWS

Sacramento National Wildlife Refuge requires leashes. There are 10,783 acres of marshland that is home to migrating birds and a wide variety of wildlife. Located off Route 57; after exiting, go approximately 6 miles on the frontage road to the entrance. For more information, call (530) 934-2801.

PETS WELCOME!

Central California

Apple Lane Inn Bed and Breakfast

Apple Lane Inn Bed and Breakfast
6265 Soquel Drive
Aptos, CA 95003
800-649-8988 ▪ 831-475-6868
Website: www.applelaneinn.com

Room Rates:	$110–$180, including country breakfast.
Pet Charges or Deposits:	$25 fee plus credit card imprint. Horses welcome. Manager's prior approval required.
Rated: 4 Paws 🐾🐾🐾🐾	5 rooms and suites with private baths, some sitting rooms and meadow views.

O ne of Santa Cruz County's oldest farmhouses is also among its first bed and breakfast inns. The Apple Lane Inn is a charming Victorian house and barn, lovingly restored to reflect its original 1872 character and set on three acres amid fields and apple orchards.

Guests may choose from five private rooms with romantic decor, antique furniture, plump quilts and picturesque views of the meadows. Before heading out for a day of beachcombing and sightseeing with your four-legged friend, begin your day with an elegant country breakfast of fresh fruit, juice, pastries, a hearty main course and special coffee blends.

If you prefer to linger at the historical inn, owners Doug and Diana Groom invite you to unwind in the front parlor with a glass of wine or a book; play darts, cards, horseshoes or croquet; visit resident animals in the barn; pick apples from the orchard; or relax in the white Victorian gazebo, surrounded by the trim lawn, flowering gardens and wisteria arbors—a popular place for weddings and special gatherings.

Carmel Country Inn

Carmel Country Inn
Third Avenue and Dolores Street
P.O. Box 3756
Carmel, CA 93921
800-215-6343 ▪ 831-625-3263
Website: www.carmelcountryinn.com ▪ Email: info@carmelcountryinn.com

Room Rates:	$115–$205, including continental breakfast. AAA, AARP and AKC discounts.
Pet Charges or Deposits:	$10 per day, plus nightly room rate as deposit.
Rated: 4 Paws 🐾🐾🐾🐾	12 rooms, including suites and studios, some with fireplaces; near local attractions.

Y ou'll remember the flowers at the Carmel Country Inn—both those in the colorful gardens and the freshly cut ones placed in your room. Serving up a blend of comfort, convenience, romance and natural beauty, the inn is nestled in a quiet residential area within three blocks of the center of quaint Carmel.

Secluded in its lovely garden setting, the inn (formerly the Dolores Lodge) offers large one- and two-bedroom suites, with comfortable sitting rooms and fireplaces. Start your day off with a continental breakfast in the cheerful country kitchen before heading out to explore the village's shops, galleries and restaurants. The residential neighborhood, parks and beaches are all inviting experiences for you and your pet in this animal-friendly community.

Carmel Mission Inn – Best Western

Carmel Mission Inn Best Western
3665 Rio Road
Carmel, California 93923
800-348-9090 ▪ 831-624-1841
Website: www.bestwestern.com

Room Rates:	$89–$219. AAA and AARP discounts.
Pet Charges or Deposits:	$25 per stay. Manager's prior approval required.
Rated: 3 Paws 🐾🐾🐾	165 newly remodeled rooms and suites with terraces and guest rooms, full-service restaurant, room service, secretarial services, bicycle rentals; minutes from shopping, beaches and local attractions.

Perched at the mouth of pastoral Carmel Valley, within a private garden setting, is the Carmel Mission Inn Best Western. Here guests will find the amenities and meeting facilities of a large hotel wrapped in the intimacy and warmth of a country inn.

The historic Carmel Mission is a must-see, especially when it's only a mile away. While the inn is mere minutes from downtown Carmel's shops, art galleries, restaurants and pristine beaches, the surrounding neighborhood offers plenty of opportunities, too, for a stroll through shops and restaurants in the adjacent Barnyard and Crossroads shopping areas. If you prefer to dine in, Sassy's Bar and Grill boasts a varied menu and cocktail lounge.

To keep pets engaged during your stay, the inn offers a choice of dog runs, exercise areas and a pet playground. And remember, Carmel Beach at the end of Ocean Avenue allows supervised dogs to run free.

Cypress Inn

Cypress Inn
Lincoln Street and Seventh Avenue
P.O. Box Y
Carmel, CA 93921
800-443-7443 ▪ 831-624-3871
Web Site: www.cypress-inn.com ▪ Email: info@cypress-inn.com

Room Rates:	$125–$350, including continental breakfast
Pet Charges or Deposits:	$20 per day.
Rated: 4 Paws 🐾🐾🐾🐾	34 guest rooms.

S ince fellow animal-lover Doris Day is one of its owners, it's of little sur-prise that the historic Cypress Inn is open to pets. Built in 1929 in the heart of Carmel-by-the-Sea, the 34-room inn is known for its classic, state-ly interior and brilliant white Mediterranean exterior, with Spanish-tiled roof and intimate garden courtyard.

Each room is distinct in its character and charm, offering a choice of sitting rooms, verandahs or ocean views. While the accommodations may vary, the staff's warmth and personal attention to detail are constants here. Guests awake to a generous continental breakfast, served in the warmth of the sunny breakfast room or in the serenity of the garden courtyard. In the evening, relax in the elegant "living room" lobby with its overstuffed sofas, soft music and cozy fire.

Forest Lodge and Suites

Forest Lodge and Suites
Ocean Avenue and Torres Street
P.O. Box 1316
Carmel, CA 93921
831-624-7023

Room Rates:	$149–$240, including breakfast. Call for discounts.
Pet Charges or Deposits:	$5–$10 per stay, depending on size.
Rated: 3 Paws 🐾🐾🐾	1 deluxe room in the main house, plus 3 cottages with fireplaces and full baths (1 includes full kitchen), garden setting; near town and beach.

T ucked away in the quaint village of Carmel is the charming Forest Lodge and Suites, built in the early 1920s by Dutch immigrant and horticulturist, Johan Hagemeyer. Two of the spaces, the Garret and the Manor House, were later set up as a studio and workshop for his photography. His subjects included such famous visitors to Carmel as Salvador Dali and Albert Einstein.

Majestic oak trees and lush, flowering English gardens surround these unique accommodations. The Garret is a spacious loft in the main house, featuring a king-sized bed and fireplace. The Cottage-in-the-Glen offers a queen bed and fireplace, while the Garden House has two queen-sized beds and fireplace. The Manor House features a full kitchen, fireplace and two queen-sized beds.

Spend the day exploring the many shops, galleries and restaurants in the village. And don't forget to head down to leash-free Carmel Beach with your dog for an oceanfront romp.

Lincoln Green Inn

Lincoln Green Inn
Carmelo Street between 15th and 16th Avenues
P.O. Box 2747
Carmel, CA 93921
800-262-1262 ▪ 831-624-1880

Cottage Rates:	$95–$165.
Pet Charges or Deposits:	$20 per day. Manager's prior approval required.
Rated: 4 Paws 🐾🐾🐾🐾	4 separate cottages with kitchens, full baths, large living areas and ocean views.

Ensconced on picturesque Carmel Point, a mere stone's throw from River Beach, is the Lincoln Green Inn. As you enter the English country garden setting of this romantic, Shakespearean-style inn, you'll discover four steep-peaked, white English cottages with forest-green shutters. Each cottage has a cathedral ceiling, a large living area and bedroom, a Carmel-stone fireplace, kitchen, full bath and ocean views.

Relax on the sun deck and drink in the scenic view of the Big Sur Mountains and Carmel Point, or stroll through the wild bird reserve and lagoon adjacent to the property. Take advantage of the no-leash law on Carmel Beach for a picnic or an afternoon walk on the sandy shores with your dog.

Quail Lodge Resort and Golf Club

Quail Lodge Resort and Golf Club
8205 Valley Greens Drive
Carmel, CA 92923
888-828-8787 ▪ 831-624-2888

Room Rates:	$225 and up. AAA discount.
Pet Charges or Deposits:	None.
Rated: 5 Paws 🐾🐾🐾🐾🐾	100 luxury rooms, suites and Executive Villas; conference and banquet facilities; 18-hole golf course and four tennis courts with professional golf and tennis instructors; two pools; croquet court; hot tub; sauna; jogging, hiking and bicycling paths; picnic areas; bicycle rentals.

S et in the sunny part of Carmel among lush fairways, oak-studded meadows, rolling hills and sparkling lakes, the Quail Lodge Resort and Golf Club combines natural beauty with five-star resort elegance. From private decks and patios, each room overlooks either the lakes, the golf course or lush gardens.

Recreational pursuits include golf on the championship course, tennis, swimming, jogging or hiking with your dog. Or spend your day exploring the many shops and galleries in the quaint village of Carmel-by-the-Sea.

Start the day with breakfast at the Country Club dining room, with its scenic views of the resort. For evening dining, the award-winning Covey Restaurant has unveiled a new menu based on the abundance of fresh ingredients found on the Central Coast. With views of the lake, with its arched footbridge and lighted fountain, as well as live entertainment Wednesday through Sunday, it's a comfortable place to sit back and enjoy refreshments and the view.

Sunset House Bed and Breakfast

Sunset House Bed and Breakfast
Camino Real between Ocean and Seventh Avenues
P.O. Box 1925
Carmel, CA 93921
831-624-4884
Website: www.sunset-carmel.com • Email: sunsetbb@redshift.com

Room Rates:	$160–$190, including expanded breakfast. AAA discount.
Pet Charges or Deposits:	$20 per stay. Sorry, no cats.
Rated: 3 Paws 🐾🐾🐾	4 rooms with fireplaces, some with sitting areas, ocean views, canopy beds and kitchenettes; close to town and beach.

L ocated only a few blocks from Carmel Beach, in the heart of Carmel, this romantic inn captures the essence of this quaint town. Guests may choose from four cottage-style rooms, with their antique decor, charm and wood-burning fireplaces.

The South Room offers tree-top views with a glimpse of the blue Pacific. For privacy, try the West Room and its beamed cathedral ceiling. The North Room offers a king-sized "Hans Christian Anderson" bed, cozy sitting area and ocean view. Finally, there is the romantic canopy bed and Jacuzzi tub in the Patio Room.

No matter which accommodation you choose, you'll enjoy the uniquely decorated rooms, private baths and the pampering touch of a breakfast tray brought to your room each morning.

Vagabond House Inn

Vagabond House Inn
Fourth Avenue and Dolores Street
P.O. Box 2747
Carmel, CA 92921
800-262-1262 ▪ 831-624-7738

Room Rates:	$95–$185, including continental breakfast.
Pet Charges or Deposits:	$20 per day.
Rated: 4 Paws 🐾🐾🐾🐾	11 rooms with fireplaces, some kitchens and courtyard.

N estled in the heart of Carmel is the Vagabond House Inn, a charming brick and half-timbered English Tudor country inn. Your experience begins as you enter the delightful courtyard with its ancient oak tree, cascading waterfall, hanging plants, camellias, rhododendrons, ferns and flowers creating an almost magical atmosphere.

This is an ideal spot to daydream or relax with an intriguing book and a glass of local wine. Accommodations include guest rooms with fireplaces and traditional country decor. The guest parlor offers a variety of collections, including toys and books from the '20s, '30s and '40s. The charming courtyard is the setting for your continental breakfast, or you may have it served in your room. Then put on your walking shoes, grab the dog's leash and head out for a day of exploring the village.

Wayside Inn

Wayside Inn
Seventh Avenue and Mission Street
P.O. Box 1900
Carmel, CA 93921
800-433-4732 ▪ 831-624-5336

Room Rates:	$124–$279, including continental breakfast. AAA and AARP discounts.
Pet Charges or Deposits:	Manager's prior approval required.
Rated: 3 Paws 🐾🐾🐾	22 rooms and suites, some with wood-burning fireplaces and kitchens.

Conveniently set in the heart of downtown Carmel is the charming, Colonial Williamsburg-style Wayside Inn. Accommodations include homey furnishings, wood-paneled walls, spacious rooms and suites big enough for the entire family, including your pets. Many rooms include a wood-burning fireplace and a full kitchen.

The inn kicks off your day with a complimentary continental breakfast and newspaper delivered to your door each morning. After you have enjoyed your breakfast, take a walk around the artistic village or head to the beach with your dog, where he can run free along the sandy shoreline.

Carmel Valley Lodge

Carmel Valley Lodge
Carmel Valley Road at Ford Road
P.O. Box 93
Carmel Valley, CA 93924
800-641-4646 ▪ 831-659-2261
Website: www.valleylodge.com ▪ Email: info@valleylodge.com

Room Rates:	$119–$309, including continental breakfast. AAA and AARP discounts.
Pet Charges or Deposits:	$10 per day. Sorry, no cats.
Rated: 4 Paws 🐾🐾🐾🐾	31 guest rooms and studios and 8 cottages with fireplaces and kitchens, antique furnishings, meeting rooms, pool, sauna, whirlpool, exercise room and landscaped grounds.

When looking for a lush and relaxing setting in the sun belt of the Monterey Peninsula, the Carmel Valley Lodge has plenty to offer. Tucked into the rolling hills of sunny Carmel Valley, this quiet country inn makes a peaceful retreat for guests wishing to escape the crowds. Choose from a garden patio room, fireplace studios or individual one- and two-bedroom fireplace cottages, individually decorated with classic Shaker furniture and quilted bedspreads, with open-beamed ceilings and modern conveniences. The cottages offer the added bonus of wood-burning stoves and kitchens with microwaves.

Start each morning with freshly brewed coffee and a generous continental breakfast before heading out to explore the shops in Carmel Valley Village or wandering through the shops and galleries of Carmel. If you are feeling adventurous, you can hike through the hills with your dog, play golf or tennis, swim, ride horses or relax in the lush garden setting. The resident lodge dog, "Lucky," will gladly show you around.

Harris Ranch Inn and Restaurant

Harris Ranch Inn and Restaurant
24505 West Doris Avenue
P.O. Box 777
Coalinga, CA 93210
800-942-2333 ▪ 559-935-0717
Website: www.harrisranch.com ▪ Email: TheInn@harrisranch.com

Room Rates:	$80–$250. AAA and AARP discounts.
Pet Charges or Deposits:	$10 per day. Manager's prior approval required.
Rated: 5 Paws 🐾🐾🐾🐾🐾	123 rooms and suites, Olympic-style pool, Jacuzzis, fitness facility, conference and party rooms, grand ballroom, private airstrip, country store, restaurants, bar and lounge.

Built in 1937, the Harris Ranch Inn exudes early California charm and family hospitality. Guests may choose from 123 deluxe rooms and 28 luxury suites with a patio or balcony, overlooking the courtyard, the pool or a view of the ranch lands.

The hacienda setting beckons travelers to lounge in the courtyard by the pool, relax in the spa, work out at the fitness center or explore the spacious, landscaped grounds with a four-legged friend.

When it comes to tempting dining, guests may opt for the Ranch Kitchen, featuring the ranch's renowned beef and ranch-style meals. The Jockey Club, with a decor that pays tribute to the ranch's equestrian history and award-winning thoroughbreds, serves up beef specialties and other country favorites. Guests may also take a lunch or dinner break in The Bar and Lounge's western atmosphere.

Yosemite View Lodge

Yosemite View Lodge
11136 Highway 140
El Portal, CA 95318
800-321-5261 ▪ 209-379-2681
Web Site: www.yosemite-motels.com ▪ Email: res@yosemite-motels.com

Room Rates:	$109–$149.
Pet Charges or Deposits:	$5 per day.
Rated: 3 Paws 🐾🐾🐾	278 rooms with refrigerators and microwaves. Indoor and outdoor pools, spa. Facilities for the disabled. Fine dining, lounge and pizza parlor on premises.

T he Yosemite View Lodge offers many rooms with river views, spa tubs for two, kitchenettes and fireplaces. Refrigerators and microwaves are available in most units.

Yosemite National Park is two miles west and Badger Pass ski area is a short 35 minutes away. The Lodge is located on the Merced River, with fishing and river-rafting nearby in season.

Tenaya Lodge at Yosemite

Tenaya Lodge at Yosemite
1122 Highway 41
P.O. Box 159
Fish Camp, CA 93623
888-514-2167 ▪ 559-683-6555
Website: www.tenayalodge.com

Room Rates:	$109–$339. AAA and AARP discounts.
Pet Charges or Deposits:	$50 cleaning fee.
Rated: 4 Paws 🐾🐾🐾🐾	244 nonsmoking rooms and suites, some sunken tubs and wet bars, indoor and outdoor pools, sauna, steam room, whirlpool, data ports, conference and banquet facilities, laundry facilities, restaurant, coffee shop and cocktail lounge.

Y osemite's natural splendor has inspired the photographs of Ansel Adams and the writings of John Muir, as well as captivated millions of visitors. Just two miles from the national park's south entrance, visitors to the area will find the Tenaya Lodge.

Surrounded by acres of Sierra National Forest, this smoke-free resort invites guests to escape the hustle and bustle of the outside world. Spend the day exploring the natural wonders of the area with your pet, before escaping to the spa to relieve stress with a relaxing massage. With three restaurants on premises, guests may enjoy informal snacks or fine dining. They'll even pack a picnic for you to savor al fresco on a hike through the redwoods. The Guest Experience Center will arrange outings, too, from mountain biking to a ride on a steam-driven logging train.

For business and executive needs, the lodge has over 8,000 square feet of conference and banquet facilities.

Garden Court Inn – Best Western

Garden Court Inn – Best Western
2141 North Parkway Drive
Fresno, CA 93705
800-437-3766 ▪ 559-237-1881
Website: www.bestwestern.com

Room Rates:	$48–$62. AAA, AARP, AKC and ABA discounts.
Pet Charges or Deposits:	$10 per day. Pets under 40 pounds.
Rated: 3 Paws 🐾🐾🐾	103 spacious rooms with coffeemakers, microwaves and refrigerators, some with garden view, spacious landscaped courtyard, meeting rooms, pool and whirlpool, dog runs.

Set on 10 lusciously landscaped acres in the heart of the Central Valley is the charming Garden Court Inn – Best Western. Here travelers will find spacious accommodations overlooking the garden courtyard, with four acres of undeveloped land adjacent to the inn.

Spend part of the day relaxing in the outdoor spa or swimming pool. If land games are more your style, try your hand at shuffleboard or take the dog for a quick jog around the grounds. Be sure to ask desk personnel to direct you to the Chaffee Zoological Gardens in Roeding Park, within walking distance of the inn.

For dining, the Gaslight Steakhouse serves up prime rib, charcoal-broiled steaks, seafood, fresh-baked breads and tantalizing desserts. Try the full-service coffee shop for a more casual meal any time of the day.

Groveland Hotel

Groveland Hotel
18767 Main Street
P.O. Box 289
Groveland, CA 95321
800-273-3314 ▪ 209-962-4000
Website: www.groveland.com ▪ Email: info@groveland.com

Room Rates:	$125–$200. AAA discount.
Pet Charges or Deposits:	Manager's prior approval required.
Rated: 3 Paws 🐾🐾🐾	17-room bed and breakfast hotel, all rooms with private baths, European antiques, down comforters.

F ounded in 1849, the Groveland Hotel was once part of a thriving gold mining town. Today the original adobe hotel has been combined with an adjacent Queen Anne-style hostelry, originally built in 1914 to house VIP guests. The elegant, 17-room bed and breakfast hotel has recently undergone a million-dollar renovation, yet has retained its 19th-century character ensuring travelers a look into the past while they enjoy modern comforts.

Groveland offers guests and their pets the luxury of wide-open spaces. Go fishing, hiking, try white-water rafting on the Tuolumne River, visit the nearby Gold Rush towns or explore the natural bounty of Yosemite National Park. After a day of adventure in this slice of small-town California, amidst the spectacular scenery of the Sierra Nevada, relax in the courtyard with a glass of spirits from the saloon before sampling the hotel restaurant's seasonal cuisine.

The Groveland Hotel Restaurant features outstanding cuisine prepared from California seasonal ingredients. Most herbs are from the hotel's garden.

Zaballa House Bed and Breakfast

Zaballa House Bed and Breakfast
324 Main Street
Half Moon Bay, CA 94019
650-726-9123
Website: www.zaballahouse.com • Email: info@zaballahouse.com

Room Rates:	$105–$265, including full breakfast. AAA and AARP discounts.
Pet Charges or Deposits:	$10 per stay. Manager's prior approval required. Sorry, no cats.
Rated: 3 Paws 🐾🐾🐾	19 guest rooms and 4 suites with private baths, some with whirlpool tubs and fireplaces.

O n historic Main Street, within walking distance of shops and restaurants, stands the historic Zaballa House. Built in 1859, it is the oldest building in Half Moon Bay.

This friendly inn offers guests a casual, homey atmosphere. Put your feet up and relax in front of the fire with a book or magazine in the parlor or enjoy the privacy of your room, decorated with antiques, original oil paintings and wallpaper. All rooms offer private baths, some with double-sized whirlpool tubs, and fireplaces.

Sample the large breakfast menu before heading out for a day of beachcombing or hiking with your dog, or go bicycling, horseback riding, shopping or sightseeing. In the evening, you're invited to relax and socialize with the other guests, with complimentary beverages and hors d'oeuvres in the front parlor.

Madera Valley Inn – Best Western

Madera Valley Inn – Best Western
317 North G Street
Madera, CA 93637
559-673-5164
Website: www.bestwestern.com

Room Rates:	$65–$88. AAA, AARP, AKC and ABA discounts.
Pet Charges or Deposits:	Small pets only.
Rated: 3 Paws 🐾🐾🐾	93 rooms and suites, some with refrigerators; secluded, heated pool, laundry service, coffee shop and cocktail lounge.

Madera Valley Inn – Best Western is set in the nation's fruit bowl, just minutes from Yosemite National Park, Kings Canyon and Sequoia National Park. Guests will appreciate spacious rooms and the convenience of the coffee shop, open for any meal of the day. Vacationers heading to the lake with boats and trailers will find ample parking here.

Since the inn is near the western Sierra Nevada Mountains, it's a convenient winter destination with access to ski areas. In the spring and summer, the allure is fishing, boating, water skiing, hiking or exploring nearby Yosemite, Kings Canyon and Sequoia parks, where you and your dog can enjoy nature at its best.

Katherine's House Bed and Breakfast Retreat

Katherine's House Bed and Breakfast Retreat
201 Waterford Avenue
Mammoth Lakes, CA 93546
760-934-2991
Web Site: www.katherineshouse.com ▪ Email: katherine@katherineshouse.com

Room Rates:	$95–$205, including full breakfast and evening wine and hors d'oeuvres.
Pet Charges or Deposits:	$10 per day; includes biscuits and walking.
Rated: 3 Paws 🐾🐾🐾	2 guest suites and 2 cottages.

Katherine's House is a vintage Mammoth chalet-style home nestled in a quiet residential neighborhood and surrounded by massive Jeffrey pines. The modern and elegant interior is decorated with antiques and boasts original artwork. The home faces southeast, toward the distant White Mountains of Nevada and the nearby Sherwin Mountain Range. Ski lifts are a short five-minute drive.

The Morning Suite offers a large master bedroom with a king-sized bed, fireplace and large expanse of windows. Luxuriate in the marble-and-glass block bath, complete with Jacuzzi tub.

The cottages are self contained with full kitchen and living rooms and have TVs and VCRs. All the beds are luxuriously comfortable, with down comforters and flannel sheets.

Sequoia Inn – Best Western

Sequoia Inn – Best Western
1213 V Street
Merced, CA 95340
800-735-3711 ▪ 209-723-3711
Website: www.bestwestern.com

Room Rates: $45–$85. AAA and AARP discounts.
Pet Charges or Deposits: Small pets only.
Rated: 3 Paws 🐾🐾🐾 98 remodeled rooms, heated pool, cable and color TV, free
HBO, 85 miles to Yosemite National Park.

A Central Valley landmark and favorite resting stop for travelers heading to Yosemite National Park, the Sequoia Inn offers visitors comfortable accommodations with a selection of guest-room amenities such as complimentary coffee, microwaves, refrigerators and free in-room movies. Business travelers will be pleased with the moderate rates and the convenient meeting and conference facilities. The restaurant and lounge offer California cuisine in comfortable, pleasant surroundings. Pets and children stay free.

Bay Park Hotel

Bay Park Hotel
1425 Munras Avenue
Monterey, CA 93940
800-338-3564 • 831-649-1020
Website: www.bayparkhotel.com • Email: info@bayparkhotel.com

Room Rates:	$85–$160. AAA discount.
Pet Charges or Deposits:	$5 per day.
Rated: 3 Paws 🐾🐾🐾	80 rooms; meeting rooms, pool and restaurant, near shopping and local attractions.

S et among the Monterey pines at the crest of Carmel Hill, Bay Park Hotel stands midway between the quaint charm of Carmel-by-the-Sea and the history of Monterey, affording views of the bay and wooded hillside. The rustic allure of its natural wood decor comes packaged with modern amenities such as remote-control TV, air conditioning, clock radios and morning coffee.

Priding itself on its "family style" operation, the hotel is across the street from a city park for you and your pet to enjoy, as well as the Del Monte Shopping Center for an afternoon of shopping. For relaxing after a day of local adventures, guests have the option of a bricked spa, full-sized pool, gazebo or the hotel's Crazy Horse Restaurant and Bar.

Monterey Beach Hotel – Best Western

Monterey Beach Hotel – Best Western
2600 Sand Dunes Drive
Monterey, CA 93940
800-242-8627 ▪ 831-394-3321
Website: www.montereybeachhotel.com ▪ Email: reservations@montereybeachhotel.com

Room Rates:	$89–$219. AAA and AARP discounts.
Pet Charges or Deposits:	$25 per stay.
Rated: 3 Paws 🐾🐾🐾	196 large rooms; ocean views, conference and meeting facilities, pool, whirlpool, restaurant and cocktail lounge.

The Monterey Beach Hotel is the area's only beachfront hotel. As such it affords guests miles of California's most scenic views of the white dunes and sandy beaches encircling Monterey Bay.

Many rooms come equipped with microwaves and refrigerators for in-room snacks, or you can enjoy a meal any time of the day or night from the hotel's restaurant, perched on the top floor with a grand view. The new lounge on the main floor invites guests to enjoy afternoon hors d'oeuvres and spirits while watching a colorful sunset.

Monterey Fireside Lodge

Monterey Fireside Lodge
1131 Tenth Street
Monterey, CA 93940
800-722-2624 ▪ 831-373-4172

Room Rates:	$69–$299, including continental breakfast.
Pet Charges or Deposits:	$10–$20 per day. Manager's prior approval required.
Rated: 3 Paws 🐾🐾🐾	23 rooms and 1 suite with wood-burning fireplace and wet bar.

L ocated one mile from downtown Monterey and Fisherman's Wharf, the Monterey Fireside Lodge offers clean, comfortable rooms at affordable rates.

All rooms include coffeemakers, free movies, refrigerators and cable TV.

Lake El Estero is a convenient block away, offering Fido an opportunity to run in the park and on the lakeside paths.

Victorian Inn

Victorian Inn
487 Foam Street
Monterey, CA 93940
800-232-4141 ▪ 831-373-8000

Room Rates:	$169–$449, including continental breakfast and afternoon wine and cheese reception. AAA, AARP and AKC discounts.
Pet Charges or Deposits:	$100 deposit of which $25 is nonrefundable. Manager's prior approval required.
Rated: 3 Paws ❖❖❖	68 rooms with fireplaces, private patios, balconies or window seats; hot tub, walking distance to local attractions; "Pooch Package" given upon check-in.

L ocated on Monterey's historic Cannery Row, the Victorian Inn combines the best of old and new in what it calls "an oasis of tranquillity." Guests step into hospitality and classic luxury upon entering any of the 68 guest rooms, which include marble fireplaces and honor bars, with either a private patio, balcony or window seat.

To make guests feel welcome, the inn plays host to an afternoon wine and cheese reception in the parlor, a lavish continental breakfast and, for the canine guests, presents a "Pooch Package" containing a bowl with the inn's logo, filled with dog cookies, bottled water and a postcard for Fido to send to a friend back home.

Andril Fireplace Cottages

Andril Fireplace Cottages
569 Asilomar Boulevard
Pacific Grove, CA 93950
831-375-0994
Website: www.andrilcottages.com ▪ Email: inquiries@andrilcottages.com

Cottage Rates:	$58–$300. Call for discounts.
Pet Charges or Deposits:	$14 per day.
Rated: 3 Paws 🐾🐾🐾	16 cottages with separate living areas and kitchens, fireplaces, some with decks or yards, and a 5-bedroom ranch house, all in a private setting near the beach.

L ocated on a quiet corner in a residential area near the beautiful Pacific Ocean is the charming Andril Fireplace Cottages. This relaxing hideaway consists of sixteen separate cottages set among the pine trees, within walking distance of Asilomar State Beach. Each cottage offers a woodburning fireplace, homey, comfortable furnishings, a fully equipped kitchen, color television with cable and a private telephone.

For your recreational pleasure there is Ping Pong, a spa and barbecues. Take advantage of your location for a leisurely stroll along the beach with your dog, explore the numerous tidepools, or merely take a few moments to enjoy the breathtaking sunset. Everything is within easy reach of your accommodations. After your day sightseeing and visiting all the local shops and galleries, you will appreciate the comfortable, homey feeling of a cozy fire in your private cottage.

Lighthouse Lodge and Suites

Lighthouse Lodge and Suites
1150 Lighthouse Avenue
Pacific Grove, CA 93950
800-858-1249 ▪ 831-655-2111
Web Site: www.lhls.com ▪ Email: jsmith7303@aol.com

Room Rates:	$79–$149, including expanded continental breakfast and daily afternoon Barbecue. AAA discount.
Pet Charges or Deposits:	None.
Rated: 3 Paws 🐾🐾🐾	63 guest rooms. Outdoor heated pool, spa and sauna.

As a guest of either property you are located at the corner of Lighthouse and Asilomar Avenues, adjacent to Point Pinos Lighthouse and just a one-block stroll from the ocean.

The Lodge sits amongst the pine trees and backs up to the city's 18-hole, ocean-side golf course. A good choice for family budgets, guest rooms include remote-controlled cable TV, in-room coffee service and a complimentary, extended continental breakfast buffet. Afternoon include a complimentary poolside barbecue, weather permitting.

Each five-star suite includes a king-sized bed with down pillows, in-room fireplaces, over-sized Jacuzzi tubs and plush terry robes, mini-kitchenettes with stocked honor bars, large-screen televisions with cable and remote control. Optional living room and larger suites are available as well.

EdgeWater Inn

EdgeWater Inn
1977 West Manning Avenue
Reedley, CA 93654
800-479-5855 ▪ 559-637-7777

Room Rates:	$49–$125. AAA and AARP discounts.
Pet Charges or Deposits:	$7 per day. Small pets only.
Rated: 3 Paws 🐾🐾🐾	50 rooms and master suites, heated pool, whirlpool, air conditioning and some refrigerators. Close to national parks and lakes.

F resno County's Blossom Trail is a 63-mile, self-guided driving tour showcasing the beauty of California's wildflowers and agriculture. Located on the Blossom Trail, a mere 500 feet from the sparkling Kings River, the EdgeWater Inn offers guests comfort and convenience framed in scenic surroundings.

You and your travel companion, human or canine, may laze next to the river under large trees or partake of this Sierra river's different personalities, with white-water rafting or a quiet canoe tour. The inn boasts a large swimming pool and spa, and for the younger set, there is an adjacent toddler's lot. Large master suites provide home-like amenities, including spacious living rooms and dining rooms, as well as microwaves and refrigerators.

This little river town, dubbed "The World's Fruit Basket," also features some of the oldest homes in Fresno County, while the Mennonite Quilting Center and downtown shops offer turn-of-the-century charm. The EdgeWater is the closest inn to Kings Canyon and Sequoia parks.

Barlocker Rustling Oaks Ranch Bed and Breakfast

Barlocker Rustling Oaks Ranch Bed and Breakfast
25252 Limekiln Road
Salinas, CA 93908
831-675-9121

Room Rates:	$100–$250, including breakfast.
Pet Charges or Deposits:	$20 per day. Horse boarding available. Manager's prior approval required.
Rated: 3 Paws 🐾🐾🐾	3 guest rooms and 1 cottage. Outdoor pool.

R elax under the old rustling oaks in lush, green Steinbeck Country, as you imagine cowboys working on this cattle ranch, which was built in the 1940s. Surrounded by fertile Salinas Valley agricultural lands, Barlocker's is located within a short drive of many of Monterey County's award-winning wineries.

Enter the spacious serenity of the Barlocker home and you'll find a friendly, quiet living room just perfect for curling up and reading your favorite novel. Continuing through the old ranch house, the paneled, knotty-pine family room offers a warm, inviting fireplace, large-screen television with satellite, and a pool table. Your host, Margaret Barlocker, will serve you a full breakfast in the sunny dining room or outside, overlooking the picturesque hillside.

Horseback riding, trail rides and horse boarding are also available.

Homewood Suites Hotel

Homewood Suites Hotel
10 West Trimble Road
San Jose, CA 95131
800-225-5466 ▪ 408-428-9900
Website: www.homewood-suites.com

Room Rates:	$89–$262, including expanded continental breakfast. AAA and AARP discounts.
Pet Charges or Deposits:	$275 deposit of which $200 is refundable. Pets under 30 pounds.
Rated: 3 Paws 🐾🐾🐾	140 suites, business center, conference facilities, secretarial services, heated pool, whirlpool, sports court, exercise room, laundry facilities, in-room data ports, airport transportation, convenience store, manager's reception.

T he spacious, apartment-style accommodations of Homewood Suites offer guests separate living and sleeping areas, furnished with the amenities of home such as remote-controlled televisions, a VCR, data ports, voice-mail message system and a fully equipped kitchen. The expanded continental breakfast and evening social hour in the lodge are opportunities to mingle with other guests.

After breakfast, guests may choose to lounge by the pool or swim a few laps, work out in the exercise center, join in a game at the sports/activity court or head out for a day of thrills at the nearby Paramount's Great America Theme Park.

Business travelers will appreciate the 24-hour executive center, with use of personal computers, modem and copier, secretarial services, free incoming faxes, discounted outgoing faxes and Federal Express drop-off sites.

Westin Santa Clara

Westin Santa Clara
5101 Great America Parkway
Santa Clara, CA 95054
800-WESTIN-1 ▪ 408-986-0700
Website: www.westin.com ▪ Email: clara@westin.com

Room Rates:	$275–$325. AAA discount.
Pet Charges or Deposits:	Small pets only.
Rated: 4 Paws 🐾🐾🐾🐾	505 rooms and suites, business center, conference facilities, heated pool, sauna, whirlpool, 18-hole golf course, tennis courts, exercise facilities, restaurant and cocktail lounge, 24-hour room service, in-room coffeemakers, honor bars and refrigerators.

Located in the heart of Silicon Valley, next to Paramount's Great America Theme Park and near the Santa Clara Valley vineyards, the Westin Santa Clara is a popular destination for both business and leisure travelers. The 14-story facility offers rooms and suites equipped with the creature comforts of home and a luxury hotel. Eight Westin Guest Offices outfit business travelers with high-tech office setups and services.

Enjoy the flavor and activities of the area by visiting Northern California's pre-eminent theme park, featuring rides and entertainment. If golf or tennis is more your style, the Santa Clara Golf and Tennis Club is next door and features a par-72 championship golf course and tennis center, both with professional instructors. To keep fit away from home, guests can work out in the hotel's private fitness center with exercise equipment, sauna and heated outdoor pool with whirlpool spa. There are even jogging and hiking trails nearby. For your dog's enjoyment, there is an exercise area at the hotel and a park nearby.

Ocean Front Vacation Rental House

Ocean Front Vacation Rental
Mailing Address: 1741 Wilcox Way, San Jose, CA 95125
1600 West Cliff Drive
Santa Cruz, CA 95060
800-801-4453 ▪ 408-266-4453
Website: www.oceanfronthouse.com ▪ Email: reservations@oceanfronthouse.com

House Rates:	$300 and up per night. AARP discount. Call for weekly rates.
Pet Charges or Deposits:	$200 refundable deposit. Manager's prior approval required. Sorry, no cats.
Rated: 4 Paws 🐾🐾🐾🐾	3 bedroom/2 bath home sleeps up to eight people; full kitchen.

I f you're looking for a real "home away from home" for a relaxing family vacation at the beach or an extended business trip, this furnished Ocean Front Vacation Rental may be ideal. Many vacationers choose these accommodations because they enjoy cooking for themselves and prefer the homelike surroundings, with enclosed back yard and ocean views. Pets are welcome, but should not to be left alone in the house or yard. A list of pet sitters is available.

Guests may venture along miles of shoreline flanked by prestigious West Cliff Drive and explore secluded beaches with their pets. Or, if you like amusement parks, head over to the Santa Cruz Beach and Boardwalk for a day of entertainment before returning to relax in front of a roaring fire as you watch the sun go down.

Ocean Pacific Lodge

Ocean Pacific Lodge
120 Washington Street
Santa Cruz, CA 95060
800-995-0289 ▪ 831-457-1234
Email: oceanpac@infopoint.com

Room Rates:	$70–$176, including continental breakfast. AAA and AARP discounts.
Pet Charges or Deposits:	$20 per stay. Small pets only.
Rated: 3 Paws 🐾🐾🐾	68 rooms and suites, heated pool, meeting and banquet facilities, laundry facilities, exercise room; close to the ocean and boardwalk.

Located just two blocks from the beach, Ocean Pacific Lodge offers comfortable accommodations in the heart of Santa Cruz's beach resort community. For guests mixing business with pleasure, the lodge offers in-room fax and computer hookups and fully equipped meeting facilities. The lodge features large rooms and suites, many with in-room micro-fridges, as well as a complimentary continental breakfast.

Walk to the Santa Cruz Beach and Boardwalk for a day of sun, fun, midway games and amusement park rides, or visit the downtown area's restaurants and unique shops. The area boasts numerous parks and beaches for a picnic, a day of beachcombing or a game of catch with your dog.

The Redwoods In Yosemite – Year-Round Vacation Home Rentals

The Redwoods In Yosemite – Year Round Vacation Home Rentals
8038 Chilnualna Falls Road
P.O. Box 2085 Wawona Station
Yosemite National Park, CA 95389
209-375-6666
Website: www.redwoodsinyosemite.com ▪ Email: info@redwoodsinyosemite.com

Room Rates:	$82–$438.
Pet Charges or Deposits:	$15 per stay. Manager's prior approval required.
Rated: 3 Paws 🐾🐾🐾	Over 130 fully equipped rustic cabins and modern homes, spacious decks and fireplaces, located in Yosemite National Park.

T he Redwoods In Yosemite offers lodging choices ranging from rustic one-bedroom cottages and cabins to spacious, modern six-bedroom homes, all nestled among the forest and mountain streams of Wawona.

In winter, visitors revel in spectacular downhill and cross-country skiing at Badger Pass. Spring brings rebirth to the park's natural beauty, especially their own Chilnualna Falls. Summer is the perfect time to take a trail or stagecoach ride at Wawona Stables, play a round of golf at Wawona Golf Course, take a refreshing dip or wet your fishing line in one of the many streams and creeks. In the fall, enjoy the crisp days and colorful changes in the foliage and nights around a campfire. No matter what the season, nature is at your doorstep in Yosemite.

Central California

Leashes are required unless otherwise stated.

APTOS

Rio Del Mar Beach is a wide, sandy strip of beach on Rio Del Mar Boulevard. There is plenty of room for you and Rover to stretch your legs and get your feet wet. For more information, call (831) 688-3222.

BIG SUR

Pfeiffer Big Sur State Beach is off Highway 1 on narrow, winding Sycamore Canyon Road. Enjoy the awe-inspiring view from the white sand beaches as the treacherous waves of the Pacific Ocean crash against the rocks, sea caves and natural arches. Leashes are required. For more information, call (831) 648-3130.

CARMEL

Carmel City Beach is off Highway 1 at the bottom of Ocean Avenue. Here you and your pet can enjoy a leash-free romp, a dip in the water or a stroll along the cypress-lined walking path together. For more information, call (831) 624-3543.

CARMEL VALLEY

Garland Ranch Regional Park, off Highway 1 on Carmel Valley Road, is great if wide-open spaces are more to your liking. This leash-free paradise has 9 miles of scenic trails and 4,500 acres of oak, willow and maple trees. It's an out-door experience you and your pup will never forget. For more information, call (831) 659-4488.

ELKHORN SLOUGH NATIONAL WETLANDS RESERVE AND SANCTUARY

Situated near Moss Landing (between Castroville and Watsonville) off Highway 1, you can take several hours to explore this vast home to native flora and fauna. There are hundreds of species of birds, small mammals and fish. A visitors' center demonstrates both the history of the sanctuary and the uses of wetlands throughout the United States. You and your pet walk on boardwalks that are slightly above the wetlands themselves. Take plenty of film for this adventure. Nearby Moss Landing, commercial fishing hub of Monterey Bay, has numerous antique shops, excellent seafood restaurants and the ambiance of an Italian fishing village. For more information, call (831) 728-5939.

FRESNO

Kearney Park was formerly a 225-acre estate and is now a scenic park. The exquisite mansion and ancient trees are a sight to behold. The park is 7 miles west of Fresno on Kearney Boulevard. There is a small fee.

Kings River Special Management Area is a wild trout fishery on the Kings River. This exceptional recreation area consists of 49,000 acres in the Sierra and Sequoia National Forests. Take Belmont Avenue east, which turns into Trimmer Springs Road, and continue around Pine Flat Reservoir, past Kirch Flat Campground, over the bridge and along Kings River to the Special Management Area. For more information, call (559) 855-8321.

Pine Flat Lake is a wonderful area for a day of picnicking and playing with your dog. Here you will find incredible views, a trickling stream, ancient oak trees and a beautiful blue lake. If you are a fisherman, you might want to wet your line. To reach the lake, take Belmont Avenue east, which turns into Trimmer Springs Road, and follow it for 35 miles to the lake. For more information, call (559) 787-2589.

Woodward Park consists of 300 acres of lush fields, woods, lakes and streams to explore. The park is also a bird refuge, so you may want to bring your binoculars, too. Take Highway 41 and exit at Friant Road, head northeast, then turn left on East Audubon Drive and continue to the main entrance. There is a parking fee. For more information, call (559) 498-1551.

HALF MOON BAY

Bean Hallow State Beach is off Highway 1, 18 miles south of town. There is a level projection above the beach where you can explore and watch the sea lions. For more information, call (415) 879-0832.

Davenport Beach is full of untouched sand dunes and breathtaking ocean views. This is a chance for your dog to run leash-free. Head south on Highway 1, past Ano Nuevo State Park for 9 miles to Davenport. There you will find plenty of parking along the highway. For more information, call (831) 462-8333.

McNee Ranch State Park has spectacular views from several trails, ranging from sea level to nearly 2,000 feet. It can get warm, so bring enough water for both you and your pooch. For more information, call (916) 653-6995.

MERCED

There are several neighborhood parks with plenty of running room:

Ada Givens Park, at Hawthorn Avenue and Ada Givens School
Applegate Park, between M and R Streets
Burbank Park, at Olive Avenue and Burbank School
Circle Drive Park, at East 23rd Street and Circle Drive
Courthouse Park, at 21st and M streets
Fahrens Park, at Buena Vista Drive
Flanagan Park, at East Cone Avenue
Gilbert Macias Park, at Child Avenue and G Street
Joe Herb Park, at Yosemite Parkway and Parsons
McNamara Park, at 11th and Canal streets
McReady Park, at Grogan Avenue and McReady Drive
Rahilly Park, at Parsons Avenue and Flying Circle
Santa Fe Strip Park, at Buena Vista Drive and M Street
Stephen Leonard Park, at 7th and T streets

MONTEREY

Jack's Peak Regional Park, off Highway 68 on Jacks Peak Road, offers 8.5 miles of paths and trails to wander, plus panoramic views of Carmel Valley and Monterey Bay, from Monterey Peninsula's highest point. For more information, call (831) 755-4899.

Monterey and Pacific Grove share a wonderful, scenic walking/jogging and bike path that stretches from Lovers Point on Sunset Drive in Pacific Grove, around the cliffs that hug the Monterey Bay, through Monterey's famed Cannery Row, and on past Fisherman's Wharf along Del Monte Avenue, ending at Canyon Del Rey.

PACIFIC GROVE

Asilomar State Beach, on Sunset Drive between Monterey and Pebble Beach, offers a stretch of rugged coastline to explore and remarkable tide pools. For more information, call (831) 372-4076.

George Washington Park is leash-free from sunrise to 9 a.m. and 4 p.m. to sunset. It is full of tall pine trees and picnic tables and is a popular hangout for locals and their dogs. It is bordered by Melrose Avenue, Short Street, Alder Street and Pine Avenue. For more information, call (831) 648-3100.

Lynn "Rip" Van Winkle Open Space is leash-free from sunrise to 9 a.m. and 4 p.m. to sunset. There is plenty of open space and lots of trails to explore. Located across from Forest Grove Elementary School, just outside the non-toll section of Seventeen Mile Drive, the entrance is a small, dirt parking lot on your right.

Take Sunset Drive, turn right on Congress Avenue. The unmarked parking area is on the right, just past the school.

REEDLEY

Hillcrest Tree Farm is a peaceful little park for you and your dog to explore. It is on Reed Road at Adams, north of Reedley.

Pioneer Park is a nice place to pack a lunch and spend the day with your four-legged friend. This neighborhood park is on the corner of G and 8th streets.

SAN JOSE

Almaden Quicksilver County Park has 3,600 acres and 15 miles of trails to explore. There is a wonderful picnic area and lots of wildflowers. Take Highway 85 to the Almaden Expressway, then exit south for 4.5 miles to Almaden Road to Mockingbird Hill Lane, turn right and follow it to the parking area. For more information, call (408) 268-3883.

Anderson Lake Park is 2,365 acres of open space. Here you will find a great 15-mile pathway that wanders along Coyote Creek through the trees and abundant wildlife. If you like fly-fishing, you will enjoy trying your luck at Coyote Creek, which is open for fishing from April to November. Anderson Reservoir is a great place to wet your line, too. The park can be accessed from Cochrane Road in Morgan Hill, east of Highway 101 to Monterey Road until you reach Burnett Avenue. There is an entry fee posted at the gate. For more information, call (408) 779-3634.

Calero Park has wonderful views of the Santa Cruz Mountains. It is a great place for a picnic and is full of wildflowers in the spring. It is good place for fishing if you like to catch and release; it is not advisable to eat the fish. Dogs are not allowed on the beach, but there is plenty of room to explore. Take Almaden Expressway south to Harry Road, turn right, then left on McKean Road to reach the park entrance. For more information, call (408)268-3883.

Coyote Hellyer Park is 223 beautiful acres west of the Hellyer Avenue exit from Highway 101. Wander along the stream, through the tall trees, and get back to nature. It is a great place for a picnic or a barbecue with the family. A 15-mile hike along Coyote Creek leads to Anderson Park. The entrance fee is posted at the ranger station. For more information, call (408) 225-0225.

Joseph D. Grant County Park is in the Diablo Range of the Coastal Mountains. The views are spectacular and so is the wildlife. It is a wonderful place to hike in the spring, when the wildflowers are in bloom. Fees are posted at the park entrance. The areas that allow dogs are posted, too. To reach the park, take Mount Hamilton Road to the east for 8 miles, to Alum Rock Avenue. For more information, call (408) 274-6121.

Kelley Park is popular with the locals. There are great walking paths for you and your dog to explore. There is a parking fee on holidays and weekends. The park is on Senter Road, between Tully Road and Keyes Street.

Lexington County Park encompasses a 450-acre lake where you can spend the day boating or fishing or just enjoying the surrounding scenery with your dog. The fees are posted at the entrance. Dogs are restricted to certain areas. To reach the park, take Interstate 880 to Old Santa Cruz Highway and continue on to Aldercroft Heights Road. This leads to Alma Bridge Road; follow that to the parking area. For more information, call (408) 867-0190.

At Penitencia Creek County Park, several small parks were combined to make an 83-acre park along Penitencia Creek. It is great for a relaxing picnic with your dog. Fees are posted at the entrance. The park is bounded by Noble Avenue, Jackson and Mabury streets. Dogs are restricted to certain areas. For more information, call (408) 358-3741.

SANTA CLARA

Central Park, off Kiely Boulevard, has 52 acres of trails to wander. It is a great place to soak up some sun or have a picnic.

Lexington Reservoir, off Highway 17 at Alma Bridge Road, is a lovely park where you and your dog can fish, swim or spend the day exploring the park. For more information, call (408) 358-3741.

Santa Clara Dog Park, the only leash-free park in Santa Clara, is at 3445 Lochinvar Avenue, near Lawrence Expressway and Homestead Road. This is a dog's paradise. Here he can run and play with other dogs. There are pooper scoopers, fresh water and a small enclosed dog run with benches for the humans.

SANTA CRUZ

Bonny Doon Beach, off Highway 1 on Bonny Doon Road, is an isolated, peaceful beach surrounded by high bluffs. It is a great place to spend the day beachcombing, playing fetch with your dog or picnicking. For more information, call (831) 462-8333.

East Cliff Drive offers access at several points to dog-friendly beaches. From around 12th Street to 41st Street, there are streets leading to several beaches. Try the beach off Seabright between the Boardwalk and the Yacht Harbor.

Mitchell's Cove Beach, on West Cliff Drive between Almar and Woodrow avenues offers you and your dog an opportunity to romp the beach leash-free from dawn to 10 a.m. and 4 p.m. to sunset.

Pleasure Point Beach is off East Cliff Drive on Pleasure Point Drive. This is a surfers' paradise, but your pooch will love it, too. Climb down the staircase to reach the sandy beach or walk the trail around the cliff for a bird's-eye view.

West Lighthouse Beach, on West Cliff Drive, is leash-free from dawn to 10 a.m. and 4 p.m. to sunset. It is a nice stretch of beach for a run or just a good game of Frisbee. For more information, call (831) 429-3777.

SEQUOIA AND KINGS CANYON NATIONAL PARK

The park's 1,139,519 acres are scattered with the largest living sequoia trees, many reaching 30 feet in diameter and more than 200 feet tall, as well as with magnificent forests of ponderosa and sugar pine trees. The park extends from the foothill of the San Joaquin Valley to the crest of the High Sierras with the highest point reaching 14,494 feet. The wildlife ranges from mule deer to the common chipmunk, so your dog will have a ball with all the creature smells. Here you and your dog can go camping, picnicking, hiking, boating, fishing, swimming or horseback riding. There also are nature programs and a visitors' center. Dogs are not allowed on trails or in public buildings. There are several ways to access the park and many more things to see and do. It is recommended that you call the superintendent of the park for directions, recreation and camping information at (559) 565-3134.

YOSEMITE NATIONAL PARK

Set aside as the nation's first state park by Abraham Lincoln on June 30, 1864, Yosemite became a national park 26 years later. This region of unusual, breathtaking, natural beauty lies in Central California on the western slope of the Sierra Nevada and consists of 1,169 square miles of land. There are more than 800 miles of trails to explore and more streams, creeks and rivers than you could fish in a week. The main paved route to Yosemite is State Route 140 from Merced. At the park, you can go camping, hiking, fishing, boating, bicycling, swimming, river rafting and horseback riding. There are plenty of food service areas, visitors' centers, lodges and different types of cabins. Dogs and cats are welcome in the park in the Upper Pines, in Yosemite Valley, the west end of the campgrounds at Tuolumne Meadows, at White Wolf, Bridal Veil Falls, Crane Flat, Wawona, Hodgdon Meadows, and Yosemite Creek campgrounds. They are not allowed on trails or in public buildings. For information on the park, its restrictions on pets and accommodations, call the park superintendent at (209) 372-0200 or 372-0265.

Southern California

Residence Inn by Marriott

Residence Inn by Marriott
1700 South Clementine Street
Anaheim, CA 92802
800-331-3131 ▪ 714-533-3555
Website: www.residenceinn.com

Suite Rates:	$178–$224, including breakfast buffet. AAA and AARP discounts.
Pet Charges or Deposits:	$40 per stay. $10 per day.
Rated: 3 Paws 🐾🐾🐾	200 suites with fully equipped kitchens and some fireplaces, daily maid service, grocery shopping service, heated pool, whirlpool, Sport Court, health club privileges, meeting facilities, complimentary evening beverage.

L ocated near major Southern California attractions, the Residence Inn by Marriott will appeal to business travelers and vacationers alike. From the spacious accommodations with separate sleeping and living areas, the fully equipped kitchens, grocery shopping service, laundry facilities, room service from any of the local restaurants, work areas and meeting facilities, to the manager-hosted continental breakfast buffet and informal hospitality hour, the inn seems more like a home than a hotel.

For recreation, the retreat offers a heated swimming pool, whirlpool, toddlers' pool, barbecue areas and a Sport Court where you can play a game of basketball, volleyball or tennis. Your pet can join you for a stroll around the groomed grounds.

Residence Inn by Marriott

Residence Inn by Marriott
321 East Huntington Drive
Arcadia, CA 91006
800-331-3131 ▪ 626-446-6500
Website: www.residenceinn.com

Suite Rates:	$101–$139, including breakfast buffet. AAA and AARP discounts.
Pet Charges or Deposits:	$40 per stay. $10 per day.
Rated: 3 Paws 🐾🐾🐾	120 suites, some with fireplaces, fully equipped kitchens, meeting rooms, heated pool, whirlpool and Sport Court.

I f you're looking for that "at home" feeling, look no further than the Residence Inn by Marriott. Whether you choose an oversized studio or a penthouse suite, all accommodations offer a fully equipped kitchen, microwave and comfortable living area. Guests will enjoy the complimentary grocery shopping service, satellite television, laundry facilities, valet service, curbside parking, shuttle service and more.

After a hard day at work or play, unwind with a game of basketball or tennis on the Sport Court, take a swim in the heated pool, relax in the whirlpool or take the dog for a stroll on the pet walk. The evening hospitality hour, weekly manager's barbecue and neighborhood setting add a social flavor to your stay.

Residence Inn by Marriott

Residence Inn by Marriott
4241 Chester Lane
Bakersfield, CA 93309
800-331-3131 • 661-321-9800
Website: www.residenceinn.com

Suite Rates:	$115–$135, including breakfast buffet. AAA discount.
Pet Charges or Deposits:	$40 per stay. $6 per day.
Rated: 4 Paws 🐾🐾🐾🐾	114 suites, some with fireplaces, central courtyard, meeting rooms, putting green, exercise room and Sport Court.

Consistently rated among the top 20 hotels in the nation, Residence Inn by Marriott is a leader in extended stay lodging for families and business travelers. You'll discover a warm, homey feeling the minute you walk into the townhouse-like building.

With amenities such as a complimentary breakfast buffet, evening hospitality hour, weekly barbecue or dinner, spacious suites with full kitchens, guest laundry facilities and computer hookups, you will feel right at home. The landscaped grounds, walkways and central courtyard foster a community setting. For recreation, there is a pool with heated spa, a Sport Court for tennis, basketball and volleyball and a putting green so you can get in some practice before you hit the course. There are also dog runs and exercise areas for your pet's recreational and exercise needs.

Rio Bravo Resort

Rio Bravo Resort
11200 Lake Ming Road
Bakersfield, CA 93306
888-517-5500 ▪ 661-872-5000
Web Site: www.riobravoresort.com ▪ Email: relax@riobravoresort.com

Room Rates:	$68–$225. AAA and AARP discounts.
Pets Charges or Deposits:	$50 refundable deposit. Sorry, no cats.
Rated: 3 Paws 🐾 🐾 🐾	103 guest rooms and 7 suites. Pool, spa, lighted tennis courts. Restaurant and lounge.

R io Bravo Resort offers spectacular views of the southern Sierras for a romantic interlude or a peaceful retreat. Private balconies and patios overlook rolling hills, panoramic vistas, Lake Ming and the Kern River.

Guest rooms are generously sized, each with coffeemaker and patio balcony. Rio Bravo features an Olympic-sized heated pool, a smaller lodge pool, 3 Jacuzzis, saunas in both the men's and women's locker rooms and a fully equipped fitness center with personal training available, as well as a variety of exercise classes. Professionally ranked Rio Bravo Tennis Club offers 19 lighted courts for competition or pleasure.

A myriad of activities await, including sand volleyball, whitewater rafting, wind-surfing, sailing, power-boating, kayaking, fishing, hiking and nature tours on the Kern River and on Lake Ming. Public and private golf courses are minutes from the resort, which is conveniently located near downtown Bakersfield.

Regent Beverly Wilshire

Regent Beverly Wilshire
9500 Wilshire Boulevard
Beverly Hills, CA 90212
800-545-4000 ▪ 310-275-5200

Room Rates:	$325 and up.
Pet Charges or Deposits:	Small pets only.
Rated: 4 Paws 🐾🐾🐾🐾	275 elegant rooms and suites, business center, meeting and conference facilities, heated pool, saunas, whirlpool, health club, valet laundry service, 24-hour room service, coffee shop, restaurant and cocktail lounge.

L ocated in the heart of Beverly Hills, the historic Regent Beverly Wilshire generously proportioned guest rooms have housed dignitaries, celebrities and discerning travelers since 1928. The attention to detail is evident by the services of the 24-hour personal room attendants, the attentive concierge staff, the oversized and understated rooms, the use of natural fabrics and hues, the opulent bathrooms with their deep soaking tubs and separate showers, the plush terry robes, premium toiletries, dual phone lines and executive-sized desks.

Nothing is overlooked, including your pet. Upon arrival, canine guests receive a dish of biscuits and bottled water to make their stay more comfortable.

For your dining pleasure, select from the creative California-Continental cui-

sine in the Dining Room, have cappuccino overlooking Rodeo Drive in the Café, high tea or cocktails in the European ambiance of the Lobby Lounge or a brandy in The Bar.

Shore Acres Lodge

Shore Acres Lodge
40090 Lakeview Drive
P.O. Box 110410
Big Bear Lake, CA 92315
800-524-6600 ▪ 909-866-8200
Web Site: www.bigbearvacations.com ▪ Email: shoreacres@bigbear.net

Cottage Rates:	$85–$500. Call for discounts.
Pet Charges or Deposits:	$5 per day.
Rated: 3 Paws 🐾🐾🐾	100 cottages. Private boat dock, swimming, barbecues, volleyball and badminton. Close to village and ski slopes.

Big Bear Lake is located in the San Bernardino mountains, about a two-hour drive from Los Angeles. Here you will find two world-class ski resorts in the winter and a wide variety of outdoor activities, including boating, hiking, mountain biking and jet skiing in the summer.

Shore Acres Lodge is one of Big Bear's finest lakefront lodges, offering a warm, family atmosphere with easy access to all activities for summer and winter getaways.

In addition, Shore Acres Vacation Rentals features many fine homes and cabins that include living rooms with fireplaces, large, fully equipped kitchens, washers and dryers and scenic decks to enjoy the views. All rentals are fully equipped with bed linens, towels, kitchen utensils, telephones and VCRs.

Timberline Lodge

Timberline Lodge
39921 Big Bear Blvd.
Big Bear Lake, CA 92315
800-803-4111 ▪ 909-866-4141
Web Site: www.thetimberlinelodge.com ▪ Email: timberline@bigbear.com

Room Rates:	$71–$260. AAA and AARP discounts.
Pet Charges or Deposits:	$10 per day. $100 refundable deposit. Manager's prior approval required. Sorry, no cats.
Rated: 3 Paws 🐾🐾🐾	13 cabins, 2 private homes offering wood-burning fireplaces, color cable TV and many with full kitchens. Heated pool, barbecue with picnic tables, large fire-pit bonfires, volleyball, horseshoes, basketball and spacious children's playground.

Nestled in the pines of Big Bear Lake, The Timberline Lodge is a resort for all seasons, offering individual, beautiful lakeview cabins. Close to Big Bear Village and ski slopes, this area offers fishing, boating, hiking and horseback riding right next door.

The cabins feature fireplaces, private phones, full kitchens and daily maid service.

Wildwood Resort

Wildwood Resort
40210 Big Bear Boulevard
P.O. Box 2885
Big Bear Lake, CA 92315
888-294-5396 ▪ 909-878-2178
Web Site: www.wildwoodresort.com ▪ Email: info@wildwoodresort.com

Room Rates: $60–$150.
Pet Charges or Deposits: $10 per day. Manager's prior approval required.
Rated: 3 Paws 🐾🐾🐾 15 individual cabins and 4 mini-suites. Heated outdoor pool and spa.

Wildwood Resort is located on more than an acre of grassy tree-shaded grounds with picnic tables, barbecues, and a playground for the children. You are within walking distance of restaurants, shopping and the Alpine Slide, and minutes from ski resorts, the village and the lake.

Each of the cabins features complete kitchens with refrigerators, stoves and ovens, as well as cable TV and phones. Many offer wood-burning fireplaces. All linens are provided, as well as maid service.

Walker River Lodge

Walker River Lodge
100 Main Street
Bridgeport, CA 93517
800-688-3351 ▪ 760-932-7021

Room Rates:	$60–$125
Pet Charges or Deposits:	None.
Rated: 3 Paws 🐾🐾🐾	36 rooms and suites, landscaped grounds, whirlpool, heated pool, refrigerators, some microwaves, gift shop.

Walker River Lodge is nestled in a valley of the Eastern Sierras in the historic town of Bridgeport. Located right on East Walker River, many rooms face the riverfront, where guests may take advantage of some of the finest trout fishing in the Sierras.

Guests will appreciate the large, comfortable accommodations, satellite television, heated pool and spa. For non-fishing guests, there are plenty of sights to see: Bodie Ghost Town, Mono Lake, Twin Lakes, Virginia Lakes, snow skiing in the winter, the natural hot springs and Yosemite National Park. Or opt to relax by the peaceful river with a picnic lunch or barbecue.

Hilton Burbank Airport and Convention Center

Hilton Burbank Airport and Convention Center
2500 Hollywood Way
Burbank, CA 91505
800-445-8667 ▪ 818-843-6000
Website: www.hilton.com

Room Rates: $121–$480. AAA and AARP discounts.
Pet Charges or Deposits: $50 deposit refundable. Pets under 50 pounds.
Rated: 3 Paws 🐾🐾🐾   403 guest rooms and 83 suites, some with fireplaces and
                                         mountain views, 2 pools, exercise room, meeting facilities,
                                         airport transportation, cocktail lounge, dining room and coffee
                                         shop.

T he Burbank Airport Hilton and Convention Center, near Southern California attractions, offers guests hospitality, spacious suites with panoramic mountain views, meeting facilities and convenience.

The hotel is 10 minutes from Universal Studios, 30 minutes from Magic Mountain and 50 minutes from Disneyland. Before or after taking in the local attractions, enjoy the hotel's saunas, spas or pools. Or if you are up for a workout, head to the hotel's fitness center.

For dining and entertainment, visit famous Daily Grill. Here you can enjoy casual dining while listening to live music from the piano bar.

La Quinta Inn

La Quinta Inn
150 Bonita Road
Chula Vista, CA 91910
800-687-6667 ▪ 619-691-1211
Website: www.laquinta.com

Room Rates:	$61–$175, including First Light™ breakfast. AAA and AARP discounts.
Pet Charges or Deposits:	$25 refundable deposit. Small pets only.
Rated: 3 Paws 🐾🐾🐾	142 rooms, expanded in-room entertainment system, refrigerators and microwaves.

For business travelers or vacationers, La Quinta Inn offers spacious rooms with plenty of amenities. From the crisp white exterior, softly colored lobby and relaxing atmosphere, guests will feel right at home in quiet, comfortable accommodations.

Kids of all ages will enjoy the latest video games and in-room, first-run movies viewed on the expanded entertainment system. You and your dog will appreciate the landscaped, spacious grounds.

Included in the price of your accommodations is a complimentary breakfast, featuring your choice of cereal, fresh fruit, bagels, pastries, juice, milk and coffee. You can work off your breakfast at the health club.

Crown City Inn

Crown City Inn
520 Orange Avenue
Coronado, CA 92118
800-422-1173 ▪ 619-435-3116
Web Site: www.crowncityinn.com

Room Rates:	$85–$199. AAA and AARP discounts.
Pet Charges or Deposits:	$8 per day. Manager's prior approval required.
Rated: 3 Paws 🐾🐾🐾	32 guest rooms, some with kitchens. Outdoor pool. Restaurant.

T his intimate Inn is centrally located within the resort community of Coronado Island. You are just a pleasant walk from the beach, the Hotel Del Coronado and the Old Ferry Landing.

Guest rooms are newly redecorated and feature refrigerators, microwaves, color televisions with HBO, and in-room coffee service. The Café Bistro restaurant, known for its French and American entrées, is open for breakfast, lunch and dinner.

Residence Inn by Marriott

Residence Inn by Marriott
881 Baker Street
Costa Mesa, CA 92626
800-331-3131 ▪ 714-241-8800
Website: www.residenceinn.com

Suite Rates:	$119, including breakfast buffet. AAA, AARP, AKC and ABA discounts.
Pet Charges or Deposits:	$10 per day. $40 per stay.
Rated: 3 Paws 🐾🐾🐾	144 suites with fully equipped kitchens, oversized living areas, many with fireplaces, large work desks, grocery shopping service, fitness center, Sport Court, barbecue grills, pet exercise area.

N ear Disneyland and beaches, the Residence Inn affords a home-away-from-home type of environment. The spacious rooms and suites, many with wood-burning fireplaces, fully equipped kitchens, oversized living area, separate sleeping areas and daily housekeeping service make this inn a convenient place to stay, whether you are traveling for business or pleasure.

A great way to get to know your neighbors and enjoy a meal is to take advantage of the breakfast buffet and complimentary hospitality hour during the week, with a light buffet dinner and drinks, which are both included as part of your room rate. Barbecue grills located throughout the property are an opportunity for a dining change of pace.

The expansive, beautifully landscaped grounds and selected exercise areas are a welcome relief from ordinary hotels for both you and your pet.

Westin South Coast Plaza

Westin South Coast Plaza
686 Anton Boulevard
Costa Mesa, CA 92626
800-WESTIN-1 ▪ 714-540-2500
Website: www.westin.com ▪ Email: south@westin.com

Room Rates:	$145–$225. AAA and AARP discounts.
Pet Charges or Deposits:	$50 refundable deposit. Small pets only. Manager's prior approval required.
Rated: 4 Paws ☙☙☙☙	373 deluxe rooms and 17 luxury suites, all with honor bars, coffeemakers, large work desks, data ports, irons and ironing boards, hair dryers, children's recreation program, outdoor heated pool, sun deck, lighted tennis courts, fitness center, valet and laundry service, 24-hour room service, meeting and conference facilities, grand ballroom, covered and valet parking, gift shop, restaurant and lounge.

S ituated in the heart of Southern California's cultural and entertainment area, the Westin South Coast Plaza offers guests oversized guest rooms, world-class luxury suites with all the amenities and personalized service.

For leisure, there's a children's recreation program, pool and sun deck, jogging trails, tennis courts and a fully equipped fitness center. Or take advantage of the guest access to the Spa at South Coast Plaza, only a short stroll from the hotel, across the Unity Bridge.

With more than 50 restaurants within walking distance of the hotel, there are dining options for every palate. Pinot Provence brings the flavor and feeling of Southern France to Costa Mesa. The Lobby Lounge is the place to unwind with a cocktail and appetizers before dinner.

Embassy Suites Hotel

Embassy Suites Hotel
8425 Firestone Boulevard
Downey, CA 90241
800-EMBASSY ▪ 562-861-1900
Website: www.embassy-suites.com

Suite Rates:	$125–$169, including full breakfast. AAA and AARP discounts.
Pet Charges or Deposits:	$15 per day.
Rated: 3 Paws 🐾🐾🐾	219 suites with private bed and living rooms, refrigerators and microwaves; indoor pool, sauna, steam room, whirlpool, exercise room, meeting rooms, secretarial services, complimentary evening beverages, restaurant, laundry service, gift shop, exercise area for dogs.

L ocated in the heart of Southern California, the Embassy Suites Hotel offers guests the convenience and luxury of a first-class hotel at an affordable rate. The spacious, two-room suites give you that homey feeling while offering all the added amenities a business traveler or vacationing family needs. Relax in the lush tropical gardens of the eight-story atrium courtyard with its rock waterfall and koi-filled ponds as you enjoy the manager's reception.

Awake to a complimentary morning newspaper and a full cooked-to-order breakfast. For an intimate dinner, Gregory's Restaurant overlooks the hotel's atrium and features such main dishes as Chicken Jerusalem and Steak Dijon. Top off your evening with a nightcap at Gregory's Lounge.

Welk Resort Center

Welk Resort Center
8860 Lawrence Welk Drive
Escondido, CA 92026
800-932-9355 ▪ 760-749-3000
Website: www.welkresort.com

Room Rates:	$160–$190. AAA, AARP, AKC and ABA discounts.
Pet Charges or Deposits:	$50 refundable deposit. Manager's prior approval required.
Rated: 3 Paws 🐾🐾🐾	132 rooms, some with refrigerators, meeting facilities, putting green, 18-hole executive golf courses, pro shop, 2 pools, whirlpools, valet laundry, Lawrence Welk Resort Theater and Museum, coffee shop, deli, buffet dinner theater, restaurant and lounge.

T he Welk Resort Center is set on 1,000 scenic acres of rugged, unspoiled hills and valleys. Each of the spacious rooms has a panoramic view of the golf course and surrounding hills, a private patio or balcony, a micro-fridge and many other amenities.

The resort offers guests their choice of endless activity or complete serenity. Play golf on one of three meticulously maintained 18-hole courses, relax in the sun by the pool or in one of the spas, enjoy a tennis match or take your dog for a hike in the surrounding hills.

At the Lawrence Welk Resort Theater and Museum you can enjoy lunch or dinner, as well as entertaining Broadway musicals with professional casts. For dining any time of the day, the Resort Restaurant offers an extensive selection of home-cooked entrées.

Joshua Tree Inn Bed and Breakfast

Joshua Tree Inn Bed and Breakfast
61259 Twenty-Nine Palms Highway
P.O. Box 340
Joshua Tree, CA 92252
800-366-1444 ▪ 760-366-1188
Website: www.joshuatreeinn.com ▪ Email: inn@joshuatreeinn.com

Room Rates:	$65–$220. AAA, AARP, AKC and ABA discounts.
Pet Charges or Deposits:	$10 per day. Horse corrals are available.
Rated: 3 Paws 🐾🐾🐾	10 comfortable rooms and semi-suites, with private showers, full suites with complete kitchens and baths, all furnished with antiques and Old West memorabilia, a main living room, dining room, study, patio and pool.

Minutes from the gateway of the scenic 500,000-acre Joshua Tree National Park is the Joshua Tree Bed and Breakfast Inn. This high-desert retreat strives to make you feel right at home with its charming antique furnishings and gourmet home-cooked breakfast prepared from scratch.

If you and your dog are feeling adventurous, box lunches are available for the asking, so you can spend the day exploring Joshua Tree National Park with its mines, man-made dam, endless trails for hiking or horseback riding, and even geological tours.

For a romantic evening, a candlelight dinner under the stars can be arranged. The desert nights are famous for their clear skies and panoramic views. For an evening of entertainment, the Hi-Desert Playhouse is right next door and is known for first-rate theatrical productions.

La Jolla Marriott

La Jolla Marriott
4240 La Jolla Village Drive
La Jolla, CA 92037
800-228-9290 • 619-587-1414
Website: www.marriott.com

Room Rates:	$198–$650. AARP discount.
Pet Charges or Deposits:	Small pets only.
Rated: 4 Paws 🐾🐾🐾🐾	360 rooms and 16 luxury suites, whirlpool, saunas, indoor and outdoor pools, health club, game room, restaurants, cocktail lounge, valet parking, ballroom, meeting and conference facilities, gift shop, close to major attractions.

S ituated in the heart of La Jolla's business district and minutes from major attractions, the La Jolla Marriott offers impeccable service and striking elegance combined with business and banquet facilities. The climate-controlled rooms and luxury suites offer guests amenities that range from the basics to Concierge Level upgrades.

Dining options include the Garden Court, with indoor and outdoor seating, or Character's Bar and Grill for sports action. The La Jolla Marriott prides itself on being a hotel big enough for an impressive reception or business conference, yet small enough for personal service.

Residence Inn by Marriott

Residence Inn by Marriott
8901 Gilman Drive
La Jolla, CA 92037
800-531-5900 ▪ 858-587-1770
Website: www.residenceinn.com

Suite Rates:	$155–$275, including breakfast buffet. AAA and AARP discounts.
Pet Charges or Deposits:	$10 per day. $75 per stay.
Rated: 3 Paws 🐾🐾🐾	288 suites, all with living rooms and separate sleeping areas, some with fireplaces; meeting facilities, 2 heated pools, whirlpool, Sport Court, complimentary evening beverages, laundry facilities, airport transportation, pet exercise area.

When it comes to relaxation and affordable accommodations with all the amenities of home, look no further than Residence Inn by Marriott. And since pet owners would not feel at home unless the "entire family" was along, the inn has allocated certain Pet Suites. Here await comfortable rooms and suites more inviting than an ordinary hotel. That's likely due to the wood-burning fireplace, separate sleeping and living areas, the grocery shopping service and the complimentary hospitality hours during the week.

Start the day with the breakfast buffet served at the Gatehouse, followed by a day of sightseeing or a visit to some of the major attractions—or stay where you are and relax by the pool, swim a few laps or venture to the Sport Court for a game of tennis, volleyball or basketball. Pets have their own exercise area, too.

Residence Inn by Marriott

Residence Inn by Marriott
14419 Firestone Boulevard
La Mirada, CA 90638
800-331-3131 ▪ 714-523-2800
Website: www.residenceinn.com

Suite Rates:	$115–$140, including breakfast buffet. AAA, AARP, AKC and ABA discounts.
Pet Charges or Deposits:	$6 per day. $75 per stay. Pets under 35 pounds.
Rated: 3 Paws 🐾🐾🐾	146 suites with fully equipped kitchens, pool, Jacuzzi, exercise room, Sport Court, laundry facilities, meeting facilities, business services, room service, manager-hosted evening hospitality, near all major attractions.

I f you need accommodations for a short business trip or an extended family vacation that offer plenty of space and the comforts of home, then La Mirada's Residence Inn fits the bill. Here your suite will be larger than the normal hotel room, with the convenience of a fully equipped kitchen and private sleeping area.

Start your morning with a refreshing Gatehouse breakfast. For aquatic relaxation, the pool or the Jacuzzi may call to you. For a workout, the inn's exercise room has all the equipment you will need, or join some of the other guests in a game of basketball or tennis on the Sport Court. You and your pet can enjoy a stroll through the manicured grounds before you head out for a day of business, sightseeing or visiting some of the area's major attractions. Top off your day with complimentary evening beverages and hors d'oeuvres served either in the Gatehouse or poolside.

Casa Laguna Bed and Breakfast Inn

Casa Laguna Bed and Breakfast Inn
2510 South Coast Highway
Laguna Beach, CA 92651
800-233-0449 ▪ 949-494-2996

Room Rates:	$79–$249, including continental-plus breakfast, afternoon tea and wine. AAA discount.
Pet Charges or Deposits:	$5 per day. Manager's prior approval required.
Rated: 3 Paws 🐾🐾🐾	15 guest rooms and 5 suites with ocean views, tropical garden and heated pool.

T erraced on a hillside amid tropical gardens and flower-splashed patios, the Casa Laguna Inn exudes an ambiance of bygone days, when Laguna Beach was developing its reputation as an artists' colony and hideaway for Hollywood film stars.

The mission-style architecture features guest rooms and suites that are decorated in a mixture of antique, collectable and contemporary furnishings. The many beautiful garden areas include the aviary patio, beneath a family of queen palms, the bougainvillea-splashed courtyard and the ocean-view pool deck with its banana and avocado trees.

Two beaches are located across from the Casa. This property is very popular with pet owners, as there are several walkways and other areas to exercise your pet.

Prophets Paradise Bed and Breakfast

Prophets Paradise Bed and Breakfast
26845 Modoc Lane
Lake Arrowhead, CA 92352
800-987-2231 ▪ 909-336-1969

Room Rates:	$100–$160, including gourmet breakfast.
Pet Charges or Deposits:	$20 per day. Small pets only. Manager's prior approval required.
Rated: 3 Paws 🐾🐾🐾	4 spacious rooms with private baths, some with fireplaces, decorated with antiques; game room, gym, exercise area for pets.

Set in the beautiful mountain resort of Lake Arrowhead is Prophets Paradise Bed and Breakfast. This multi-level inn offers four uniquely decorated rooms with antiques, oak and wicker furnishings, stained glass, featherbeds and intimate decks from which to enjoy your gourmet breakfast. All rooms have private baths, some have wood-burning fireplaces, refrigerators and wet bars.

Having been in the motion picture business for years, the innkeepers kindly share their collection of memorabilia and artifacts with their guests. You are welcome to enjoy the billiard room, work out in the gym, play horseshoes or swing under the giant oak tree. There are wonderful winding paths for you and your dog to explore, with hewn-log benches to stop for rest or repose.

Saddleback Inn

Saddleback Inn
300 South State Highway 173
P.O. Box 1890
Lake Arrowhead, CA 92352
800-858-3334 ▪ 909-336-3571
Web Site: www.lakearrowhead.com/saddleback ▪ E-mail: info@saddlebackinn.com

Room Rates: $90–$225, including breakfast. AAA discounts.
Pet Charges or Deposits: $8 per day.
Rated: 3 Paws 🐾🐾🐾 28 guest rooms and 6 suites, with fireplaces and Jacuzzi tubs. Restaurant and bar.

Located in the mile-high resort of Lake Arrowhead, the Inn is situated in the San Bernardino National Forest, providing year-round recreation.

Saddleback Inn features guest rooms and cottages with queen- or king-sized beds, stone fireplaces, double whirlpool baths, heated towel racks and refrigerators. Varieties of suite combinations afford excellent lodgings for families and groups, as well as for individuals and couples.

The Inn's architecture and furnishings are a blending of Victorian mountain and country styles, complimented by Laura Ashley prints and fabrics.

Quails Inn at Lake San Marcos Resort

Quails Inn at Lake San Marcos Resort
1025 La Bonita Drive
Lake San Marcos, CA 92069
800-447-6556 ▪ 760-744-0120
Website: www.quailsinn.com ▪ Email: info@quailsinn.com

Room Rates:	$99–$299. AAA and AARP discounts.
Pet Charges or Deposits:	$10 per day. Manager's prior approval required.
Rated: 3 Paws 🐾🐾🐾	142 lakeside rooms and apartments with balconies or patios, 16 with wet bars, refrigerators, whirlpool baths; meeting rooms, 2 heated pools, boating, tennis courts, exercise room, golf courses.

San Diego's only lakeside resort, the Quails Inn offers distinctive lakeside rooms and comfortable suites.

There are a variety of activities to keep you entertained, including tennis, swimming, boating and canoeing on the mile-long lake. If golf is your game, try the resort's 72-par championship course or the hilly, par-58 executive course.

Spacious one- or two bedroom lakeside apartments, complete with kitchenettes, dining and sitting areas, are near Southern California attractions and the heart of San Diego. For on-site dining, guests may choose either the acclaimed Quails Inn Dinnerhouse or the Country Club Restaurant.

Quality Inn and Executive Suites

Quality Inn and Executive Suites
1621 North H Street
Lompoc, CA 93436
800-224-6530 ▪ 805-735-8555
Website: www.qualitysuites.com

Room Rates:	$69–$109. AAA discount.
Pet Charges or Deposits:	$25 per stay.
Rated: 3 Paws 🐾🐾🐾	218 rooms, some larger efficiency rooms, 91 executive suites, meeting rooms, heated pool, whirlpool, exercise area for dogs.

A t the southern end of the Central Coast Mountain Range, the Quality Inn and Executive Suites is set in the scenic Lompoc Valley. Surrounded by historic missions, fields of colorful flowers, blue skies and friendly people, guests may choose from several distinctive rooms and suites.

When choosing the deluxe room, guests enjoy the added bonus of a microwave and refrigerator. The executive suite adds a sitting area and kitchenette. Of course, all rooms and suites include in-room coffee, guest laundry facilities, full health club privileges, massage salon and use of the heated pool and spa. For guests traveling with their animals, there is a pet exercise area.

Century Plaza Hotel and Tower

Century Plaza Hotel and Tower
2025 Avenue of the Stars
Los Angeles, CA 90067
800-WESTIN-I • 310-277-2000
Website: www.centuryplazala.com • Email: centu@westin.com

Room Rates:	$300–$435. AAA discount.
Pet Charges or Deposits:	Small pets only.
Rated: 4 Paws ❧❧❧❧	1,072 rooms and suites with ocean and city views, wet bars, stocked refrigerators, twice-daily maid service, 24-hour concierge and room service, laundry and valet service, complimentary Town Car service, international business center, pool, guest passes for the Century Plaza Spectrum Club and the Century City Tennis Club; multilingual staff.

A djacent to Beverly Hills, in the heart of the fashionable Westside of Los Angeles and minutes from major attractions is the Century Plaza Hotel and Tower. Here you'll find spacious accommodations with private lanais or balconies, magnificent views and amenities galore.

Whether in town on business or pleasure, travelers will appreciate the opportunity to relax by the garden swimming pool, work out the stresses of the day at one of the poolside fitness centers or take a relaxing stroll among the acres of lush gardens with the dog.

For a diversion from the ordinary dining fare, the Terrace il ristorante features Mediterranean cuisine fused with a Northern Italian flair. The Café Plaza offers casual indoor or outdoor dining for any meal of the day.

Four Seasons – Regent Hotel

Four Seasons – Regent Hotel
300 South Doheny Drive
Los Angeles, CA 90048
800-332-3442 ▪ 310-273-2222
Website: www.fourseasons.com

Room Rates:	$325 and up. AAA discount.
Pet Charges or Deposits:	Small pets only. Pets under 15 pounds. Pets older than 1 year.
Rated: 4 Paws 🐾🐾🐾🐾	285 guest rooms and suites with private bar, VCR, fax machine, voice mail, multi-line phones and computer hookups; heated pool, whirlpool, exercise room, massage, twice-daily maid service, 24-hour concierge services, meeting rooms, exercise area for pets, complimentary limousine service to Rodeo Drive, 24-hour room service and award-winning restaurants.

O verlooking Beverly Hills and greater Los Angeles, the Four Seasons – Regent Hotel features residential-style guest rooms and suites decorated with floral, Oriental, contemporary or eclectic designs. All rooms offer amenities such as refrigerated bars, computer hookups, 24-hour room and laundry service and twice-daily maid service. Situated among a lush garden on the fourth floor are the outdoor swimming pool and Jacuzzi, with a tented exercise and massage center.

For award-winning dining, Gardens Restaurant offers contemporary California cuisine. For an informal menu, there's The Café or the Poolside Terrace. Top off your evening at the Windows Lounge, featuring nightly entertainment and cocktails.

Your pets will be treated to dinner service, offering a choice of personal favorites prepared to their specifications, before a pet care specialist takes charge of the dog-walking duties.

Hotel Nikko at Beverly Hills

Hotel Nikko at Beverly Hills
465 South La Cienega Boulevard
Los Angeles, CA 90048-4001
800-NIKKO-US ▪ 310-247-0400

Room Rates:	$245 and up.
Pet Charges or Deposits:	$100 deposit. Pets under 5 pounds. Manager's prior approval required.
Rated: 4 Paws 🐾🐾🐾🐾	300 contemporary rooms with CD stereo system, in-room fax, business and conference facilities, data ports, secretarial services, valet laundry, heated pool, saunas, exercise room, airport transportation, restaurant and cocktail lounge.

Situated at the edge of Beverly Hills, the Hotel Nikko is only minutes from major area attractions. When entering the lobby, visitors will likely be struck by the contrast and beauty of another world. The advanced technology of this highly automated hotel is discreetly hidden by the soothing colors and simple elegance. Business travelers will appreciate the extra thought put into the design of the luxurious work environment; the perfect place for a small conference or intimate business dinner.

Upon entering your room, you will be greeted by the aroma of a fresh bouquet of flowers. The neutral palette of colors and hand-made artwork make an immediate visual impression. Guests are offered the ultimate in amenities, a generous living room, a spacious bedroom, a luxurious bath and powder room, walk-in closet and private dining area.

Dining choices include the Hana Lounge and Bar for casual dining or the

Pangaea Restaurant and Private Dining Room, with its use of fresh exotic ingredients, prepared in the finest tradition of European artistry.

Hotel Sofitel Los Angeles

Hotel Sofitel Los Angeles
8555 Beverly Boulevard
Los Angeles, CA 90048
800-521-7772 ▪ 310-278-5444
Web Site: www.hotelsofitel.com

Room Rates:	$189–$550. AAA and AARP discounts.
Pet Charges or Deposits:	$25 per stay.
Rated: 4 Paws 🐾🐾🐾🐾	311 guest rooms and 13 suites. Le Club Fitness, heated outdoor pool, sun deck and sauna. Restaurant and lobby bar piano lounge.

You are welcomed by the warmth and elegance of a small French-style hotel with Mediterranean architectural details. Many of the guest rooms and suites offer spectacular views of the Hollywood Hills. Relax in the cozy comfort and style of Pierre Deux French country decor, while surrounded by every amenity you might desire.

The new Le Club Fitness offers state-of-the-art equipment available to you 24 hours a day. The Hotel Sofitel is conveniently located across the street from the Beverly Center on Restaurant Row, minutes from the world-class shops of Rodeo Drive, trendy Melrose Place and the hottest nightspots on Sunset Boulevard.

Barnabey's Hotel

Barnabey's Hotel
3501 Sepulveda Boulevard
Manhattan Beach, CA 90266
800-552-5285 ▪ 310-545-8466
Web Site: www.calanderlive.com/barnabeyshotel

Room Rates:	$129–$169. AAA discount.
Pet Charges or Deposits:	None.
Rated: 3 Paws ❧ ❧ ❧	120 guest rooms. Heated outdoor covered pool with fireplace and hot tub, complimentary access to local fitness center. Restaurant and lounge.

Barnabey's is a charming blend of Victorian elegance with modern-day convenience. This full-service boutique hotel is built around beautiful gardens, yet is only a short 10-minute drive from Los Angeles International Airport.

Located in the oceanside community of Manhattan Beach, you are one mile from the beach and within walking distance of shops, movies and restaurants.

The award-winning Auberge Restaurant serves breakfast, lunch and dinner in a private setting, decorated with antiques and crystal chandeliers. The Pub, a lively setting for cocktails and casual dining, features live dance music and a big-screen TV.

Colorado River Inn – Best Western

Colorado River Inn – Best Western
2371 Needles Highway
Needles, CA 92363
800-528-1234 ▪ 760-326-4552
Website: www.bestwestern.com ▪ Email: hotel@ctaz.com

Room Rates:	$45–$75. AAA and AARP discounts.
Pet Charges or Deposits:	Small pets only.
Rated: 3 Paws 🐾🐾🐾	63 rooms, some with refrigerators and microwaves, heated indoor pool, sauna and whirlpool.

When looking for a desert oasis set among palm trees, the Colorado River Inn – Best Western has 63 comfortable rooms from which to choose, some with microwaves and refrigerators. Guests may opt to refresh themselves in the indoor heated swimming pool or relax in the sauna or whirlpool.

Located between Barstow and Kingman, Arizona, near the Colorado River, the inn's location is convenient to water skiing, wind surfing and swimming. There is plenty of room for you and your pet to get your daily exercise, not only around the inn, but along the riverbank, too. If you like to gamble, the Laughlin Casinos are only 25 minutes from the inn.

Four Seasons Hotel

Four Seasons Hotel
690 Newport Center Drive
Newport Beach, CA 92660
800-332-3442 ▪ 949-759-0808
Web Site: www.fourseasons.com

Room Rates:	$315 and up. AAA and AARP discounts.
Pet Charges or Deposits:	Pets under 15 pounds. Manager's prior approval required.
Rated: 4 Paws 🐾🐾🐾🐾	285 guest rooms including 96 suites. Tennis courts, pool, spa and fitness center. Two restaurants and lounge.

Amidst lush gardens, a sparkling pool and magnificent palms, the Four Seasons Newport Beach has been honored by AAA with their highest award, Five Diamonds. It is minutes from endless beaches and Southern California's wealth of cultural, sports, family and entertainment attractions.

Rising above the blue Pacific, 19 levels offer distinguished accommodations, many with panoramic views from private balconies. Guest rooms are exceptionally spacious, with fully stocked refrigerated bars, thick terry robes and twice-daily maid service.

The Pavilion Restaurant features inviting cuisine of Italy and the Mediterranean, artfully presented with a fresh California influence.

Hyatt Newporter

Hyatt Newporter
1107 Jamboree Road
Newport Beach, CA 92660
800-233-1234 ▪ 949-729-1234
Website: www.hyattnewporter.com

Room Rates: $159 and up. AAA discount.
Pet Charges or Deposits: $50 per stay. Pets up to 50 lbs.
Rated: 4 Paws ❤❤❤❤ 405 rooms and suites, plus 4 private villas with private
          pools and fireplaces, tennis courts, 9-hole golf course, 3 pools,
          3 spas, health club, jogging and bicycling trails, business center,
          secretarial services, laundry, beauty salon and dress shop,
          restaurants and lounges, dog runs and exercise areas; near
          major attractions.

Set on 26 acres of lush gardens, the Hyatt Newporter overlooks the bay of Newport Beach. Enjoy the panoramic view of the bay from your balcony as the fresh sea air washes over you. At this luxury resort, guests may relax by one of the heated pools, play tennis or a few rounds of golf, jog or bike on the trails or visit the health club. Take some time out for a game of fetch with your dog at the beach or explore the gardens of this paradise. If amusement parks are for you, you will appreciate the convenient proximity to major area attractions.

The casual atmosphere of the hotel's Jamboree Café features American classic cuisine, while Italian dishes are in store at Ristorante Cantori. Join other guests for cocktails, fun and conversation at the Lobby Bar.

Ojai Valley Inn

Ojai Valley Inn
Country Club Road
Ojai, CA 93023
800-422-6524 ▪ 805-646-5511
Website: www.ojairesort.com

Room Rates:	$235 and up. AAA discount.
Pet Charges or Deposits:	$25 per day. Small pets only.
Rated: 4 Paws 🐾🐾🐾🐾	207 deluxe rooms and suites with balconies or patios, fireplaces and mini-bars, 18-hole golf course, tennis courts, 2 pools, fitness center, whirlpool, steam rooms and saunas, conference rooms, horseback riding, petting farm.

Nestled on 220 enchanted acres is the mountain resort of Ojai Valley Inn. Built in 1923 in traditional Spanish style as a golf clubhouse, the building is now the focal point of the new and updated inn. The stunning setting fosters relaxation, inspiration, exhilaration, adventure and romance.

There are activities for all ages: a children's petting farm and Camp Ojai program, tennis courts, an 18-hole championship golf course, horseback riding, biking, hiking, swimming and an exercise area for the dog.

For real relaxation, try the 31,000-square-foot luxury spa facilities, where you will be pampered with a facial or massage, or relax in one of the steam rooms or whirlpools. The art studio is a wonderful place for self-discovery, or if you prefer, relax and meditate in the beautiful wooded landscape surrounding the village plaza.

Residence Inn by Marriott

Residence Inn by Marriott
2025 Convention Center Way
Ontario, CA 91764
800-331-3131 ▪ 909-937-6788
Website: www.residenceinn.com

Suite Rates:	$140–$175, including breakfast buffet. AAA and AARP discounts.
Pet Charges or Deposits:	$6 per day. $50–$75 per stay.
Rated: 3 Paws 🐾🐾🐾	200 suites with fully equipped kitchens and some fireplaces, heated swimming pool, whirlpool, Sport Court, health club privileges, meeting facilities, complimentary dog bowls, complimentary evening beverage.

I f you're looking for that "at home" feeling, that's the trademark of Residence Inn by Marriott. Whether you choose an oversized studio or a penthouse suite, the professional staff knows how to make you feel welcome. All accommodations offer a fully equipped kitchen, microwave and separate living and sleeping areas. Upon check-in, your dog will receive bowls with the inn's logo to make their stay more comfortable.

Guests will appreciate the complimentary grocery shopping service, satellite television, laundry facilities, valet service, curbside parking and more. After a hard day at work or play, unwind with a game of basketball or tennis on the Sport Court, take a dip in the heated pool or relax in the whirlpool. The landscaped grounds invite a stroll with your dog. The evening hospitality hour, weekly manager's barbecue and neighborhood setting will make you feel right at home.

Estrella Inn at Palm Springs

Estrella Inn at Palm Springs
415 South Belardo Road
Palm Springs, CA 92262
800-237-3687 ▪ 760-320-4117
Website: www.estrella.com ▪ Email: info@estrella.com

Room Rates:	$79–$300, including daily California breakfast. AAA, AARP, Entertainment and Quest discounts.
Pet Charges or Deposits:	$20 per day. Sorry, no cats.
Rated: 4 Paws 🐾 🐾 🐾 🐾	64 guest rooms, suites and bungalows, three pools and two spas, outdoor barbecues, shuffleboard and volleyball courts, golf and tennis arrangements.

T he Estrella Inn is a desert hideaway that is still one of Palm Springs best-kept secrets, but with $4 million in restorations, the cat will soon be out of the bag. Built in the 1930s and once host to stars of Hollywood's golden era, the entire inn has been remodeled. Most rooms are adorned with antiques and unusual beds and one-of-a-kind pieces, while others boast a desert feel with Southwestern tile and embellishments, and still others with a roaring '20s theme. The bungalows have fireplaces and full kitchens. Suites are equipped with kitchenettes, and guest rooms have wet bars and refrigerators. All guest quarters have balconies, patios or poolside views.

Outside, three acres of land are separated into three special environments, each with a pool: a rose garden, a fountain court and an original area maintained since the mid-'30s. There's even a pet exercise area.

The inn is in the heart of historic Palm Springs "village," just one block from famous Palm Canyon Drive and within walking distance of restaurants, bistros, boutiques and art galleries.

Place in the Sun Garden Hotel

Place in the Sun Garden Hotel
754 San Lorenzo Road
Palm Springs, CA 92264
800-779-2254 ▪ 760-325-0254

Room Rates: $49–$159. AAA, AARP and AKC discounts.
Pet Charges or Deposits: $10 per day. Small pets only.
Rated: 3 Paws 🐾🐾🐾 16 bungalows with garden patios or courtyards with barbecues, air-conditioning, fully equipped kitchens, swimming pool, whirlpool, putting green, conference room.

R esting on an acre of lush lawns and spacious gardens in the heart of Palm Springs, the "Place in the Sun" Garden Hotel offers guests personal hospitality for a luxurious yet casual vacation. The single-story studio and one-bedroom bungalows accommodate up to four guests and offer a living room, equipped kitchen, telephone and television. Add to that exceptional mountain views, landscaped private patios, courtyards, a pool and barbecue.

The grounds, dotted with fruit trees and adjacent to a riverbed, provide you and your pet a scenic place to explore.

Riviera Resort and Racquet Club

Riviera Resort and Racquet Club
1600 North Indian Canyon Drive
Palm Springs, CA 92262
800-444-8311 ▪ 760-327-8311

Room Rates:	$99–$850. AAA discount.
Pet Charges or Deposits:	$200 credit card refundable deposit.
Rated: 4 Paws 🐾🐾🐾🐾	480 deluxe rooms and luxury suites, all with refrigerators, microwaves and coffeemakers, 5 rooms with private outdoor hydrotherapy pools; 2 heated pools, wading pool, exercise room, basketball and volleyball courts, lighted putting green, tennis courts, croquet, business and meeting facilities, data ports, valet laundry, restaurant.

S urrounded by mountains and drenched by the Southern California sun, the Palm Springs Riviera Resort and Racquet Club offers deluxe rooms and luxury suites, all with oversized beds, individual climate control and in-room movies. The staff promises to lavish you and your pet with prompt, courteous service.

Guests may linger poolside, tone up in the fitness center, relax with a massage, try a friendly game of croquet, perfect their stroke on the putting course, join in a game of basketball or volleyball or play a few games of tennis, day or night on the lighted courts. To get a bird's-eye view of the scenic area, take a ride on the famous aerial tram. The spacious grounds offer plenty of opportunity for you and your pet to explore the desert setting.

The Grill at the resort features poolside cuisine for lunch and dinner, with live evening entertainment on weekends.

Oxford Suites Resort

Oxford Suites Resort
631 Five Cities Drive
Pismo Beach, CA 93449
800-982-7848 ▪ 805-773-3773

Suite Rates:	$69–$129, including full breakfast and welcoming reception. AAA and AARP discounts.
Pet Charges or Deposits:	$10 per stay. Pets under 50 pounds.
Rated: 3 Paws 🐾🐾🐾	133 suites with microwaves, refrigerators, VCRs, large work areas, putting green, heated pool, wading pool, guest laundry, valet services, business services, conference facilities, convenience shop, video rentals, complimentary evening reception.

S et in the charming seaside village of Pismo Beach, the Oxford Suites Resort is known for its comfort and convenience. Guests will appreciate the in-room microwaves and refrigerators and separate sleeping areas in the executive-king or family suites.

Start the morning with the complimentary breakfast buffet. After that, you may enjoy the resort's spa, pool or putting green, or strike out on your own adventures. You and your dog might enjoy taking a walk around the landscaped grounds or resting under the shade trees in the courtyard.

After a busy day, top off the evening with the manager's complimentary evening reception with beverages and light hors d'oeuvres.

Spyglass Inn

Spyglass Inn
2705 Spyglass Drive
Pismo Beach, CA 93449
800-824-2612 ▪ 805-773-4855
Website: www.spyglassinn.com ▪ Email: info@spyglassinn.com

Room Rates:	$69–$189. AAA and AARP discounts.
Pet Charges or Deposits:	$10 per day. Designated rooms only.
Rated: 3 Paws 🐾🐾🐾	82 comfortable rooms and suites, many with ocean views, some with kitchens; miniature golf, shuffleboard, heated pool, whirlpool, restaurant and lounge; near beaches, wineries and Hearst Castle.

Designed for comfort and enjoyment, the oceanfront Spyglass Inn offers guests freshly decorated rooms, many with views of the dramatic coastline, set amidst meticulously landscaped grounds. This quiet refuge beckons relaxation. Take a walk on the beach with your dog and drink in the beauty of the ever-changing tides, swim in the heated pool, soak your cares away in the spa, play a few rounds of miniature golf or a game of shuffleboard before heading out for an afternoon of sightseeing, wine tasting, fishing, sailing or other water sports.

For dining, the nautical theme of the Spyglass Inn Restaurant is carried out on an oceanfront deck where guests may sit and watch the sun seemingly sink into the ocean while they enjoy a cocktail before dinner. Live entertainment is offered nightly.

Sheraton Suites Fairplex

Sheraton Suites Fairplex
601 West McKinley Avenue
Pomona, CA 91768
800-722-4055 ▪ 909-622-2220
Website: www.sheraton.com

Suite Rates:	$165, including full breakfast buffet. AAA, AARP and AKC discounts.
Pet Charges or Deposits:	$10 per day. $75 refundable deposit.
Rated: 3 Paws 🐾🐾🐾	247 full-sized suites, business center, fitness center, sauna, pool, spa, gift shop, airport shuttle, dog exercise area; near major attractions.

S ituated on 487 acres with on-site business center, in-room computer hookups, meeting room and banquet facilities, the Sheraton Suites Fairplex is the first all-suites hotel in San Diego. The full-sized, spacious suites provide guests with a living room and separate bedroom area, plus the conveniences of a microwave, wet bar and refrigerator.

Start your day with the complimentary full breakfast buffet before heading out for the fitness facilities for a workout, or relax in the sauna or pool. Once you and your pet have explored the landscaped grounds, head across the street for a good run in the neighborhood park.

For your dining pleasure, the Sheraton offers gourmet dining at the Brass Ring Restaurant and nightly entertainment at Banner's Lounge.

Panamint Springs Resort

Panamint Springs Resort
P.O. Box 395
Ridgecrest, CA 93556
775-482-7680
Web Site: www.deathvalley.com
E-mail: panamint@ix.netcom.com

Room Rates:	$56.50–$129.50. AAA and AARP discounts.
Pet Charges or Deposits:	None.
Rated: 3 Paws 🐾🐾🐾	14 rooms and 1 cottage. Campgrounds, RV park, store, restaurant and bar.

P anamint Springs Resort is located inside the west entrance to Death Valley National Park. The resort overlooks the stunning geological formations and sand dunes of the Panamint Valley.

If you are planning on doing some exploring, you'll find this small, Western-style resort makes a great base camp for exploring the neighboring ghost towns, abandoned mines and waterfalls. The location is ideal for four-wheel-drive exploring, hiking, biking, or just relaxing.

La Quinta Inn

La Quinta Inn
205 East Hospitality Lane
San Bernardino, CA 95814
800-687-6667 ▪ 909-888-7571
Website: www.laquinta.com

Room Rates:	$62–$75, including First Light™ breakfast. AAA and AARP discounts.
Pet Charges or Deposits:	None.
Rated: 3 Paws 🐾🐾🐾	153 rooms, cable television, movies on demand, outdoor heated pool, fitness club privileges.

Located near ski areas, Lake Arrowhead, California State University, Loma Linda University and Medical Center and the Civic Light Opera is the La Quinta Inn. The inn has a new look that goes beyond the crisp white exteriors and new landscaping to bigger rooms, oversized desks and data ports, comfy recliners and colorful decor.

Start the day with the complimentary light breakfast, featuring your choice of cereal, fresh fruit, bagels, pastries, juice, milk and coffee.

Top off your busy day at the pool, take advantage of the fitness club privileges or enjoy a stroll through the groomed grounds with your pooch.

DoubleTree Hotel
San Diego Mission Valley

DoubleTree Hotel San Diego Mission Valley
7450 Hazard Center Drive
San Diego, CA 92108
800-222-TREE ▪ 619-297-5466
Website: www.doubletree.com

Room Rates:	$119. AAA and AARP discounts.
Pet Charges or Deposits:	Small pets only.
Rated: 3 Paws 😺😺😺	300 rooms and suites, 2 pools, sauna, whirlpool, tennis courts, exercise room, valet laundry, conference facilities, restaurant and lounge.

When it comes to California dreaming, one of the best places to while away your day might just be the DoubleTree Hotel, mere minutes from shopping, beaches and Southern California attractions. Guests are welcomed with DoubleTree's signature greeting of freshly baked chocolate chip cookies. You may wish to spend the day pampering yourself in the spa or indoor/outdoor pools, playing tennis or working off those tasty cookies at the fitness center. Busy executives will appreciate the in-room data ports, mini-bar, room service, laundry and valet services. You and your pet are sure to enjoy the trails along the riverbank adjacent to the hotel.

Diners may choose from the casual dining at the Fountain Café or heat up the night with entertainment, dinner and dancing at Club Max, before topping off the evening with a nightcap at Windows Lobby Bar.

Hanalei Hotel

Hanalei Hotel
2270 Hotel Circle North
San Diego, CA 92108
800-882-0858 ▪ 619-297-1101
Website: www.hanaleihotel.com

Room Rates:	$79–$169. AAA, AARP and AKC discounts.
Pet Charges or Deposits:	$25 per stay.
Rated: 3 Paws 🐾🐾🐾	402 rooms and 14 suites with Polynesian atmosphere, pool and whirlpool, restaurant and coffee shop, conference facilities; close to major attractions.

E scape to a Hawaiian paradise right in the heart of San Diego at the Hanalei Hotel. Surrounded by a lush landscape, spend your day relaxing on your private lanai or sun yourself by the inviting crystalline pool.

You and your dog will appreciate the tropical setting, with plenty of open space to explore before you take in one of the many local attractions or head out for a day of sightseeing.

The Hanalei is home to the Islands Restaurant, serving Hawaiian, Oriental and American cuisine. For lighter, more casual dining, there's the Peacock Cafe. The Islands Lounge is perfect for an exotic drink, dancing and entertainment.

During the summer, enjoy a sumptuous feast and an authentic Hawaiian show. You'll find excellent golf courses and complete health facilities nearby. Also only minutes away are Sea World, the San Diego Zoo, Old Town, San Diego Mission de Acala and famed shopping areas.

Hilton Beach and Tennis Resort

Hilton Beach and Tennis Resort
1775 East Mission Bay Drive
San Diego, CA 92109
800-HILTONS ▪ 619-276-4010
Website: www.hilton.com

Room Rates:	$155–$295. AAA, AARP, AKC and ABA discounts.
Pet Charges or Deposits:	$50 per stay. Pets under 20 pounds. Sorry, no cats.
Rated: 4 Paws 🐾🐾🐾🐾	357 rooms and suites with panoramic views, refrigerators, mini-bars, coffeemakers, 60-channel "on command" in-room movie system, children's recreation program, heated pool, sauna, whirlpools, wading pool, beach access, putting green, conference facilities, laundry facilities, airport transportation, 18 acres of Mediterranean-landscaped grounds.

O verlooking Mission Bay, the San Diego Hilton Beach and Tennis Resort is set on 18 tropical acres. This exotic, Mediterranean vision offers guests panoramic views of the bay, with amenities such as mini-bars, coffeemakers, a 60-channel movie system and refrigerators.

For dining, choose the casual atmosphere of Café Picante, serving breakfast, lunch and dinner, or the Banana Cabaña, which offers poolside snacks and light meals. For dinner, try Cavatappi's Italian cuisine or take in the sunset from the terrace at Fundido's, which offers live entertainment as well.

Guests may choose from recreational activities such as swimming, beach-combing, scuba diving, water skiing, windsurfing, boating, canoeing, paddleboating, bicycling or jogging. There also are tennis tournaments, health club facilities and a private dock. For the truly indulgent, spend a day at the full-service spa, where you will be pampered with facials, massage therapy, manicures and pedicures.

For your pet, there are 18 acres of land and beachfront to explore.

Holiday Inn – South Bay

Holiday Inn – South Bay
700 National City Boulevard
San Diego – National City, CA 91950
800-HOLIDAY ▪ 619-474-2800
Email: hisouthbay@worldnet.att.net

Room Rates:	$59–$69. AAA and AARP discounts.
Pet Charges or Deposits:	$25 refundable deposit. Small pets only.
Rated: 3 Paws 🐾🐾🐾	180 rooms, some with bay views, meeting rooms, data ports, outdoor pool and spa, valet service, airport transportation, full-service restaurant, cocktail lounge with live entertainment.

Centrally located near major Southern California attractions, just off Interstate 5, the South Bay Holiday Inn offers guests deluxe rooms, including nonsmoking and handicapped accommodations. Plus, youths under 18 stay free with parents. Amenities include Spectravision movies and concierge service.

After a day of sightseeing and local attractions, guests can enjoy the heated pool or whirlpool. Business travelers will appreciate the conference and banquet facilities, featuring more than 6,000 square feet of meeting space for groups of up to 300 people.

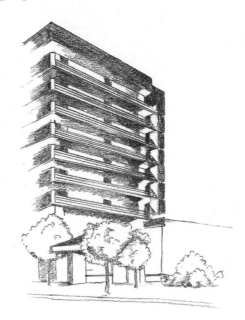

La Quinta Inn

La Quinta Inn
10185 Paseo Montril
San Diego, CA 92129
800-531-5900 ▪ 858-484-8800
Website: www.laquinta.com

Room Rates:	$52–$71, including First Light™ breakfast. AAA and AARP discounts.
Pet Charges or Deposits:	Credit card imprint only.
Rated: 3 Paws 🐾🐾🐾	120 rooms with refrigerators, large work areas with data ports, heated pool, landscaped grounds; near major attractions.

With Sea World and the San Diego Zoo nearby, La Quinta Inn is a bargain for families on a budget. In addition to its proximity to major Southern California businesses and attractions, the inn offers spacious rooms, oversized bathrooms and large work areas.

Start your day with the complimentary First Light™ breakfast, with your choice of cereal, fresh fruit, bagels, pastries, juice, milk and coffee.

There's an exercise area on site, too, for your pet.

Lamplighter Inn and Suites

Lamplighter Inn and Suites
6474 El Cajon Boulevard
San Diego, CA 92115
800-545-0778 • 619-582-3088
Website: www.lamplighter-inn.com

Room Rates:	$50–$140. AAA and AARP discounts.
Pet Charges or Deposits:	$5 per day.
Rated: 3 Paws 🐾🐾🐾	54 guest rooms and 9 suites. Pool.

The Lamplighter Inn offers a wide selection of rooms, all at exceptional prices. All of the rooms are tastefully appointed, featuring air conditioning and remote-controlled cable TV with HBO. The studio suites enjoy the convenience of fully equipped kitchens and sitting areas.

The grounds of the Inn are lushly landscaped with tropical palms, flowering bougainvillea and hibiscus, creating a very peaceful setting. Enjoy the warm sunshine by the heated swimming pool or relax under the magnolia tree in the shady picnic area.

The Lamplighter Inn is within walking distance to San Diego State University, a wide selection of restaurants and movie theaters, and, is near convenient public transportation.

Marriott Hotel and Marina

Marriott Hotel and Marina
333 West Harbor Drive
San Diego, CA 92101-7700
800-228-9290 ▪ 619-234-1500
Website: www.marriott.com

Room Rates: $215–$235. AAA, AARP and AKC members.
Pet Charges or Deposits: Small pets only.
Rated: 4 Paws 🐾🐾🐾🐾 1,355 rooms and suites with harbor views, 2 heated pools,
                       sauna, whirlpools, health club, tennis courts, marina,
                       conference facilities, restaurants, coffee shop and lounge, gift
                       shops, hair salon, room service, laundry and dry cleaning; near
                       major attractions; Honored Guest Program.

The dockside ambiance and resort setting of the San Diego Marriott Hotel and Marina invite you to indulge yourself. Whether visiting for business or pleasure, you'll enjoy the spacious guest rooms and stunning views of the harbor and the 446-slip marina.

Guests may spend time working out at the health club, playing tennis, sailing the harbor, enjoying a leisurely bike ride, jogging with the dog, sunning by the pool or relaxing in the sauna or hydrotherapy pools.

When mealtime arrives, there's Las Cascadas or the Yacht Club, both featuring American favorites; Molly's for specialty dining; and for appetizers and libations, D.W.'s pub and the Lobby Bar.

Mission Valley Hilton

Mission Valley Hilton
901 Camino Del Rio South
San Diego, CA 92108
800-733-2332 ▪ 619-543-9000
Website: www.hilton.com

Room Rates:	$124–$209. AAA and AARP discounts.
Pet Charges or Deposits:	$50 per stay. Pets under 25 pounds.
Rated: 3 Paws ❅❅❅	350 rooms, coffeemakers, fully stocked armoire cafés, in-room movies, heated pool with poolside food service, spa and dry sauna, exercise room, health club nearby, valet laundry service, covered parking.

Simply put, the luxurious, award-winning accommodations of the Mission Valley Hilton will impress you. From the spacious rooms with their overstuffed chairs, cheerful lighting and comfortable beds, to the remote-controlled cable televisions and two in-room telephones, you will appreciate all the effort put into these welcoming touches.

Once you're settled in your room, take advantage of the heated pool for a relaxing diversion, or work out at the full-service health club located nearby and then wind down in the dry sauna.

The two on-site restaurants provide a choice of fine and fun dining. Choose the Monterey Whaling Company for any meal. The menu features a daily variety of fresh fish, pasta, salads and steaks. The adjacent Pub offers the latest sports action on 11 television monitors to enjoy with your complimentary happy hour hors d'oeuvres and libations.

Residence Inn by Marriott

Residence Inn by Marriott
5400 Kearny Mesa Road
San Diego. CA 92111
800-331-3131 ▪ 858-278-2100
Website: www.residenceinn.com

Suite Rates:	$100–$155, including breakfast buffet. AAA and AARP discounts.
Pet Charges or Deposits:	$6 per day. $50 nonrefundable deposit.
Rated: 3 Paws ❖❖❖	144 suites with kitchens and some fireplaces, heated pool, whirlpool, Sport Court, health club privileges, meeting facilities, complimentary evening beverage, concierge services, pet bowls with inn's logo and exercise area for pets; near major attractions.

Convenient to major Southern California attractions, San Diego's Residence Inn by Marriott dispels the myth that there's no place like home. When you have to be away from home on business or vacation, you will appreciate the inn's comforts and conveniences.

From the spacious accommodations, some with fireplaces, separate sleeping and living areas, fully equipped kitchens, laundry facilities, room service from any of the local restaurants, work areas and meeting facilities, to the manager-hosted continental breakfast buffet and informal hospitality hour, you're bound to feel at home here.

For recreation, this retreat offers a heated pool, two whirlpools, three barbecue areas, Marriott's trademark Sport Court, where you can play basketball, volleyball or tennis, landscaped grounds and an exercise area for your pet.

San Diego Paradise Point Resort

San Diego Paradise Point Resort
1404 West Vacation Road
San Diego, CA 92109
800-344-2626 ▪ 619-274-4630
Website: www.paradisepoint.com ▪ Email: info@paradisepoint.com

Room Rates:	$170–$405. AAA discount.
Pet Charges or Deposits:	$20 per day.
Rated: 3 Paws 🐾🐾🐾	462 rooms and bungalows with refrigerators and coffeemakers, 5 pools, sauna, whirlpool, 18-hole putting course, lighted tennis courts, marina, health club, recreational program, canoeing, paddleboats, bicycles, conference facilities, secretarial services.

If you ever dreamed of vacationing on a tropical island, then the Paradise Point Resort might just be a dream come true. Located in the heart of San Diego's Mission Bay, this island resort is in a world of its own. The exotic setting is ablaze with color, with sparkling waterfalls, winding lagoons and pathways weaving throughout the island for you and your dog to explore. The single-story guest rooms and suites offer comfort and panoramic views, making this an ideal place for an exotic family weekend, a romantic getaway or a business meeting.

Guests may practice their putt on the 18-hole putting links; work out at the fitness center; tour the island by bicycle; jog on the 1.3-mile course; play video games, tennis, croquet, volleyball or shuffleboard; swim; sail; or relax with a sauna and massage.

For dining, try the casual elegance of Dockside, dine poolside at Tropics or enjoy the live entertainment at the Barefoot Bar and Grill.

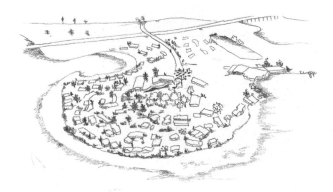

U.S. Grant Hotel

U.S. Grant Hotel
326 Broadway
San Diego, CA 92101
800-HERITAGE ▪ 619-232-3121

Room Rates:	$145 and up. AAA, AARP and AKC discounts.
Pet Charges or Deposits:	None.
Rated: 4 Paws 🐾🐾🐾🐾	340 rooms and suites, antique furnishings, restaurant and cocktail lounge. "Pampered Pet Program" for dogs and cats.

Built in 1910 by Ulysses S. Grant Jr. in memory of his father, the 340 rooms and suites of the historic U.S. Grant Hotel have housed 12 visiting presidents. Exquisitely restored and listed with Preferred Hotels Worldwide, the hotel is known for its Queen Anne reproduction furniture, comfortable and spacious rooms and four-star amenities. For fine dining, you need look no further than the Grant Grill, winner of numerous awards for excellence. A companion lounge features a variety of cocktails.

Four-legged guests will enjoy the "Pampered Pet Program," in which your cat will be offered a beckoning feast of warm milk, a scratching post, catnip and squeaky toys. Vacationing dogs will be indulged with soft pillows for naps, chef-prepared gourmet dinners, rawhide toys and turn-down service with a dog biscuit.

Capistrano Inn – Best Western

Capistrano Inn – Best Western
27174 Ortega Highway
San Juan Capistrano, CA 92675
800-441-9438 ▪ 949-493-5661
Website: www.bestwestern.com

Room Rates:	$69–$99, including breakfast on weekdays. AAA and AARP discounts.
Pet Charges or Deposits:	Small pets only.
Rated: 3 Paws 🐾🐾🐾	108 rooms, some with balconies, honor bars, microwaves and refrigerators, some efficiency kitchens, heated pool, whirlpool, complimentary evening beverages, meeting facilities, valet laundry.

S ituated on a knoll overlooking picturesque Capistrano Valley is the Capistrano Inn – Best Western. Conveniently located near Mission San Juan Capistrano, Dana Point, the Pacific Ocean and major Southern California attractions, this charming inn offers guests comfortable rooms (some with balconies), a heated swimming pool and spa.

Stop by the desk and get directions to the nearby park, where you and your dog can enjoy a game of fetch. At the end of your busy day, return to the inn for a free beverage at the complimentary happy hour.

Fess Parker's DoubleTree Resort

Fess Parker's DoubleTree Resort
633 East Cabrillo Boulevard
Santa Barbara, CA 93103
800-879-2929 ▪ 805-654-4333
Website: www.fessparkersdoubletree.com ▪ Email: reservations@fessparkersdoubletree.com

Room Rates:	$179 and up. AAA, AARP, AKC and ABA discounts.
Pet Charges or Deposits:	$50 deposit.
Rated: 4 Paws 🐾🐾🐾🐾	337 guest rooms and 23 suites with balcony or patio, in-room honor bar, coffeemakers, putting green, pool, sauna, whirlpool, tennis courts, exercise room, shuffleboard and basketball court, data ports, conference facilities, airport transportation, 24-hour room service, coffee shop, cocktail lounge, spacious landscaped grounds, located across from the beach.

L ocated on the beautiful Santa Barbara coastline is Fess Parker's 25-acre resort. Here guests will find a coastal paradise, featuring guest rooms with amenities such as mini-bars, large bathrooms, 24-hour room service and a patio or balcony with a view of the ocean or the majestic Santa Ynez Mountains.

For fine dining, try the Café Los Arcos or Barra Los Arcos, both offering California cuisine brimming with fresh seafood.

Enjoy the beach activities, such as swimming, volleyball and sailing, all just steps from the resort. In addition to the beach, there's also an on-site exercise area for dogs.

Four Seasons Biltmore

Four Seasons Biltmore
1260 Channel Drive
Santa Barbara, CA 93108
800-332-3442 ▪ 805-969-2261

Room Rates:	$380 and up. AAA discount.
Pet Charges or Deposits:	None.
Rated: 5 Paws 🐾🐾🐾🐾🐾	234 luxury oceanfront rooms and suites, with private bar, in-room safes, 24-hour room service, multilingual concierge, twice-daily maid service, laundry and dry cleaning service, video library, beauty salon, business center, restaurants and cocktail lounge.

S anta Barbara is known for its sun-drenched oceanfront of celebrity estates, terraced vineyards, mountain canyons and sandy beaches overlooked by coastal bluffs. In the '20s, a copper baron claimed 20 acres of Pacific-front paradise for his lavish residence. Since then, it has been reborn as an adobe and terra cotta hotel flanked by private cottages, known as the Santa Barbara Biltmore.

The dramatic landscape and amenable climate, backdrop for luxury guest rooms and suites and a cluster of guest cottages, have made this classic estate a popular retreat for celebrities and dignitaries for years.

Your pet will receive a five-paw welcome at check-in with a complimentary dog bowl with snacks and a special toy. The spacious grounds, beach and nearby park offer several places to explore. Pet sitters are available upon request.

San Ysidro Ranch of Santa Barbara

San Ysidro Ranch of Santa Barbara
900 San Ysidro Lane
Santa Barbara, CA 93108
800-368-6788 ▪ 805-969-5046
Website: www.sanysidroranch.com ▪ Email: ressyr@west.net

Room Rates:	$399 and up.
Pet Charges or Deposits:	$75 per stay. Horses welcome. Privileged Pet Program.
Rated: 5 Paws 🐾🐾🐾🐾🐾	39 luxury rooms and suites, 21 cottages with private terraces, fireplaces and ocean views, health club facilities, tennis courts, restaurant, pub, dog runs and exercise areas; near major attractions.

Situated on 500 acres in the foothills of the Santa Ynez Mountains, the San Ysidro Ranch for more than a century has offered guests rustic, elegant accommodations in a country setting, blending the charm of yesterday with the tastes of today. Here you can roam colorful flower gardens, swim in the ocean-view pool, join in a friendly tennis match, try your hand at lawn bowling, or pamper yourself with a therapeutic massage, facial or body wrap at the spa.

Animals love the "Privileged Pet Program." They receive complimentary dog bowls, dog cookies and bagels, bottled water, a dog bed and turn-down service with a dog bone every evening. There are dog runs and exercise areas, plus 500 acres of oceanfront property to explore. After only one visit you and your pet will know why many guests throughout the years have called this their favorite retreat.

Big America Hotel – Best Western

Big America Hotel – Best Western
1725 North Broadway
Santa Maria, CA 93454
800-426-3213 ▪ 805-922-5200
Website: www.bestwestern.com

Room Rates:	$55–$90, including continental breakfast. AAA, AARP, AKC and ABA discounts.
Pet Charges or Deposits:	Small pets only. Manager's prior approval required.
Rated: 3 Paws 🐾🐾🐾	106 rooms and suites, in-room refrigerators, cable TV, heated pool, whirlpool, meeting and conference facilities, restaurant and lounge.

Midway between Los Angeles and the Central Coast, in scenic Santa Maria, is the Big America Hotel – Best Western. This hotel offers business travelers and vacationers comfortable rooms and a family atmosphere at an affordable price.

Each of the guest rooms features a wet bar, deluxe bathroom with separate dressing area and large, comfortable beds. Choose from 50 specially designed rooms with motifs reflecting each of the states, from Alaska to Wyoming.

For aquatic leisure, the hotel offers a heated outdoor pool and whirlpool. Stop by the front desk for directions to a nearby park, where you and your dog can stretch your legs.

Whether dining with a business associate or your family, check out the famous Strawberry Patch restaurant, featuring home-style cooking at popular prices.

Georgian Hotel

Georgian Hotel
1415 Ocean Avenue
Santa Monica, CA 90401
800-538-8147 • 310-395-9945
Website: www.georgianhotel.com ▪ E-mail: reservations@georgianhotel.com

Room Rates:	$210–$500, including full breakfast. AAA and AARP discounts.
Pet Charges or Deposits:	$200 deposit of which $100 is non-refundable. Pets under 25 lbs. Manager's prior approval required.
Rated: 3 Paws 🐾🐾🐾	56 guest rooms and 28 suites.

Your reservation at the Georgian Hotel also includes the attractions of its spectacular location. You are within walking distance of the ocean, the historical Santa Monica Pier, Third Street Promenade, many of Los Angeles' finest restaurants and its most avant-garde shopping.

The Georgian Hotel boasts an art deco design, recalling the colorful architecture of historic beach resorts during the 1920s and '30s. The hotel faces Ocean Avenue and overlooks Palisade Park and Santa Monica Bay. The lobby has an intimate atmosphere and the large verandah offers a spectacular view of the ocean.

The guest rooms and suites evoke a sense of ambiance and luxury, with most offering spectacular ocean sunset views. All have windows, that open to let in the ocean breezes.

Loews Santa Monica Beach Hotel

Loews Santa Monica Beach Hotel
1700 Ocean Avenue
Santa Monica, CA 90401
800-23-LOEWS ▪ 310-458-6700
Website: www.loewshotels.com ▪ Email: loewssantamonicabeach@loewshotels.com

Room Rates:	$245 and up. AAA and AARP discounts.
Pet Charges or Deposits:	$500 refundable deposit. Pets under 25 pounds.
Rated: 4 Paws 🐾🐾🐾🐾	350 deluxe rooms and suites, ocean views, twice-daily maid service, valet laundry, conference and banquet facilities, business center, health club, heated indoor/outdoor pool, playground, child care, restaurant, coffee shop, entertainment.

A five-story atrium of shimmering glass frames a panoramic view of the blue Pacific at Loews Santa Monica Beach Hotel. Guest rooms are a blend of California casual, with bleached rattan and wicker furniture in a palette of cool colors. The luxury suites offer living and dining areas, wet bar, outdoor patio, master bedroom and marble bathroom with Jacuzzi and skylight.

For dining, the Lavande offers ocean views and French Provincial-style seafood. For casual alfresco dining, try the Ocean Café. The Lobby Bar and Lounge provide live entertainment nightly.

Venture down the private pathway from the hotel to the inviting golden sands, where you and your pet can enjoy the sun and surf.

Summit Travelodge

Summit Travelodge
500 Steuber Road
Tehachapi, CA 93561
800-578-7878 ▪ 661-823-8000

Room Rates: $49–$59. AAA and AARP discounts.
Pet Charges or Deposits: None.
Rated: 3 Paws 🐾🐾🐾   81 rooms, conference facilities, pool, Jacuzzi, on-site gas
                         station, mini-mart and deli, Summit Dining Hall and Saloon.

The city of Tehachapi, with an elevation of 4,000 feet, has become a popular place for glider planes, sky diving and golf. Centrally located from Bakersfield, Mojave and Edwards Air Force Base, the Tehachapi Summit Travelodge is the place to stay when visiting the area on business or pleasure.

Try the hotel's Summit Dining Hall and Saloon for breakfast, lunch or dinner. Sample the Cowboy Sunrise for breakfast—sliced tri-tip, outlaw beans, skillet potatoes, two eggs, tortillas and salsa. The lunch menu offers a variety of sandwiches and burgers. For dinner, select from one of the many mouthwatering steaks, oak-grilled chicken or ribs.

Your pet is bound to love the open space that surrounds the hotel.

Residence Inn by Marriott

Residence Inn by Marriott
3701 Torrance Boulevard
Torrance, CA 90503
800-331-3131 ▪ 310-543-4566
Website: www.residenceinn.com

Suite Rates:	$99–$168, including breakfast buffet. AAA and AARP discounts.
Pet Charges or Deposits:	$6 per day. $40-$60 per stay.
Rated: 3 Paws 🐾🐾🐾	247 suites, some with fireplaces, full kitchens, meeting facilities, heated pool, whirlpool, exercise room and Sport Court, complimentary evening beverages, Japanese suites and amenities.

When searching for spacious accommodations or a convenient location for a business meeting, look to the local Residence Inn by Marriott. Choose from a studio or a one- or two-bedroom suite, some with fireplaces, and 50 percent more space than traditional hotel rooms. Enjoy the conveniences of valet service, laundry facilities, daily housekeeping and fully equipped kitchens. There is even a complimentary continental breakfast served daily at the Gatehouse and a weekly manager's barbecue and social hour to get to know your neighbors.

Your dog will appreciate the pet exercise area, where he'll have plenty of room to explore. When your day is over, relax with a swim or whirlpool or play basketball, racquetball or volleyball on the Sport Court.

For those guests who enjoy Japanese accommodations, there are suites available with slippers, rice bowls, chopsticks, miso soup, green tea, rice cookers, rice and information and brochures in Japanese. There is even an AT&T in-room translator available 24 hours a day.

La Quinta Inn

La Quinta Inn
5818 Valentine Road
Ventura, CA 93003
800-687-6667 ▪ 805-685-6200
Website: www.laquinta.com

Room Rates:	$59–$99, including First Light™ breakfast. AAA and AARP discounts.
Pet Charges or Deposits:	Small pet only. Limit one pet only.
Rated: 3 Paws ❀❀❀	142 rooms, many with refrigerators; meeting facilities, heated pool, whirlpool, driving range and putting green.

The La Quinta Inn offers families on vacation and business travelers the comfort and convenience of home at a reasonable price. From the over-sized bathrooms and the large work areas with data-port phones, to the comfortable recliners and king-sized beds in all rooms, the accommodations are suitable for a week or a weekend.

You and your dog will enjoy roaming the landscaped grounds, perfect for a morning stroll. Then continue your morning with the complimentary First Light™ breakfast, featuring your choice of cereals, fresh fruit, pastries, bagels, juice, milk and coffee, before heading out for the day.

La Quinta Inn

La Quinta Inn
630 Sycamore Avenue
Vista, CA 92083-7910
800-531-5900 ▪ 760-727-8180
Website: www.laquinta.com

Room Rates:	$59–$79, including First Light™ breakfast. AAA and AARP discounts.
Pet Charges or Deposits:	Small pets only.
Rated: 3 Paws 🐾🐾🐾	106 large rooms with spacious work areas with data ports, expanded bathrooms, laundry and dry cleaning service, heated outdoor pool, workout privileges.

When looking for a place to unwind after a day of sightseeing or a hectic business meeting, the San Diego-Vista La Quinta Inn has everything you need. If you are traveling on business, the large rooms offer spacious work areas with data ports for your laptop computer, 24-hour fax and message services, with meeting space for up to 45 people.

If you are in the Southern California area to take in the local attractions with your family, you will also appreciate the spacious Gold Medal rooms, featuring fresh decor with expanded bathrooms and the daily continental breakfast. Plus, kids stay free.

You and your family, including your dog, can play and explore at the nearby park. Just stop by the desk and ask for directions.

Hampton Inn

Hampton Inn
3145 East Garvey North
West Covina, CA 91791
800-HAMPTON ▪ 626-967-5800
Website: www.hamptoninn.com

Room Rates:	$49–$69, including continental breakfast. AAA, AARP and Lifestyle 50 discounts.
Pet Charges or Deposits:	Small pets only.
Rated: 3 Paws ❤❤❤	124 rooms and suites with work areas, modem hookups, valet services, health spa, hospitality and meeting rooms.

L ocated near major attractions and Cal Poly Pomona, the Hampton Inn offers friendly service and comfortable surroundings for business travelers and vacationers, from the hospitality and meeting rooms to the complimentary continental breakfast and morning newspaper.

If you love golf, there are several golf courses nearby, as well as tennis and racquetball courts. Guests may spend the day lounging by the pool, take advantage of the adjacent fitness center or head out for a day of sightseeing or excitement at one of the theme parks located only minutes away. When you add the fact that your pets and children under 18 stay free to the inn's guarantee of 100 percent satisfaction, what more do you need?

Le Montrose Suite Hotel De Gran Luxe

Le Montrose Suite Hotel De Gran Luxe
900 Hammond Street
West Hollywood, CA 90069
800-776-0666 ▪ 310-855-1115

Suite Rates:	$185–$475. AAA, AARP and AKC discounts.
Pet Charges or Deposits:	$75 per stay. Pets under 14 pounds.
Rated: 4 Paws 🐾🐾🐾🐾	125 suites with fireplaces, refrigerators and kitchenettes, meeting rooms, whirlpool, sauna, pool, tennis court, exercise room, restaurant; near major attractions.

N estled in a quiet residential area one block east of Beverly Hills sits Le Montrose Suite Hotel De Gran Luxe. This celebrity hideaway offers guests a departure from ordinary accommodations. Charming, comfortable suites feature a sunken living room, cozy fireplace, refrigerator, color TV with VCR, maid service and, for the business traveler, multi-line phone, data port, voice mail and in-suite fax.

The friendly staff and the attention to detail will remind you of a fine European hotel. Guests may relax in the heated rooftop pool and spa, play tennis, work out in the fitness center or enjoy a massage. Diners may choose the rooftop terrace with its panoramic view or an intimate dinner at the Library Restaurant.

Le Parc Suite Hotel

Le Parc Suite Hotel
733 North West Knoll Drive
West Hollywood, CA 90069
800-5-SUITES • 310-855-8888
Web Site: www.leparcsuites.com • E-mail: info@leparcsuitehotel.com

Suite Rates:	$185–$425, including breakfast. AAA and AARP discounts.
Pet Charges or Deposits:	$75 per stay. Manager's prior approval required.
Rated: 4 Paws 🐾🐾🐾🐾	154 suites featuring kitchenettes with refrigerators and microwaves. Fireplaces, mini-bars and private balconies. Tennis courts, swimming pool and restaurant.

L e Parc Suite Hotel could very well be Los Angeles' best-kept secret. Located on a quiet, tree-lined street in West Hollywood, Le Parc is an all-suite luxury hotel with 154 one-bedroom Deluxe and Premier suites.

Each of the spacious and comfortable suites features special touches such as fine art, twice-daily maid service, multi-line data phone with voice mail, remote TV, and in-room movies and Nintendo.

The well-regarded Café Le Parc is a Mediterranean-style café resembling a cozy living room and features a separate bar area. The chef and his staff make all meals to order and in many cases take special requests for the more particular person who may be on a special diet. Meals are served either in the suites, in the intimate dining room, or al fresco on the rooftop, with the backdrop of Sunset Strip winding its way through the Hollywood Hills.

WHERE TO TAKE YOUR PET IN
Southern California

Leashes are required unless otherwise stated.

ANAHEIM

Yorba Regional Park is a popular, 166-acre park on La Palma Avenue off Weir Canyon Road and Yorba Linda Boulevard. There is a small fee for parking. For more information, call (714) 970-1640.

BAKERSFIELD

Kern River County Park offers you and your dog a combination of mountains and meadows to explore. Located on Alfred Harrell Highway, off Panorama Drive. For more information, call (805) 861-2345.

Tule Elk State Reserve protects a herd of dwarf elks. It's 956 acres offer plenty of room to roam. There is a natural history display, visitors' center, viewing area and a picnic area. Located off State Route 119 and Tupman Road. For more information, call (805) 765-5004.

BEVERLY HILLS

Laurel Canyon Park is in Coldwater Canyon, about 3 miles off Mulholland Drive, before the fire station. Here you will find a leash-free paradise from 6 a.m. to 10 a.m. and 3 p.m. to dusk. There are picnic tables and lots of shade trees. Even the rich and famous canines are known to come here from time to time. The park is equipped with water and pooper scoopers. For more information, call (818) 756-8190.

Will Rogers Memorial Park, across from the Beverly Hills Hotel on the corner of Canon and Beverly Drives at Sunset Boulevard, is in the center of posh Beverly Hills. It's a great place to burn off some energy after a day of shopping on Rodeo Drive. For more information, call (310) 285-2541.

BRIDGEPORT

Bodie State Historic Park consists of a 500-acre former mining town. There's enough open space for you and your dog to enjoy yourselves, if you don't mind the occasional ghost. Located off Highway 270 and Bodie Road; follow the road east for 13 miles to reach the park. There are fees for your vehicle and your dog. For more information, call (760) 647-6445.

BURBANK

Woodley Park has a wonderful exercise course. It's a great park for a picnic with your dog. From Burbank, take Ventura Freeway 134 to Ventura Freeway 101. Travel westbound to San Diego 405 and take the Burbank Boulevard exit. Make a right on Woodley Avenue. The park is on the right, past the Japanese Garden. For more information, call (818) 756-8190.

COSTA MESA

There are several neighborhood parks with plenty of running room.

Brentwood Park, 265 East Brentwood
Canyon Park, 970 Arbor Street
Del Mesa Park, 2080 Mainstee Drive
Estancia Park, 1900 Adams
Gisler Park, 1250 Gisler Street
Harper Park, 425 East 18th Street
Lions Park, 570 West 18th Street
Shiffer Park, 3134 Bear Street
Tanager Park, 1780 Hummingbird Drive
Vista Park, 1200 Victoria Street
Wakeham Park, 3400 Smalley Street
Wimbledon Park, 3440 Wimbledon Way

JOSHUA TREE

Joshua Tree National Park encompasses 870 square miles of California desert. It's north of Interstate 10 and east of Desert Hot Springs. Take Highway 60 to Interstate 10 and continue to Highway 62 northeast, approximately 39 miles to Twenty-nine Palms. The visitors' center is on Utah Trail, south of Highway 62. There is an entrance fee. There's a wide variety of wildlife, including the desert bighorn, and lots of Joshua trees. There are granite formations and mountains rising from the valley floor to about 3,000 feet above sea level. For more information, call (760) 367-7511.

LA JOLLA

There are miles of beachfront for you and your dog to explore at La Jolla Shores Beach, west of Camino del Oro. Dogs are only allowed on the beach before 9 a.m. and after 6 p.m. For more information, call (619) 221-8901.

LAKE ARROWHEAD – SAN BERNARDINO

Big Bear Lake is one of California's largest recreation areas, located about 30 miles northeast of San Bernardino. Here you and your pet may camp, picnic, go horseback riding, fishing and swimming in designated areas, or snow skiing and sledding in the winter. Call (909) 866-7000 for more information.

Accessible from the town of Lake Arrowhead is the San Bernardino National Forest, a popular location for fishing and winter sports. For directions and more information, and restrictions, contact the Chamber of Commerce at (909) 336-1547.

LOMPOC

La Purisima Mission State Historic Park, a 966-acre park, is 4 miles northeast on Purisima Road, off Highway 1. Originally founded in 1787 as a mission, it was destroyed by the 1812 earthquake and rebuilt from 1813 to 1822. The park includes nine buildings and a historic aqueduct system. There are more than 12 miles of hiking and riding trails for you and your dog to explore. There is a small entrance fee. Call (805) 733-3713 for more information.

LOS ANGELES

Elysian Park is more than 550 acres with hilltop views of the city. Located between Interstate 5, Highway 101 and Highway 110, the park is accessed from the Stadium Way exit. Follow the signs to the park, then turn left on Elysian Park Drive. For more information, call (213) 226-1402.

Griffith Park has more than 4,000 acres to roam and hundreds of different species of trees to inspect. Bounded by Highway 101, Interstate 5 and Highway 134, the park is off Interstate 5 at Los Feliz Boulevard. For more information, call (213) 665-5188.

Kenneth Hahn State Recreation Area, off the Santa Monica Freeway at La Cienega Boulevard, is where the 1932 Olympics were held. There is a lovely lake and stream, plus lots of hiking trails for you and your dog to explore. For more information, call (213) 291-0199.

Santa Monica Mountains National Recreation Area has more than 65,000 acres of nature with everything from waterfalls, meadows and creeks to forests and beaches. The park runs from Beverly Hills to Ventura. Contact the ranger's office at (818) 597-9192 for directions and more information.

There are several neighborhood parks with plenty of running room:

Arroyo Seco Park, 5566 Via Marisol Street
Barnsdall Park, 4800 Hollywood Boulevard
City Hall Park, 200 North Main Street

Crestwood Hills Park, 1000 Hanley Avenue
Harold A. Henry Park, 890 South Lucerne Avenue
Hollenbeck Recreation Center, 415 South St. Louis Street
Holmby Park, 601 Club View Drive
Jim Gillam Recreation Center, South La Brea Avenue
Leimert Plaza, 4395 Leimert Boulevard
Lincoln Park Recreation Center, 3501 Valley Boulevard
Norman O. Houston Park, 4800 South La Brea Avenue
Northridge Park, 10058 Reseda Boulevard
Pershing Square Park, 532 South Olive Street
Silverlake Park, 1850 West Silverlake
South Park, 345 East 51st Street
Sycamore Grove Park, 4702 N. Figueroa Street
Temescal Canyon Park, 15900 Pacific Coast Highway
Westwood Recreation Center, 1350 Sepulveda Boulevard

NEEDLES

Jack Smith Park, at Interstate 40 and Park Moabi Road, is on the Colorado River. Here you and your pooch can spend the day lazing on the riverbanks and dipping your toes in the water.

Moabi Regional Park is 1,027 acres on the Colorado River. You can rent houseboats and explore the river or check out the desert region in the surrounding area. The entrance is at Interstate 40 and Park Moabi Road. There is a vehicle fee and a fee for your dog. For more information, call (760) 326-3831.

NEWPORT BEACH

Newport Harbor is probably one of the most scenic small harbors in the world. Your dog will love exploring the sand dunes. The harbor office is at 1901 Bayside Drive. For more information, call (949) 723-4511.

OJAI

Foster Park is 205 acres of open space, off Highway 33, south of Ojai. For more information, call (805) 654-3951.

Libbey Park consists of 15 acres of oak trees. It is in downtown Ojai, across from the Arcade.

Los Padres National Forest starts in the Ojai Valley in the town of Goleta. The park is made up of 1,750,000 acres of pine trees, desert, coastal areas and a condor sanctuary. For more information, call (805) 683-6711.

Soule Park, east of downtown Ojai on Boardman Road, is a beautiful county park.

PALM SPRINGS

Idyllwild County Park is 202 acres of open space, located at the north end of County Park Road, a mile off Highway 243. There is an entrance fee for you and your dog.

Palm Springs Indian Canyons has three separate canyons to explore. This secluded area is off South Palm Canyon Drive. For more information, call (760) 325-5673.

PISMO BEACH

The area was once known for the Pismo clam, but today butterflies reign as the local attraction from November to March as thousands of monarchs fill the trees. The beach area lies off scenic Highway 101. Entrance fees are paid at the Grand Avenue entrance, but there is no entry fee if you head west on Highway 1, park and walk in at the Grand Avenue entrance. Here you and your pet will discover dunes to explore, beaches to comb and miles of trails to roam. For more information, call (805) 927-4509 or (805) 773-4382.

RANCHO MIRAGE

Salton Sea State Recreation Area is 234 feet below sea level and is the largest inland body of water in the world. There are 16 miles of shoreline and five beaches to explore. Take Highway 111 southeast of Mecca to the visitors' center on the west side of the highway. Call (760) 393-3502 for more information.

SAN BERNARDINO – see Lake Arrowhead

SAN DIEGO

Fiesta Island, a paradise for man and his best friend, is on Fiesta Island Road off Interstate 5 at the Sea World Drive exit. Here you can enjoy a leashless romp in the surf or a walk on the beach, enjoying the outstanding views of downtown San Diego and Mission Bay. So bring your picnic lunch and don't forget the ball. For more information, call (619) 221-8901.

Los Penasquitos Canyon Preserve, off Interstate 15 on Black Mountain Road, offers groves of shady oak trees for a relaxing picnic. Then venture on to the creekside trails leading to the waterfalls and pools of water at the bottom of the canyon. In the spring there are magnificent fields of wildflowers to behold. For more information, call (619) 685-1350.

Mission Beach and Pacific Beach, on West Mission Bay Drive and Mission Park Boulevard, offer miles of coastline to enjoy, but dogs are limited to the hours before 9 a.m. or after 6 p.m.

Mission Trails Regional Park consists of 5,700 acres, making it the largest urban park in the United States. Hike up to Cowles Mountain for terrific summit views or make your way to the Old Mission Dam, built by Native Americans. Located off Interstate 8 at the College Avenue exit on Navajo Road. Park at Goldcrest Drive, where the trail to Cowles Mountain begins. For more information, call (619) 533-4051.

Mount Woodson is a haven for rock climbers. This leashless refuge offers peace, serenity and gorgeous views of the Pacific. Located off Interstate 15 north of San Diego, the entrance is at the California Division of Forestry Fire Station off Highway 67. For more information, call (619) 695-1400.

Ocean Beach Park is the most popular beach in the area for dog lovers. Referred to as "Dog Beach," the off-leash section at the north end of the beach will be your dog's favorite place to run. Take Interstate 5 to the Interstate 8 exit. Follow the signs to Sunset Cliffs Boulevard and bear right to reach the entrance. For more information, call (619) 221-8901.

Wooded Hill Nature Trail, off Sunrise Highway, has the highest wooded summit in the Laguna Mountains. No leashes are required, allowing you and your dog a vigorous hike up the vista for a superb view of San Diego and Catalina Island. For more information, call (619) 445-6235.

SANTA BARBARA

Arroyo Burro County Beach, 2981 Cliff Drive, west of Las Positas Road, is a wonderful place for you and your dog to chase some waves. It also has a small outdoor café, where you and your dog can dine together. For more information, call (805) 963-7109.

Santa Barbara Botanic Gardens is 65 acres with more than 1,000 species of native California plants. Located on Mission Canyon Drive off Foothill Road, this constantly blooming garden has more than 5 miles of trails to explore. There is an admission fee. Call (805) 563-2521 for more information.

There are several neighborhood parks with acres of running room:

Alameda Park, 1400 Santa Barbara Street
Mission Park, Laguna and Mission Drives
San Antonio Canyon Park, San Antonio Creek Road
Shoreline Park, Marina and Shoreline Drives

SANTA MARIA

Adam Park, 600 West Enos Drive, has 30 acres of grass, where you and your dog can play a game of Frisbee.

Preisker Park is a 40-acre park with a delightful pond full of ducks and geese. The Grandchildren's Grove has monarch butterflies in season. Located at 2301 North Broadway.

Waller Park, at South Broadway and Goodwin Road, is a wonderful park full of tall pine trees, a tranquil lake and room for your dog to exercise. For more information, call (805) 934-6211.

There are several neighborhood parks with acres of running room:

Alice Trefts Park, 510 E. Park Avenue
Armstrong Park, 1000 E. Chapel Street
Atkinson Park, 1000 N. Railroad Avenue
Buena Vista Park, 800 S. Pine Street
Central Plaza Park, 100 N. Broadway
Grogan Park, 1155 W. Rancho Verde
Joe White Park, 500 S. Pine Street
Maramonte Park, 620 E. Sunrise Drive
Memorial Park, 200 N. Pine Street
Oakley Park, 1300 N. Western Avenue
Rice Park, 700 E. Sunset Avenue
Russell Park, 1000 W. Church Street

SOLVANG

Hans Christian Andersen Park, off Highway 246 at Atterdag Road, is a 52-acre park left in its natural, rugged state. A 164-foot-high waterfall cascades over the cliffs in the rainy season. There are trails to the falls, picnic areas, a ball field and a volleyball court. Call 800-468-6765 for more information.

TEHACHAPI

Tehachapi Mountain Park has wonderful scenic trails for you and your dog to explore. Located off Highway 202; exit south, head west and stay on Tucker Road until you reach Highline Road. Follow that for about 1½ miles, then turn left on Water Canyon Road and follow it for two miles until you reach the park.

VENTURA

Grant Memorial Park has some wonderful views of the Channel Islands from the grassy knoll area. There is plenty of room to roam, but not much in the way of shade. Located two blocks east of Ventura Avenue on Ferro Drive.

PETS WELCOME!

National and State Parks and Beaches

CALIFORNIA'S PARKS, FORESTS, RECREATION AREAS, PRESERVES AND SEASHORE AREAS THAT ALLOW PETS

PLEASE NOTE

Pets must be on leash at all times and may be restricted to certain areas. For directions, use fees, pet charges and general information contact the numbers listed below.

NATIONAL PARKS GENERAL INFORMATION

National Park Service
Fort Mason, Building 201
Bay and Franklin streets
San Francisco, CA 94123
(415) 556-0560

NATIONAL PARKS

Death Valley National Park
Superintendent's Office
P.O. Box 579
Death Valley, CA 92328
(760) 786-2331

Joshua Tree National Park
Superintendent's Office
74485 National Park Drive
Twenty-nine Palms, CA 92277-3597
(760) 367-7511

Lassen Volcanic National Park
Superintendent's Office
P.O. Box 100
Mineral, CA 96063-0100
(530) 595-4444

Redwood National Park
Superintendent's Office
1111 Second Street
Crescent City, CA 95531
(707) 464-6101

Sequoia and Kings Canyon National Park
Superintendent's Office
47050 Generals Highway
Three Rivers, CA 93271
(559) 565-3134

Yosemite National Park
Park Superintendent's Office
P.O. Box 577
Yosemite National Park, CA 95389
(209) 372-0200

NATIONAL RECREATION AREAS

Golden Gate National Recreation Area
General Superintendent's Office
Fort Mason, Building 201
San Francisco, CA 94123
(415) 556-0560

Santa Monica Mountains National Recreation Area
Superintendent's Office
30401 Agoura Road, Suite 100
Agoura Hills, CA 91301
(818) 597-9192, ext. 201, or
   800-533-7275

Whiskeytown-Shasta-Trinity National Recreation Area
Off of State Route 299 near Whiskeytown,
   8 miles west of Redding
(530) 246-1225

❖
NATIONAL FOREST GENERAL INFORMATION

Pacific-Southwest Region
U.S. Forest Service
630 Sansome Street, Room 527
San Francisco, CA 94111
(415) 705-2874
800-280-CAMP (for information and
   camping reservations)

❖
NATIONAL FORESTS

Angeles National Forest
Supervisor's Office
701 N. Santa Anita Avenue
Arcadia, CA 91006
(626) 574-1613

Cleveland National Forest
Supervisor's Office
10845 Rancho Bernardo Road, Suite 200
San Diego, CA 92127
(619) 673-6180

Eldorado National Forest
100 Forni Road
Placerville, CA 95667
(530) 622-5061

Inyo National Forest
Supervisor's Office
873 North Main Street
Bishop, CA 93514
(760) 873-2400

Klamath National Forest
Forest Supervisor's Office
1312 Fairlane Road
Yreka, CA 96097
(530) 842-6131

Lassen National Forest
Supervisor's Office
55 South Sacramento Street
Susanville, CA 96130
(530) 257-2151

Los Padres National Forest
Forest Supervisor's Office
6144 Calle Real
Goleta, CA 93117
(805) 683-6711

Mendocino National Forest
Forest Supervisor's Office
825 North Humbolt Avenue
Willows, CA 95988
(530) 934-3316

Modoc National Forest
Forest Supervisor's Office
800 West 12th Street
Alturas, CA 96101
(530) 233-5811

Plumas National Forest
Ranger Station and Forest Headquarters
P.O. Box 11500
Quincy, CA 95971
(530) 283-2050

San Bernardino National Forest
Forest Supervisor's Office
1824 South Commercenter Circle
San Bernardino, CA 92408-3430
(909) 383-5588

Sequoia National Forest
Forest Supervisor's Office
900 West Grand Avenue
Porterville, CA 93257-2035
(559) 784-1500

Shasta-Trinity National Forest
Forest Supervisor's Office
2400 Washington Avenue
Redding, CA 96001
(530) 244-2978

Sierra National Forest
Forest Headquarters
1600 Tollhouse Road
Clovis, CA 93611
(209) 297-0706

Six Rivers National Forest
Forest Supervisor's Office
1330 Bayshore Way
Eureka, CA 95001
(707) 442-1721

Stanislaus National Forest
Supervisor's Office
19777 Greenley Road
Sonora, CA 95370
(209) 532-3671

Tahoe National Forest
Forest Supervisor's Office
631 Coyote Street
P.O. Box 6003
Nevada City, CA 95959
(530) 265-4531

NATIONAL PRESERVES
AND SEASHORES

Mojave National Preserve
Preserve Office
222 East Main Street
Barstow, CA 92311
(619) 255-8760 or 255-8801

Point Reyes National Seashore
Superintendent's Office
Point Reyes National Seashore
Point Reyes, CA 94956
(415) 663-1092

STATE PARK
GENERAL INFORMATION

California State Park System
Department of Parks and Recreation
P.O. Box 942896
Sacramento, CA 94296-0001
(916) 653-6995

STATE PARKS AND
RECREATION AREAS

Anderson Marsh State Park
Highway 53
Lower Lake
(707) 994-0688

Andrew Molera State Park
Off Highway 1
Big Sur
(831) 667-2315

Annadel State Park
Channel Drive, off Montgomery Drive
Santa Rosa
(707) 539-3911

Anza-Borrego Desert State Park
West Palm Canyon Drive
Borrego Springs
(760) 767-5311

Armstrong Redwoods State Park
Armstrong Woods Road, off Highway 116
Guerneville
(707) 869-2015

Auburn State Recreation Area
Highway 49, one mile south of Highway 80
Auburn
(916) 885-4527

Austin Creek State Recreation Area
Armstrong Woods Road, near Sweetwater
   Springs Road
Guerneville
(707) 869-2015

Bethany Reservoir State Park
South of Byron on Christensen Road
Byron
(209) 874-2056

Big Basin Redwoods State Park
Northwest of Boulder Creek on Highway 236
Big Basin
(831) 338-8860

Bodie State Historic Park
Southeast of Bridgeport via U.S. 395 and
    State Route 270
Bridgeport
(760) 647-6445

Bothe-Napa Valley State Park
Highway 29
Calistoga
(707) 942-4575

Brannan Island State Park
Highway 160, 13 miles north of Antioch
    Bridge
Rio Vista
(916) 777-6671

Calaveras Big Trees State Park
Highway 4
Arnold
(209) 795-2334

Castaic Lake State Recreation Area
Ridge Route and Lake Hughes Roads
Seneca Hills
(818) 880-0350

Castle Crags State Park
Off Interstate 5
Dunsmuir
(530) 235-2684

Caswell Memorial State Park
28000 South Austin Road
Ripon
(209) 599-3810

Clear Lake State Park
5300 Soda Bay Road
Kelseyville, CA 95451
(707) 279-4293

Columbia State Park
Sierra Nevada foothills
Columbia
(209) 532-0150

**Colusa-Sacramento River State
Recreation Area**
Highway 20, 9 miles east of Interstate 5
Colusa
(530) 458-4927

Cuyamaca Rancho State Park
Highway 79, between Highway 78 and
    Interstate 8
Julian
(760) 765-0755

D. L. Bliss State Park
Highway 89, 8 miles south of Tahoma
South Lake Tahoe
(530) 525-7277

Del Norte Coast Redwoods State Park
1375 Elk Valley Road
Crescent City
(707) 464-6101 x 5120

Empire Mine State Historic Park
10791 East Empire Street
Grass Valley, CA 95945
(530) 273-8522

Fremont Peak State Park
Highway 156 on San Juan Canyon Road
San Juan Bautista
(831) 623-4255

Garland Ranch Regional Park
700 W. Carmel Valley Road
Carmel Valley, CA 93924
(831) 659-4488

Grizzly Creek Redwoods State Park
16949 Highway 36
Carlotta
(707) 777-3683

Henry Cowell Redwoods State Park
Highway 9
Felton
(831) 335-4598

Humboldt Lagoons State Park
15330 Highway 101
Trinidad
(707) 488-2041

Jack London State Historic Park
2400 London Ranch Road
Glen Ellen
(707) 938-5216

Jedediah Smith Redwoods State Park
1375 Elk Valley Road
Crescent City
(707) 464-6101 x5112 or x5101

Lake Elsinore State Recreation Area
Highway 74, 3 miles west of Interstate 15 at
    Central Avenue exit
Lake Elsinore
(909) 674-3177

Lake Perris State Recreation Area
Lake Perris Drive, off Ramona Expressway
Lakeview
(909) 657-0676

Mac Kerricher State Park
Mac Kerricher Road, off Highway 1
Cleone
(707) 964-9112

Manchester Beach State Park
Kinney Road, near Highway 1
Point Arena
(707) 882-2463

**McArthur-Burney Falls Memorial
State Park**
Highway 89 and Pacific Crest National
    Scenic Trail
Burney
(530) 335-2777

Millerton Lake State Recreation Area
5290 Millerton Road
Friant
(209) 822-2332

Mount Diablo State Park
Mount Diablo Scenic Boulevard
Clayton
(925) 837-2525

Palomar Mountain State Park
Route S-6
Palomar Mountain
(760) 742-3462

Patrick's Point State Park
4150 Patrick's Point Drive
Trinidad
(707) 677-3570

Plumas-Eureka State Park
County Road A14, west of Highway 89
Blairsden
(530) 836-2380

Point Mugu State Park
9000 West Pacific Coast Highway
Malibu
(310) 457-8143

Prairie Creek Redwoods State Park
Off Highway 101
Orick
(707) 464-6101 x5301

Pyramid Lake State Park
State Route 445, off Highway 395
Sutcliffe
(702) 476-1155

Richardson Grove State Park
16000 Highway 101
Garberville
(707) 247-3318

South Yuba River Project State Park
17660 Pleasant Valley Road
Penn Valley
(530) 432-2546 or 273-3884

❖ OTHER RECREATIONAL AREAS

Anthony Chabot Regional Park and Lake Chabot Marina
9999 Redwood Road
Oakland
(510) 635-0138

Contra Loma Regional Park
Frederickson Lane, west of Empire Mine
    Road
Antioch
(510) 635-0135

Cow Mountain Recreation Area
Mill Creek Road, off Highway 101
Ukiah
(707) 468-4000

Del Valle Regional Park
7000 Del Valle Road
Livermore
(510) 373-0332

Don Pedro Lake
Bonds Flat Road, off La Grange Road
Stanislaus County
(209) 852-2396

Doran and Westside Regional Parks
Doran Park Road, off Highway 1
Bodega Bay
(707) 875-3540

Eagle Lake
Off Eagle Lake Road
Susanville
(916) 257-2151 or Ranger District, 257-4188

Gualala Point Regional Park
Highway 1
Gualala
(707) 785-2377

Lake Arrowhead
Communities Chamber of Commerce
28200 Highway 189, Building "J"
P.O. Box 219
Lake Arrowhead, CA 92352
(909) 336-6992

Lake Berryessa
Berryessa Knoxville Road off Highway 128
Yolo County, Napa
(707) 966-1419

Lake Casitas Recreation Area
Santa Ana Road and Highway 150
Ventura County
(805) 649-2233

Lake Sonoma
Visitors' Center
3333 Skaggs Springs Road
Geyserville, CA 95441
(707) 433-9483

Lake Nacimiento
Off Highway 101
Between King City and Paso Robles, Jolon
    exit
Monterey County
800-323-3839

Martinez Regional Shoreline
North Court Street, north of Ferry Street
Martinez
(510) 635-0135

Mission Bay Park
2688 East Mission Drive
San Diego
(619) 221-8900 or 276-8200

Spring Lake Regional Park
Newanga Avenue, off Summerfield Road
Santa Rosa
(707) 539-8092

Sunol – Ohlone Regional Wilderness
Geary Road, off Calaveras Road
Sunol
(510) 862-2244

**Vasona Park and Reservoir/Oak
Meadow Park**
University Avenue and Garden Hill Drive, off
   Blossom Hill Road
Los Gatos
(408) 358-3751 or 356-2729 – Vasona Park
(408) 354-6809 – Oak Meadow Park

Kennel Information For Major California Attractions

DISNEYLAND
1313 Harbor Boulevard
Anaheim, CA 92803
(714) 781-4560 or 999-4565
Kennels are on site.
Fee: $10 per day

KNOTT'S BERRY FARM
8039 Beach Boulevard
Buena Park, CA 90620
(714) 827-1776
No kennels on site. Call for a list of nearby
  kennels.

MARINE WORLD AFRICA USA
Located at Marine World Parkway, S.R. 37
  exit, off Interstate 80.
Vallejo, CA 95489
(707) 644-4000 or 643-6722
No kennels on site. Call for a list of nearby
  kennels.

PARAMOUNT'S GREAT AMERICA
Located on Great America Parkway between
  U.S. 101 and S.R. 237.
Santa Clara, CA 95054
(408) 988-1776
No kennels on site. Call for a list of nearby
  kennels.

SAN DIEGO WILD ANIMAL PARK
via Rancho Parkway off Interstate 15
Escondido, CA 92026
(619) 234-6541
No kennels on site. Call for a list of nearby
  kennels.

SAN DIEGO ZOO
P.O. Box 551
San Diego, CA 92112
(619) 234-3153
No kennels on site. Call for a list of nearby
  kennels.

SEA WORLD
1720 South Shores Road
San Diego, CA 92109
(619) 222-6363
Kennels are on site.
Fee: $5 per day

SIX FLAGS MAGIC MOUNTAIN
P.O. Box 5500
Located off Highway 5
Valencia, CA 91355
(805) 255-4100
Kennels are on site.
Fee: No charge to park visitors

UNIVERSAL STUDIO HOLLYWOOD
Lankershim Boulevard Freeway – U.S. 101
Universal City, CA 91608
(818) 508-9600
Kennels are on site.
Fee: No charge to park visitors. Stop by
  Visitor's Services.

Veterinery Care in California

Pioneer Equine Hospital
24100 North Jack Tone Road
Acampo, CA 95220
209-334-4247

Acton Veterinary Clinic
32033 Crown Valley Road
Acton, CA 93510
661-269-7060

Agoura Animal Clinic
28282 Dorothy Drive
Agoura Hills, CA 91301
818-991-1036

Sweetwater Veterinary Clinic
33324 Agua Dulce Canyon Road
Agua Dulce, CA 91350
661-268-8128

Alameda Pet Hospital
2275 Buena Vista Avenue
Alameda, CA 94501
510-523-1626

Alamo Animal Hospital
3176 Danville Boulevard
Alamo, CA 94507
925-837-7246

Hill View Pet Hospital
666 San Pablo Avenue
Albany, CA 94706
510-525-4571

Alhambra Veterinary Hospital
1501 West Mission Road
Alhambra, CA 91803
626-289-9227

Alpine Animal Hospital
3220 Alpine Boulevard
Alpine, CA 91901
619-445-5683

Alta Rancho Pet and Bird Hospital
8677 19th Street
Alta Loma, CA 91701
909-980-3575

Terra Vista Animal Hospital
10598 Baseline Road #F
Alta Loma, CA 91701
909-989-3999

Lake Avenue Animal Hospital
2519 Lake Avenue
Altadena, CA 91001
626-798-6710

Modoc Veterinary Center
501 US Highway 395 East
Alturas, CA 96101
530-233-4156

Anaheim Animal Care & Pet Hospital
116 South Magnolia Avenue
Anaheim, CA 92804
714-527-9292

Anaheim Pet Hospital
3211 West Lincoln Avenue
Anaheim, CA 92801
714-826-9380

East Hills Animal Hospital
8285 East Santa Ana Canyon Road
Anaheim, CA 92808
714-921-2500

La Palma Veterinary Hospital
1715 West La Palma Avenue
Anaheim, CA 92801
714-535-1141

Sunrise Pet Clinic
430 South Anaheim Hills Road #J
Anaheim, CA 92807
714-283-0227

Anderson Veterinary Hospital
3100 West Center Street
Anderson, CA 96007
530-365-8122

Angels Camp Veterinary Hospital
1997 Deer Creek Road
Angels Camp, CA 95222
209-736-0488

Cherry Creek Veterinary Hospital
7955 Watt Avenue
Antelope, CA 95843
916-349-2755

Antioch Veterinary Hospital
1432 West 10th Street
Antioch, CA 94509
925-757-2233

Anza Valley Veterinary Clinic
56360 Mitchell Rd Bldg 2
Anza, CA 92539
909-763-5383

Animal Care Hospital
21738 US Highway 18 #14
Apple Valley, CA 92307
760-247-0292

Apple Valley Equine Hospital
10083 Deep Creek Road
Apple Valley, CA 92308
760-247-4226

Aptos Animal Hospital
10404 Soquel Drive
Aptos, CA 95003
831-688-4242

Del Mar Pet Hospital
7525 Sunset Way
Aptos, CA 95003
831-688-2016

North Coast Veterinary Hospital
1701 Giuntoli Lane
Arcata, CA 95521
707-822-4885

Arnold Pet Clinic
1114 Blagen Road
Arnold, CA 95223
209-795-4471

Arroyo Grande Veterinary
121 Nevada Street
Arroyo Grande, CA 93420
805-481-9434

Atascadero Pet Center
9575 El Camino Real
Atascadero, CA 93422
805-466-3887

Sierra Veterinary Hospital
33041 Auberry Road #110
Auberry, CA 93602
559-855-3770

Animal Medical Center
1525 Grass Valley Highway
Auburn, CA 95603
530-823-5166

Azusa Hills Animal Hospital
333 North Citrus Avenue
Azusa, CA 91702
626-969-2266

Bakersfield Veterinary Hospital
323 Chester Avenue
Bakersfield, CA 93301
661-327-4444

Dickson Large Animal Vet Clinic
6909 Setter Court
Bakersfield, CA 93309
661-831-1515

Kern Animal Emergency Clinic
4300 Easton Drive #1
Bakersfield, CA 93309
661-322-6019

Baldwin Park Animal Hospital
14921 Ramona Boulevard
Baldwin Park, CA 91706
626-337-7246

Ballard Animal Hospital
1751 Lewis Street
Ballard, CA 93463
805-688-4881

ABC Animal Clinic
1238 East Main Street
Barstow, CA 92311
760-256-3330

Animal Care Clinic
10404 Rosecrans Avenue
Bellflower, CA 90706
562-920-1795

**Ambulatory Equine
Medicine**
501 Old County Road #K
Belmont, CA 94002
650-593-0969

Belmont Pet Hospital
539 Harbor Boulevard
Belmont, CA 94002
650-593-3161

Animal Clinic of Benicia
402 Military East
Benicia, CA 94510
707-745-5993

Benicia Cat Clinic
1410 East 2nd Street
Benicia, CA 94510
707-745-2287

Albany Veterinary Clinic
1550 Solano Avenue
Berkeley, CA 94707
510-526-2053

**Beverly Hills Animal
Hospital**
353 North Foothill Road
Beverly Hills, CA 90210
310-276-7113

**Bear City Animal
Hospital**
214 Big Bear Boulevard W
Big Bear City, CA 92314
909-585-7808

Sierra Veterinary Clinic
2640 West Line Street
Bishop, CA 93514
760-873-4824

Valley Animal Hospital
19059 Valley Boulevard #120
Bloomington, CA 92316
909-877-2384

**Circle H Veterinary
Hospital**
13165 West Hobson Way
Blythe, CA 92225
760-922-3136

**Town and Country
Animal Hospital**
4055 Bonita Road
Bonita, CA 91902
619-479-3311

**San Luis Rey Equine
Hospital**
4211 Holly Lane
Bonsall, CA 92003
760-726-4566

**Skycrest Veterinary
Clinic**
13975 Highway 128
Boonville, CA 95415
707-895-3008

**Boulder Creek
Veterinary Clinic**
12870 Highway 9
Boulder Creek, CA 95006
831-338-7205

Brawley Animal Clinic
266 West US Highway 86
Brawley, CA 92227
760-344-3531

**Founders Veterinary
Clinic**
330 North Brea Boulevard #F
Brea, CA 92821
714-990-0661

**Brentwood Veterinary
Hospital**
4519 Ohara Avenue
Brentwood, CA 94513
925-634-1177

**Brownsville Veterinary
Hospital**
16838 Willow Glen Rd
Brownsville, CA 95919
530-675-2096

**Buellton Veterinary
Clinic**
914 West Highway 246
Buellton, CA 93427
805-688-2334

Buena Park Pet Hospital
8725 Orangethorpe Avenue #C
Buena Park, CA 90621
714-523-2424

**Burbank Animal
Hospital**
123 West Burbank Boulevard
Burbank, CA 91502
818-846-7743

**Rainbow Veterinary
Hospital**
2321 West Empire Avenue
Burbank, CA 91504
818-846-1166

**Burlingame Family Pet
Hospital**
1808 Magnolia Avenue
Burlingame, CA 94010
650-697-7234

Camino Real Pet Clinic
1317 Bayswater Avenue
Burlingame, CA 94010
650-344-5711

**Discovery Bay Veterinary
Clinic**
1555 Riverlake Road #A
Byron, CA 94514
925-634-0759

C

Calabasas Animal Clinic
4937 Las Virgenes Road #101
Calabasas, CA 91302
818-880-0888

**High Desert Veterinary
Hospital**
8401 California City Boulevard
California City, CA 93505
760-373-8917

Calistoga Pet Clinic
1124 Lincoln Avenue
Calistoga, CA 94515
707-942-0404

**Camarillo Veterinary
Hospital**
258 Dawson Drive
Camarillo, CA 93012
805-482-9865

**Pleasant Valley Animal
Hospital**
2174 Pickwick Drive
Camarillo, CA 93010
805-482-8951

**Cambria Animal Medical
Center**
2501 Village Lane #A
Cambria, CA 93428
805-927-7000

**Cameron Park
Veterinary Hospital**
3931 Cambridge Road
Cameron Park, CA 95682
530-677-1671

Camino Animal Hospital
4087 Carson Road
Camino, CA 95709
530-644-6011

Bascom Animal Hospital
2175 South Bascom Avenue
Campbell, CA 95008
408-371-5630

Campbell Pet Clinic
2160 Winchester Boulevard
Campbell, CA 95008
408-378-5190

Cat Hospital
157 East Hamilton Avenue
Campbell, CA 95008
408-866-6188

All Pets Medical Center
7606 Fallbrook Avenue #1
Canoga Park, CA 91304
818-883-2600

**Canoga Park Veterinary
Center**
22323 Sherman Way #17
Canoga Park, CA 91303
818-992-8860

**West Hills Veterinary
Clinic**
23233 Saticoy Street #101
Canoga Park, CA 91304
818-592-6101

**Adobe Veterinary
Hospital**
17787 Sierra Highway
Canyon Country, CA 91351
661-251-3710

**Estrella Veterinary
Hospital**
26925 Camino de Estrella
Capistrano Beach, CA 92624
949-496-6661

**Capitola Veterinary
Clinic**
1220 41st Avenue #H
Capitola, CA 95010
831-476-7387

Pacific Veterinary Specialists
1980 41st Ave
Capitola, CA 95010
831-476-0667

Cardiff Animal Hospital
2159 San Elijo Avenue
Cardiff By Sea, CA 92007
760-436-3215

Aardvark Animal Health Center
6986 El Camino Real #I
Carlsbad, CA 92009
760-438-7766

All Cats Hospital
7040 Avenida Encinas #109
Carlsbad, CA 92009
760-431-3585

La Costa Animal Hospital
7750 El Camino Real #G
Carlsbad, CA 92009
760-944-1266

Carmel Valley Vet Hospital
13738 Center Street
Carmel Valley, CA 93924
831-659-2286

Fair Oaks Boulevard Veterinary Hospital
7348 Fair Oaks Boulevard
Carmichael, CA 95608
916-483-0492

Sacramento Cat Hospital
4115 Manzanita Avenue
Carmichael, CA 95608
916-488-4161

Animal Medical Clinic
1037 Casitas Pass Road
Carpinteria, CA 93013
805-684-8665

Torrance Animal Hospital
21617 Figueroa Street
Carson, CA 90745
310-328-4419

Castaic Animal Hospital
31573 Castaic Road
Castaic, CA 91384
661-257-6363

Canyon Veterinary Hospital
20897 Redwood Road
Castro Valley, CA 94546
510-582-6704

Castro Valley Veterinary Hospital
2517 Castro Valley Boulevard
Castro Valley, CA 94546
510-582-3656

All Creatures
243 Walker Valley Road
Castroville, CA 95012
831-633-2013

Date Palm Animal Hospital
34116 Date Palm Drive
Cathedral City, CA 92234
760-328-3330

Arrowhead Veterinary Hospital
171 State Highway 173
Cedar Glen, CA 92321
909-337-8471

Ceres Veterinary Clinic
3018 Whitmore Avenue
Ceres, CA 95307
209-538-1911

Artesia Animal Hospital
20200 Pioneer Boulevard
Cerritos, CA 90703
562-865-2677

Chatsworth Veterinary Center
21418 Devonshire Street
Chatsworth, CA 91311
818-341-7770

Animal Health Clinic
1812 Esplanade
Chico, CA 95926
530-898-9172

Animal Medical Clinic
3449 State Highway 32
Chico, CA 95973
530-343-1234

Mangrove Veterinary Hospital
1900 Mangrove Avenue
Chico, CA 95926
530-891-4818

Canyon Hills Animal Hospital
14656 Pipeline Avenue
Chino, CA 91710
909-597-4881

Chino Valley Equine Hospital
13385 Yorba Avenue
Chino, CA 91710
909-628-5545

Francis Animal Hospital
5284 Francis Avenue
Chino, CA 91710
909-591-6581

Melrose Pet Clinic
1466 Melrose Avenue
Chula Vista, CA 91911
619-427-2851

Avian Medical Center
6114 Greenback Lane
Citrus Heights, CA 95621
916-727-2663

Citrus Heights Vet Hospital
7404 Auburn Boulevard
Citrus Heights, CA 95610
916-725-2700

Greenback Auburn Pet Clinic
6110 Greenback Lane
Citrus Heights, CA 95621
916-722-4343

Sunrise Boulevard Animal Hospital
7484 Sunrise Boulevard
Citrus Heights, CA 95610
916-726-2334

Total Care Veterinary Hospital
6418 Tupelo Drive
Citrus Heights, CA 95621
916-725-2200

Claremont Veterinary Hospital
123 North Indian Hill Boulevard
Claremont, CA 91711
909-621-0900

Cat Hospital of Clayton
5435 Clayton Road #I
Clayton, CA 94517
510-672-2287

Animal Hospital of Lake County
14842 Lakeshore Drive
Clearlake, CA 95422
707-995-1138

Cloverdale Animal Clinic
150 Cherry Creek Road
Cloverdale, CA 95425
707-894-3436

Alta Animal Hospital
585 West Shaw Avenue
Clovis, CA 93612
559-298-6509

Clovis Equine Clinic
8338 North Sunnyside Avenue
Clovis, CA 93611
559-299-1661

West Hills Veterinary Clinic
195 West Glenn Avenue
Coalinga, CA 93210
559-935-5028

Coarsegold Veterinary Hospital
35335 Highway 41
Coarsegold, CA 93614
559-683-4991

Colfax Veterinary Hospital
1333 State Highway 174
Colfax, CA 95713
530-346-2297

Colton Animal Hospital
1309 North Mount Vernon Avenue
Colton, CA 92324
909-825-4335

Colusa Veterinary Hospital
1110 Bridge Street
Colusa, CA 95932
530-458-2221

Adobe Animal Hospital
3619 Clayton Road
Concord, CA 94521
925-825-3535

All Bay Animal Hospital
1739 Willow Pass Road
Concord, CA 94520
925-687-7346

Clayton Valley Pet Hospital
4801 Clayton Road
Concord, CA 94521
925-689-4600

Concord Pet Hospital
1301 Galindo Street
Concord, CA 94520
925-685-7331

Four Corners Veterinary Hospital
1126 Meadow Lane
Concord, CA 94520
925-685-0512

Cool Animal Hospital
2966 State Highway 49 #C
Cool, CA 95614
530-885-8322

Corning Veterinary Clinic
2023 Solano Street
Corning, CA 96021
530-824-2966

Aacacia Animal Hospital
939 West 6th Street
Corona, CA 91720
909-371-1002

Corona Community Vet Hospital
423 East Grand Boulevard
Corona, CA 91719
909-279-7387

Corona Del Mar Animal Hospital
2948 East Coast Highway
Corona Del Mar, CA 92625
949-644-8160

Crown Veterinary Hospital
817 Orange Avenue
Coronado, CA 92118
619-453-6281

Madera Pet Hospital
5796 Paradise Drive
Corte Madera, CA 94925
415-927-0525

Baker Bristol Pet Hospital
2976 Bristol Street
Costa Mesa, CA 92626
949-546-0010

Cat Clinic of Orange County
369 East 17th Street #19
Costa Mesa, CA 92627
949-631-1454

Costa Mesa Animal Hospital
480 East 17th Street
Costa Mesa, CA 92627
949-548-3794

Fairview Pet Hospital
1175 Baker Street #D11
Costa Mesa, CA 92626
949-556-1125

Newport Harbor Animal Hospital
125 Mesa Drive
Costa Mesa, CA 92627
949-631-1030

Cotati Large Animal Hospital
8079 Gravenstein Highway
Cotati, CA 94931
707-795-4356

Cotati Small Animal Hospital
8055 Gravenstein Highway
Cotati, CA 94931
707-795-3694

Cottonwood Veterinary Clinic
3917 Main Street
Cottonwood, CA 96022
530-347-3711

Animal Medical Center
602 North Azusa Avenue
Covina, CA 91722
626-339-5401

Covina Animal Hospital
222 East San Bernardino Road
Covina, CA 91723
626-331-5374

All Creatures Animal Hospital
1380 Northcrest Drive
Crescent City, CA 95531
707-464-7448

Crescent Animal Medical Center
1590 Northcrest Drive
Crescent City, CA 95531
707-464-8321

Indian Creek Veterinary Clinic
258 Old Arlington Rd
Crescent Mills, CA 95934
530-284-6187

Culver City Animal Hospital
5830 Washington Boulevard
Culver City, CA 90232
310-836-4551

Acadia Veterinary Clinic
10012 North Foothill Boulevard
Cupertino, CA 95014
408-996-1030

Cupertino Animal Hospital
10026 Peninsula Avenue
Cupertino, CA 95014
408-252-6380

ABC Animal Hospital
9121 Walker Street
Cypress, CA 90630
714-995-8033

College Park Animal Hospital
5839 Ball Road
Cypress, CA 90630
714-827-6861

Equine Medical Center
10542 Walker Street
Cypress, CA 90630
714-952-1134

D

McIntyre Pet Hospital
1232 El Camino Real
Daly City, CA 94014
650-755-0969

Skyline Pet Hospital
70 Skyline Plaza
Daly City, CA 94015
650-756-4877

Golden Lantern Animal Hospital
32545 Golden Lantern Street #D
Dana Point, CA 92629
949-493-1370

Oak Tree Animal Hospital
579 San Ramon Valley Boulevard
Danville, CA 94526
925-837-1632

Tassajara Veterinary Clinic
3436 Camino Tassajara
Danville, CA 94506
925-736-8387

Davis Animal Hospital
1617 Russell Boulevard
Davis, CA 95616
530-756-1766

Midtown Animal Clinic
525 Rowe Place #C
Davis, CA 95616
530-758-5650

All Creatures Hospital
3665 Via De La Valle
Del Mar, CA 92014
619-481-7992

Del Mar Heights Vet Hospital
2626 Del Mar Heights Road #B
Del Mar, CA 92014
619-792-3888

Delano Veterinary Hospital
726 South High Street
Delano, CA 93215
661-725-8614

Animal Clinic–Desert Hot Springs
13120 Palm Drive
Desert Hot Springs, CA 92240
760-329-8765

Diamond Bar Veterinary Clinic
1131 Grand Avenue
Diamond Bar, CA 91765
909-861-9561

General Pet Hospital
800 North Diamond Bar Boulevard
Diamond Bar, CA 91765
909-861-4116

Dixon Veterinary Clinic
7925 Pedrick Road
Dixon, CA 95620
916-678-2377

Downey Veterinary Hospital
11220 Brookshire Avenue
Downey, CA 90241
562-923-0763

Firestone Animal Hospital
7150 Firestone Boulevard
Downey, CA 90241
562-928-1341

All Creatures Veterinary Hospital
6612 Dublin Boulevard
Dublin, CA 94568
925-829-6260

Dublin Veterinary Hospital
7410 Amador Valley
Boulevard #D
Dublin, CA 94568
925-828-5520

Durham Veterinary Clinic
9417 Midway
Durham, CA 95938
530-891-5707

E

Animal Care Clinic
2650 Jamacha Road #159
El Cajon, CA 92019
619-670-8700

Cajon Rancho Pet Hospital
1682 Greenfield Drive
El Cajon, CA 92021
619-442-5571

East County Large Animal
10312 Quail Canyon Road
El Cajon, CA 92021
619-561-4661

Singing Hills Animal Hospital
1951 Willow Glen Drive
El Cajon, CA 92019
619-441-5850

El Cerrito Pet Hospital
11800 San Pablo Avenue
El Cerrito, CA 94530
510-234-4582

Green Valley Animal Clinic
321 Green Valley Road
El Dorado Hills, CA 95762
916-933-0527

El Monte Dog and Cat Hospital
10158 Garvey Avenue
El Monte, CA 91733
626-443-9461

El Sobrante Veterinary Hospital
401 Valley View Road
El Sobrante, CA 94803
510-223-0740

El Toro Animal Hospital
23162 El Toro Road
El Toro, CA 92630
949-837-5222

Serrano Animal Hospital
21771 Lake Forest Drive #111
El Toro, CA 92630
949-855-9744

Elk Grove Veterinary Hospital
8640 Elk Grove Boulevard
Elk Grove, CA 95624
916-685-9589

Hatton Veterinary Hospital
7615 Sheldon Road
Elk Grove, CA 95758
916-689-1688

Laguna Creek Veterinary Hospital
5060 Laguna Boulevard #129
Elk Grove, CA 95758
916-684-7300

Empire Veterinary Clinic
5132 Yosemite Boulevard
Empire, CA 95319
209-521-7305

Encinitas Veterinary Clinic
222 North Highway 101
Encinitas, CA 92024
760-753-1162

Encinitas Village Vet Clinic
119 North El Camino Real #B
Encinitas, CA 92024
760-436-1080

Encino Veterinary Clinic
17009 Ventura Boulevard
Encino, CA 91316
818-783-7387

Escalon Small Animal Clinic
1355 Escalon Avenue
Escalon, CA 95320
209-838-3512

Acacia Animal Hospital
1040 North Broadway
Escondido, CA 92026
760-745-8115

Companion Animal Clinic
1215 South Escondido
Boulevard #A
Escondido, CA 92025
760-743-2751

El Norte Veterinary Clinic
1014 West El Norte Parkway
Escondido, CA 92026
760-432-0400

Village Veterinary Hospital
316 West Mission
Avenue #113
Escondido, CA 92025
760-741-9999

Eureka Veterinary Hospital
4433 Broadway Street
Eureka, CA 95503
707-442-4885

Horse and Hound Animal Clinic
3954 Jacobs Avenue #A
Eureka, CA 95501
707-441-1249

Exeter Veterinary Hospital
251 South F Street
Exeter, CA 93221
559-592-5210

F

Greenback Veterinary Hospital
8311 Greenback Lane
Fair Oaks, CA 95628
916-969-1540

Madison Avenue Veterinary Clinic
8520 Madison Avenue
Fair Oaks, CA 95628
916-961-1541

Old Towne Animal Hospital
10530 Fair Oaks Boulevard
Fair Oaks, CA 95628
916-961-8683

Sunset Animal Medical Center
7751 Sunset Avenue
Fair Oaks, CA 95628
916-967-7768

Fairfax Veterinary Clinic
2084 Sir Francis Drake
Boulevard
Fairfax, CA 94930
415-454-8204

Animal Hospital
200 Alaska Avenue
Fairfield, CA 94533
707-422-9550

Cal West Pet Hospital
1941 North Texas Street
Fairfield, CA 94533
707-425-0292

Fairfield Animal Hospital
1325 Travis Boulevard #F
Fairfield, CA 94533
707-428-5300

Fall River Veterinary Hospital
43578 Highway 299 East
Fall River Mills, CA 96028
530-336-5528

Alvarado Veterinary Hospital
347 East Alvarado Street
Fallbrook, CA 92028
760-728-6606

Felton Veterinary Hospital
5980 Highway 9
Felton, CA 95018
831-335-3466

Ferndale Veterinary
1140 Van Ness Avenue
Ferndale, CA 95536
707-786-4200

Lakeside Pet Clinic
705 East Bidwell Street #12
Folsom, CA 95630
916-983-7387

Sierra Animal Hospital
16736 Arrow Boulevard
Fontana, CA 92335
909-350-7807

Foresthill Veterinary Clinic
24368 Main Street
Foresthill, CA 95631
530-367-3777

Covington Creek Veterinary
30303 Highway 20
Fort Bragg, CA 95437
707-964-6109

Mendocino Coast Animal Hospital
700 North Franklin Street
Fort Bragg, CA 95437
707-964-3448

Animal Medical Center
105 Main Street
Fortuna, CA 95540
707-725-6114

Fortuna Veterinary Clinic
251 North Fortuna Boulevard
Fortuna, CA 95540
707-725-6131

Animal Cove Pet Hospital
1125 East Hillsdale Boulevard #106
Foster City, CA 94404
650-377-0822

Foster City Pet Hospital
1940 Beach Park Boulevard
Foster City, CA 94404
650-574-0400

Animal Hospital– Fountain Valley
9525 Garfield Avenue #D
Fountain Valley, CA 92708
714-962-6621

Animal Medical Center
16540 Harbor Boulevard #A
Fountain Valley, CA 92708
714-531-1155

Warner Avenue Animal Hospital
8546 Warner Avenue
Fountain Valley, CA 92708
714-540-5252

Westhaven Veterinary Hospital
16161 Brookhurst Street
Fountain Valley, CA 92708
714-775-5544

Pajaro Valley Veterinary Hospital
2013 Freedom Boulevard
Freedom, CA 95019
831-722-3364

American Animal Hospital
3660 Peralta Boulevard
Fremont, CA 94536
510-791-0464

Fremont Animal Hospital
45968 Warm Springs Boulevard
Fremont, CA 94539
510-656-1852

Mission Valley Vet Clinic
55 Mowry Avenue
Fremont, CA 94536
510-797-2323

Animal Hospital and Bird Clinic
5139 North Blackstone Avenue
Fresno, CA 93710
559-227-5575

Blackstone Pet Hospital
1448 North Blackstone Avenue
Fresno, CA 93703
559-237-9054

Cedar Veterinary Hospital
1602 North Cedar Avenue
Fresno, CA 93703
559-251-7141

Dog and Cat Veterinary Clinic
4338 East Shields Avenue
Fresno, CA 93726
559-225-5233

Elm Veterinary Hospital
2338 South Elm Avenue
Fresno, CA 93706
559-233-0313

Escalon Veterinary Clinic
66 East Escalon Avenue #102
Fresno, CA 93710
559-432-3300

Fresno Cat Hospital
432 East Shaw Avenue
Fresno, CA 93710
559-222-7752

Kings Canyon Veterinary
4696 East Kings Canyon Road
Fresno, CA 93702
559-251-8482

Olive Veterinary Hospital
4677 East Olive Avenue
Fresno, CA 93702
559-255-0690

Woodward Pet Hospital
7705 North 1st Street
Fresno, CA 93720
559-449-9595

Animal Medical Clinic
3257 Associated Road
Fullerton, CA 92835
714-990-1411

Aspen Pet Clinic
1010 East Chapman Avenue
Fullerton, CA 92831
714-870-9497

East Fullerton Pet Clinic
800 East Commonwealth Avenue
Fullerton, CA 92831
714-870-9662

Tri-City Pet Hospital
1145 South Placentia Avenue
Fullerton, CA 92831
714-870-9090

G

Dry Creek Veterinary
1000 C Street #110
Galt, CA 95632
209-745-9130

Los Caballos Equine Practice
24806 Kenefick Road
Galt, CA 95632
209-334-1660

Garberville Redway Veterinary
230 Alderpoint Road
Garberville, CA 95542
707-923-2023

Boulevard Animal Hospital
8841 Garden Grove Boulevard
Garden Grove, CA 92844
714-537-6780

Community Veterinary Hospital
13200 Euclid Street
Garden Grove, CA 92843
714-537-5390

California Veterinary Hospital
230 West Victoria Street
Gardena, CA 90248
310-323-6867

Inland Animal Hospital
16116 South Western Avenue
Gardena, CA 90247
310-323-9555

All Equine Veterinary Clinic
10005 Burchell Road
Gilroy, CA 95020
408-848-8018

Gavilan Animal Hospital
7091 Monterey Street #A
Gilroy, CA 95020
408-842-0393

Mission Valley Veterinary
8418 Carmel Street
Gilroy, CA 95020
408-842-2899

Westwood Animal Hospital
7891 Westwood Drive #B
Gilroy, CA 95020
408-848-3443

Glen Ellen Veterinary Hospital
13700 Arnold Drive
Glen Ellen, CA 95442
707-996-2300

Arden Animal Hospital
407 Arden Avenue
Glendale, CA 91203
818-246-2478

Hillcrest Pet Hospital
3789 La Crescenta Avenue
Glendale, CA 91208
818-249-5594

Parkview Pet Clinic
1534 Canada Boulevard
Glendale, CA 91208
818-244-7268

**Rosemont Animal
Hospital**
2550 Foothill Boulevard #A
Glendale, CA 91214
818-957-2451

Elwood Animal Clinic
901 East Alosta Avenue #A
Glendora, CA 91740
626-914-5671

**South Glendora Animal
Hospital**
169 West Arrow Highway
Glendora, CA 91740
626-914-5717

**West Foothill Animal
Hospital**
615 West Foothill Boulevard
Glendora, CA 91741
626-335-4912

Goleta Pet Hospital
345 Rutherford Street
Goleta, CA 93117
805-967-1811

Valley Animal Hospital
102 South Fairview Avenue
Goleta, CA 93117
805-964-7755

**Balboa Veterinary
Medical Clinic**
10361 Balboa Boulevard
Granada Hills, CA 91344
818-368-2846

**North Valley Veterinary
Clinic**
11152 Balboa Boulevard
Granada Hills, CA 91344
818-366-7777

Animal Emergency Clinic
12022 La Crosse Avenue
Grand Terrace, CA 92313
909-825-9350

**Best Friends Animal
Clinic**
12509 Burma Road
Grass Valley, CA 95945
530-272-2817

**Grass Valley Veterinary
Hospital**
11101 Rough And Ready
Highway
Grass Valley, CA 95945
530-273-7272

**Nevada County
Veterinary Hospital**
12322 Nevada City Highway
Grass Valley, CA 95945
530-273-5303

Greenbrae Pet Hospital
2104 Redwood Highway
Greenbrae, CA 94904
415-924-3493

**Gridley Veterinary
Hospital**
27 East Gridley Road #A
Gridley, CA 95948
530-846-6212

Groveland Animal Clinic
18521 Main Street
Groveland, CA 95321
209-962-7058

**Grand Avenue Veterinary
Hospital**
600 Grand Avenue
Grover Beach, CA 93433
805-481-2595

**Oak Park Veterinary
Clinic**
1601 Grand Avenue
Grover Beach, CA 93433
805-481-6641

Gualala Veterinary Clinic
38460 South Highway 1
Gualala, CA 95445
707-884-3313

**Guerneville Veterinary
Clinic**
16338 1st Street
Guerneville, CA 95446
707-869-0688

H

**St. Francis Animal
Hospital**
15708 Gale Avenue
Hacienda Heights, CA 91745
626-968-4709

**Half Moon Bay
Veterinary Hospital**
719 Main Street
Half Moon Bay, CA 94019
650-726-9061

**Main Street Veterinary
Hospital**
730 Main Street
Half Moon Bay, CA 94019
650-726-0112

**Hanford Veterinary
Hospital**
9086 Lacey Boulevard
Hanford, CA 93230
559-584-4481

Lacey Animal Hospital
12181 Lacey Boulevard
Hanford, CA 93230
559-584-9251

**Laguna Vista Small and
Equine**
26333 Vermont Avenue
Harbor City, CA 90710
310-326-9371

Animal Medical Center
14138 Doty Avenue
Hawthorne, CA 90250
310-978-4065

**Avian and Exotic Animal
Hospital**
4871 West Rosecrans Avenue
Hawthorne, CA 90250
310-679-0693

**Alta Vista Veterinary
Clinic**
27641 Mission Boulevard
Hayward, CA 94544
510-537-3562

Chabot Veterinary Clinic
20877 Foothill Boulevard
Hayward, CA 94541
510-538-2330

**Haymont Veterinary
Clinic**
25886 Mission Boulevard
Hayward, CA 94544
510-537-0912

Animal Medical Center
16085 Healdsburg Avenue
Healdsburg, CA 95448
707-433-4493

Village Veterinary Clinic
15055 Vista Road
Helendale, CA 92342
760-951-9904

Animal Care Hospital
1221 West Acacia Avenue
Hemet, CA 92543
909-652-7387

Hemet Animal Hospital
130 North Girard Street
Hemet, CA 92544
909-658-3119

Hercules Pet Clinic
1511 Sycamore Avenue #B
Hercules, CA 94547
510-799-3884

**Hermosa Animal
Hospital**
1078 Aviation Boulevard
Hermosa Beach, CA 90254
310-376-8819

**VCA Coast Animal
Hospital**
1560 Pacific Coast Highway
Hermosa Beach, CA 90254
310-372-8881

Animal Medical Center
15888 Main Street #103
Hesperia, CA 92345
760-948-2497

**Hesperia Animal
Hospital**
9540 I Avenue
Hesperia, CA 92345
760-948-1553

**Ala-Palm Animal
Hospital**
8068 Palm Avenue
Highland, CA 92346
909-862-5111

**Highland Village Pet
Hospital**
7257 Boulder Avenue #A7
Highland, CA 92346
909-864-7387

Hilmar Animal Hospital
19976 Bloss Avenue
Hilmar, CA 95324
209-632-3831

**Hollister Veterinary
Clinic**
1280 Sunnyslope Road
Hollister, CA 95023
831-637-2580

Animal Hospital of Huntington
15021 Edwards Street
Huntington Beach, CA 92647
714-898-0568

Beach Boulevard Pet Hospital
16191 Beach Boulevard
Huntington Beach, CA 92647
714-847-1291

Hamilton Animal Hospital
21552 Brookhurst Street
Huntington Beach, CA 92646
714-964-4744

Huntington Harbor Clinic
16893 Algonquin Street
Huntington Beach, CA 92649
714-846-1378

Warner West Pet Clinic
6885 Warner Avenue
Huntington Beach, CA 92647
714-847-9617

Idyllwild Animal Clinic
55500 South Circle Drive
Idyllwild, CA 92549
909-659-5041

Imperial Beach Pet Hospital
538 12th Street
Imperial Beach, CA 91932
619-424-3961

Seacoast Pet Clinic
600 Palm Avenue #103
Imperial Beach, CA 91932
619-429-7387

Desert Equine Veterinary Hospital
81200 Avenue 52
Indio, CA 92201
760-398-0288

Oasis Veterinary Hospital
44840 Oasis Street
Indio, CA 92201
760-347-0718

Valley Animal Clinic
80120 Us Highway 111 #2
Indio, CA 92201
760-342-4711

Airport Cities Animal Hospital
1120 West Manchester Boulevard
Inglewood, CA 90301
310-641-8800

Ber-Mar Pet Hospital
349 East Florence Avenue
Inglewood, CA 90301
310-677-9187

Inglewood Animal Hospital
815 West Manchester Boulevard
Inglewood, CA 90301
310-649-6211

Ladera Pet Clinic
1528 Centinela Avenue
Inglewood, CA 90302
310-671-0421

Arbor Animal Hospital
14775 Jeffrey Road #F
Irvine, CA 92620
949-551-2727

Camino Pet Hospital
5408 Walnut Avenue #C
Irvine, CA 92604
949-559-1404

Northwood Animal Hospital
13925 Yale Avenue #115
Irvine, CA 92620
949-559-1992

Amador Veterinary Hospital
11071 State Highway 88
Jackson, CA 95642
209-223-2160

Foothill Veterinary Clinic
125 Peek Street #E
Jackson, CA 95642
209-223-3131

Jackson Creek Veterinary Clinic
1245 Jackson Gate Road
Jackson, CA 95642
209-223-3504

Jamestown Veterinary Hospital
9915 Victoria Way
Jamestown, CA 95327
209-984-0232

Jamul Veterinary Clinic
13910 Lyons Valley Road #A
Jamul, CA 91935
619-669-1666

Critter Care of Joshua Tree
61720 Commercial Street
Joshua Tree, CA 92252
760-366-1195

Julian Animal Hospital
2907 Washington Street
Julian, CA 92036
760-765-0500

Kensington Veterinary Hospital
400 Colusa Avenue
Kensington, CA 94707
510 528 0797

Family Animal Hospital
943 Sir Francis Drake Boulevard
Kentfield, CA 94904
415-457-3724

Kenwood Veterinary Clinic
8910 Sonoma Highway
Kenwood, CA 95452
707-833-1000

Veterinary Medical Center
547 South Madera Avenue
Kerman, CA 93630
209-846-7000

King City Veterinary Hospital
890 South 1st Street
King City, CA 93930
831-385-4878

Agate Bay Animal Hospital
8428 Trout Avenue
Kings Beach, CA 96143
530-546-7522

Kingsburg Veterinary Clinic
1991 Simpson Street
Kingsburg, CA 93631
559-897-4131

La Canada Pet Clinic
1400 Foothill Boulevard
La Canada, CA 91011
818-790-1205

Crescenta-Canada Pet Hospital
3502 Foothill Boulevard
La Crescenta, CA 91214
818-248-3963

Sunny Hills Animal Hospital
221 East Imperial Highway
La Habra, CA 90631
562-691-1698

Animal Hospital of La Jolla
7601 Draper Avenue
La Jolla, CA 92037
619-459-2665

La Jolla Veterinary Hospital
7520 Fay Avenue
La Jolla, CA 92037
619-454-6155

A Pet Emergency Clinic
5232 Jackson Drive #105
La Mesa, CA 91941
619-462-4800

Eastridge Veterinary Clinic
7750 University Avenue #A
La Mesa, CA 91941
619-465-5291

Grossmont Animal Hospital
8274 Parkway Drive #106
La Mesa, CA 91942
619-466-0501

La Mesa Pet Hospital
5336 Jackson Drive
La Mesa, CA 91942
619-469-0138

Rancho Village Veterinary Hospital
3647 Avocado Boulevard
La Mesa, CA 91941
619-670-6278

Animal Clinic-La Mirada
15808 Imperial Highway
La Mirada, CA 90638
562-943-0102

Petra Pet Clinic
14768 Beach Boulevard
La Mirada, CA 90638
562-523-1190

Hacienda Animal Clinic
1338 North Hacienda
 Boulevard
La Puente, CA 91744
626-330-4558

**All Creatures Veterinary
Care**
78359 Us Highway 111
La Quinta, CA 92253
760-564-1154

**Baldy View Animal
Hospital**
1497 Foothill Boulevard
La Verne, CA 91750
909-596-7771

Citrus Veterinary Clinic
1337 Foothill Boulevard
La Verne, CA 91750
909-596-1881

**Lafayette Animal
Hospital**
3394 Mount Diablo Boulevard
Lafayette, CA 94549
925-284-4412

Canyon Animal Hospital
20372 Laguna Canyon Road
Laguna Beach, CA 92651
949-494-1076

**Laguna Beach Animal
Hospital**
460 Forest Avenue
Laguna Beach, CA 92651
949-494-9721

**South Laguna Village
Animal Hospital**
31742 South Coast Highway
Laguna Beach, CA 92677
949-499-5378

Alicia Pet Clinic
24861 Alicia Parkway #D
Laguna Hills, CA 92653
949-699-0963

La Paz Animal Hospital
25292 McIntyre Street #J
Laguna Hills, CA 92653
949-586-9444

**Laguna Hills Animal
Hospital**
24271 El Toro Road
Laguna Hills, CA 92653
949-837-7333

**Laguna Grove Veterinary
Hospital**
28971 Golden Lantern #110a
Laguna Niguel, CA 92677
949-495-8387

**Laguna Niguel Animal
Hospital**
30001 Crown Valley
 Parkway #K
Laguna Niguel, CA 92677
949-495-0030

**San Geronimo Valley
Veterinary**
7110 Sir Francis Drake
 Boulevard
Lagunitas, CA 94938
415-488-9791

Elsinore Pet Clinic
16776 Lakeshore Drive #F
Lake Elsinore, CA 92530
909-674-7866

**Mountainview Small
Animal Hospital**
151 Diamond Drive
Lake Elsinore, CA 92530
909-674-1475

**Saddleback Animal Care
Center**
24801 Raton Drive
Lake Forest, CA 92630
714-586-4250

Plaza Pet Hospital
23684 El Toro Road
Lake Forest, CA 92630
949-581-7979

**Kern Valley Veterinary
Clinic**
14934 Highway 178
Lake Isabella, CA 93240
760-378-2486

Parker Veterinary
5104 Lake Isabella Boulevard
Lake Isabella, CA 93240
760-379-5633

Main Street Veterinary
2530 South Main Street
Lakeport, CA 95453
707-263-6232

**Northlake Veterinary
Clinic**
1351 Crystal Lake Way
Lakeport, CA 95453
707-263-8100

**Lakeside Veterinary
Hospital**
9924 Maine Avenue
Lakeside, CA 92040
619-390-2342

Desert Equine Hospital
42636 6th Street East
Lancaster, CA 93535
661-948-1113

**North Valley Veterinary
Clinic**
43619 Sierra Highway
Lancaster, CA 93534
661-945-7906

**Larkspur Landing Pet
Hospital**
1019 Larkspur Landing Circle
Larkspur, CA 94939
415-461-6133

Lawndale Pet Hospital
14700 Hawthorne Boulevard
Lawndale, CA 90260
310-679-9522

**Lemon Grove Veterinary
Hospital**
7572 North Avenue
Lemon Grove, CA 91945
619-463-0301

San Diego Pet Hospital
7368 Broadway #A
Lemon Grove, CA 91945
619-462-6600

Lemoore Animal Clinic
526 Armstrong Street
Lemoore, CA 93245
559-924-3491

Lincoln Pet Clinic
870 East Avenue
Lincoln, CA 95648
916-645-3866

**Lindsay-Westwood
Veterinary**
139 East Hermosa Street
Lindsay, CA 93247
559-562-6018

Del Valle Pet Hospital
1172 Murrieta Boulevard
Livermore, CA 94550
925-443-6000

**Livermore Country
Veterinary**
2110 Greenville Road
Livermore, CA 94550
925-449-7922

**Livermore Veterinary
Hospital**
2494 Railroad Avenue
Livermore, CA 94550
925-447-1420

Livingston Animal Clinic
2335 F Street
Livingston, CA 95334
209-394-8556

**Lockeford Veterinary
Group**
11849 East Highway 12
Lockeford, CA 95237
209-368-6668

Arbor Pet Clinic
819 North Sacramento Street
Lodi, CA 95240
209-334-4257

**Harris Veterinary
Hospital**
17112 North Highway 88
Lodi, CA 95240
209-368-8256

Lodi Veterinary Hospital
325 West Lockeford Street
Lodi, CA 95240
209-368-5166

**Lomita Animal Medical
Clinic**
1935 Pacific Coast Highway
Lomita, CA 90717
310-530-3630

Narbonne Animal Clinic
25445 Narbonne Avenue
Lomita, CA 90717
310-325-5850

**El Camino Veterinary
Hospital**
510 North I Street
Lompoc, CA 93436
805-736-5658

**St. Francis Veterinary
Hospital**
934 North H Street
Lompoc, CA 93436
805-735-8980

West Valley Veterinary Clinic
123 North V Street
Lompoc, CA 93436
805-736-1238

Belmont Heights Animal Clinic
255 Redondo Avenue
Long Beach, CA 90803
562-439-6871

Belmont Shore Animal Clinic
5313 East 2nd Street
Long Beach, CA 90803
562-433-9986

Boulevard Animal Hospital
2139 East Artesia Boulevard
Long Beach, CA 90805
562-633-6514

Cherry-South Animal Clinic
2150 East South Street #109
Long Beach, CA 90805
562-531-0973

Jaymor Animal Hospital
3449 East Pacific Coast Highway
Long Beach, CA 90804
562-597-5533

Long Beach Animal Hospital
3816 East Anaheim Street
Long Beach, CA 90804
562-434-9966

Magnolia Animal Hospital
1749 Magnolia Avenue
Long Beach, CA 90813
562-435-6331

Spring Street Animal Hospital
5858 East Spring Street
Long Beach, CA 90815
562-421-8463

Los Alamitos Animal Hospital
4102 Katella Avenue
Los Alamitos, CA 90720
562-431-6925

Adobe Animal Hospital
396 1st Street
Los Altos, CA 94022
650-948-9661

Ambassador Dog and Cat Hospital
3684 Beverly Boulevard
Los Angeles, CA 90004
213-384-1255

Animal Medical Center
2528 West Martin Luther King Jr.
Los Angeles, CA 90008
213-294-6154

Bel Air Animal Hospital
2340 South Sepulveda Boulevard
Los Angeles, CA 90064
310-479-4419

Center Sinai Animal Hospital
10737 Venice Boulevard
Los Angeles, CA 90034
310-559-3770

Eagle Glen Veterinary Clinic
4334 Eagle Rock Boulevard
Los Angeles, CA 90041
323-256-0405

Echo Park Pet Hospital
1739 Glendale Boulevard
Los Angeles, CA 90026
323-663-1107

Highland Park Animal Hospital
5210 York Boulevard
Los Angeles, CA 90042
323-254-6868

Holistic Veterinary Health
11673 National Boulevard
Los Angeles, CA 90064
310-231-4415

Laurel Pet Hospital
7970 Santa Monica Boulevard
Los Angeles, CA 90046
323-654-7060

Los Angeles Pet Clinic
5853 Melrose Avenue
Los Angeles, CA 90038
323-461-3575

Melrose Animal Hospital
7116 Melrose Avenue
Los Angeles, CA 90046
323-937-2334

Park La Brea Veterinary Care
471 South Fairfax Avenue
Los Angeles, CA 90036
323-931-1210

Plaza Pet Clinic
5211 El Verano Avenue
Los Angeles, CA 90041
323-258-2122

Shenandoah Animal Clinic
8679 West Pico Boulevard
Los Angeles, CA 90035
310-271-6186

Southwest Animal Medical Center
8481 South Western Avenue
Los Angeles, CA 90047
213-752-1120

Sunset Pet Clinic
3926 West Sunset Boulevard
Los Angeles, CA 90029
323-665-4421

Los Banos Veterinary Clinic
1900 East Pacheco Boulevard
Los Banos, CA 93635
209-826-5860

Oak Meadow Veterinary Hospital
641 University Avenue
Los Gatos, CA 95032
408-354-0838

Summit Veterinary Clinic
23291 Summit Road
Los Gatos, CA 95033
408-353-1113

Alamo Pintado Equine Medical Center
2501 Santa Barbara Avenue
Los Olivos, CA 93441
805-688-6510

Inland Equine Medical Center
2765 Corral de Quati Road
Los Olivos, CA 93441
805-688-8859

Bear Valley Animal Clinic
2021 11th Street
Los Osos, CA 93402
805-528-0693

Large Animal Practice
2245 Cimarron Way
Los Osos, CA 93402
805-528-0961

Los Osos Pet Hospital
2239 Bayview Heights Drive #A
Los Osos, CA 93402
805-528-4111

Coloma Veterinary Clinic
978 Lotus Road
Lotus, CA 95651
530-626-4164

M

Ambrose Veterinary Hospital
150 Dwyer Street
Madera, CA 93637
559-674-8869

Madera Veterinary Clinic
200 West Olive Avenue #B
Madera, CA 93637
559-675-3044

Magalia Pet Hospital
13701 Skyway
Magalia, CA 95954
530-877-1942

Malibu Animal Hospital
23431 Pacific Coast Highway
Malibu, CA 90265
310-456-6441

Pacific Coast Animal Hospital
23919 Malibu Road
Malibu, CA 90265
310-456-1783

Alpen Veterinary Hospital
217 Sierra Manor Road
Mammoth Lakes, CA 93546
760-934-2291

High Country Veterinary Hospital
148 Mountain Boulevard
Mammoth Lakes, CA 93546
760-934-3775

Animal Medical Group
1401 North Sepulveda Boulevard
Manhattan Beach, CA 90266
310-546-5731

Bay Animal Hospital
1801 North Sepulveda
 Boulevard
Manhattan Beach, CA 90266
310-545-6596

**South Bay Dog and Cat
Hospital**
333 Manhattan Beach
 Boulevard
Manhattan Beach, CA 90266
310-545-4579

Animal Clinic
406 West Yosemite Avenue
Manteca, CA 95337
209-239-4607

**Central Valley Veterinary
Hospital**
1515 West Yosemite Avenue
Manteca, CA 95337
209-239-2547

**Manteca Veterinary
Hospital**
911 Moffat Boulevard
Manteca, CA 95336
209-823-1168

Marina Pet Hospital
358 Reservation Road
Marina, CA 93933
831-384-6055

**Bay Cities Veterinary
Hospital**
13476 Washington Boulevard
Marina del Rey, CA 90292
310-821-4967

Ritter Animal Hospital
5572 State Highway 49 North
Mariposa, CA 95338
209-966-5666

**Martinez Animal
Hospital**
5055 Alhambra Avenue
Martinez, CA 94553
925-228-7100

**Village Oaks Veterinary
Hospital**
1175 Arnold Drive #D
Martinez, CA 94553
925-372-9200

**Feather River Veterinary
Hospital**
5975 Woodland Drive
Marysville, CA 95901
530-742-0919

**Marysville Veterinary
Hospital**
1530 B Street
Marysville, CA 95901
530-742-8809

**McKinleyville Animal
Care Center**
2151 Central Avenue
McKinleyville, CA 95519
707-839-1504

**Redwood Animal
Hospital**
1781 Central Avenue
McKinleyville, CA 95519
707-839-9414

Animal Doctor
2061 Avy Avenue
Menlo Park, CA 94025
650-854-1343

**Mid-Peninsula Animal
Hospital**
1125 Merrill Street
Menlo Park, CA 94025
650-325-5671

Merced Veterinary Clinic
3200 G Street
Merced, CA 95340
209-383-0555

**Yosemite Veterinary
Clinic**
2239 Yosemite Parkway
Merced, CA 95340
209-383-4722

**Middletown Animal
Hospital**
21503 Highway 29
Middletown, CA 95461
707-987-2000

Adobe Pet Hospital
265 Shoreline Highway
Mill Valley, CA 94941
415-388-4300

**Alto Tiburon Veterinary
Hospital**
25 North Knoll Road
Mill Valley, CA 94941
415-383-7700

Cat Clinic
142 Lomita Drive
Mill Valley, CA 94941
415-383-1195

**Capuchino Veterinary
Clinic**
128 Park Place
Millbrae, CA 94030
650-583-1500

Millville Veterinary Clinic
24077 Old 44 Drive
Millville, CA 96062
530-547-4457

Animal Medical Clinic
1405 North Milpitas Boulevard
Milpitas, CA 95035
408-262-7190

Bayview Equine Clinic
334 South Abel Street
Milpitas, CA 95035
408-946-6888

**Granada Veterinary
Clinic**
10838 Sepulveda Boulevard
Mission Hills, CA 91345
818-361-0125

Alisos Animal Hospital
22902 Los Alisos Boulevard #D
Mission Viejo, CA 92691
949-768-8308

**Mission Viejo Animal
Hospital**
26852 Oso Parkway
Mission Viejo, CA 92691
949-582-1220

**Muirlands Animal and
Avian Hospital**
24174 Alicia Parkway
Mission Viejo, CA 92691
949-770-9015

**Olympiad Animal
Hospital**
23032 Alicia Parkway #A
Mission Viejo, CA 92692
949-588-9339

**Coffee Road Veterinary
Clinic**
2717 Coffee Road #H
Modesto, CA 95355
209-577-4567

**Crows Landing Road Vet
Clinic**
2109 Crows Landing Road
Modesto, CA 95358
209-538-1782

Family Pet Clinic
2307 Oakdale Road #7
Modesto, CA 95355
209-551-3301

**Modesto Large Animal
Clinic**
1128 Ohio Avenue
Modesto, CA 95358
209-522-8277

**Modesto Veterinary
Hospital**
1414 9th Street
Modesto, CA 95354
209-524-4791

Huntington Pet Hospital
535 West Huntington Drive
Monrovia, CA 91016
626-357-2335

Shasta Valley Veterinary
4134 Oberlin Road
Montague, CA 96064
530-842-6045

**All Creatures Animal
Hospital**
5405 Arrow Highway #108
Montclair, CA 91763
909-946-3211

**Montclair Veterinary
Hospital**
4770 Holt Boulevard
Montclair, CA 91763
909-624-8061

**Montebello Veterinary
Hospital**
2437 West Whittier Boulevard
Montebello, CA 90640
323-726-1525

**Aguajito Veterinary
Hospital**
1221 10th Street
Monterey, CA 93940
831-372-8151

Avian and Exotic Clinic
2 Harris Court #A1
Monterey, CA 93940
831-647-1147

Purrfurably Cats
481 Cortes Street
Monterey, CA 93940
831-655-2287

Monterey Park Animal Hospital
2000 South Atlantic Boulevard
Monterey Park, CA 91754
323-722-9692

San Gabriel Animal Hospital
1829 Potrero Grande Drive
Monterey Park, CA 91755
626-280-4070

ACS Veterinary Clinic
173 East High Street
Moorpark, CA 93021
805-529-4650

Moorpark Veterinary Hospital
484 East Los Angeles Avenue
#104
Moorpark, CA 93021
805-529-7003

Contra Costa Veterinary Hospital
1025 Country Club Drive
Moraga, CA 94556
925-376-1824

Moraga Veterinary Hospital
1020 Country Club Drive
Moraga, CA 94556
925-376-1121

Animal Medical Center
25030 Alessandro
Boulevard #A
Moreno Valley, CA 92553
909-924-4181

Moreno Valley Animal Hospital
23051 Sunnymead Boulevard
Moreno Valley, CA 92553
909-242-2111

Sunnymead Veterinary Clinic
24588 Sunnymead Boulevard
Moreno Valley, CA 92553
909-242-4056

Morgan Hill Animal Hospital
16150 Monterey Street
Morgan Hill, CA 95037
408-779-7325

South County Animal Hospital
15790 Monterey Road #500
Morgan Hill, CA 95037
408-779-6867

Coast Veterinary Clinic
1060 Quintana Road
Morro Bay, CA 93442
805-772-2228

Morro Bay Veterinary Clinic
385 Quintana Road
Morro Bay, CA 93442
805-772-4411

Alpine Animal Hospital
2460 West El Camino Real
Mountain View, CA 94040
650-969-8555

Alta-View Animal Hospital
690 Showers Drive
Mountain View, CA 94040
650-948-1021

Miramonte Veterinary Hospital
1766 Miramonte Avenue
Mountain View, CA 94040
650-962-8338

Mountain View Vet Clinic
1413 Grant Road
Mountain View, CA 94040
650-967-5600

Black Butte Veterinary Hospital
5819 Truck Village Drive
Mount Shasta, CA 96067
530-926-5233

Mother Lode Veterinary Hospital
382 East US Highway 4
Murphys, CA 95247
209-728-3423

California Oaks Veterinary
40575 California Oaks Road
#D7
Murrieta, CA 92562
909-698-8919

Valley Veterinary Clinic
25095 Jefferson Avenue #101
Murrieta, CA 92562
909-677-7811

N

California Pet Hospital
3131 California Boulevard
Napa, CA 94558
707-255-6832

Lincoln Avenue Pet Hospital
501 Lincoln Avenue
Napa, CA 94558
707-224-3801

Napa Valley Veterinary Hospital
3198 Silverado Trail
Napa, CA 94558
707-224-8604

Plaza Boulevard Pet Clinic
2415 East Plaza Boulevard
National City, CA 91950
619-267-8200

Newark Pet Clinic
5454 Central Avenue #A
Newark, CA 94560
510-796-7555

Thornton Veterinary Medical
6625 Thornton Avenue
Newark, CA 94560
510-796-8535

Midtown Veterinary Clinic
3333 Kimber Drive #3
Newbury Park, CA 91320
805-498-6694

Newbury Park Vet Clinic
1240 Newbury Road
Newbury Park, CA 91320
805-498-3684

Evergreen Animal Hospital
23947 San Fernando Road
Newhall, CA 91321
661-254-5102

Newhall-Saugus Veterinary Clinic
22509 4th Street
Newhall, CA 91321
661-259-1396

Westside Animal Clinic
1225 Main Street
Newman, CA 95360
209-862-9400

Animal Clinic of Balboa
2915 Newport Boulevard
Newport Beach, CA 92663
949-675-4800

Back Bay Veterinary Hospital
4263 Birch Street
Newport Beach, CA 92660
949-756-0554

Newport Beach Veterinary Hospital
1610 West Coast Highway
Newport Beach, CA 92663
949-722-8152

Newport Hills Animal Hospital
2670 San Miguel Drive
Newport Beach, CA 92660
949-759-1911

Nipomo Animal Clinic
230 West Tefft Street
Nipomo, CA 93444
805-929-3554

All Animals Exotic Or Small
1560 Hamner Avenue
Norco, CA 91760
909-737-1242

A All Pet Hospital
3201 Orange Grove Avenue #C
North Highlands, CA 95660
916-484-7729

Highlands Veterinary Hospital
3451 Elkhorn Boulevard
North Highlands, CA 95660
916-332-2845

Berkley Pet Hospital
10908 Burbank Boulevard
North Hollywood, CA 91601
818-763-6221

Davis Animal Hospital
5425 Laurel Canyon Boulevard
North Hollywood, CA 91607
818-766-2140

Victory Veterinary Center
11739 Victory Boulevard
North Hollywood, CA 91606
818-766-8188

Northridge Veterinary Center
19462 Rinaldi Street
Northridge, CA 91326
818-832-1888

Norwalk Animal Hospital
11564 Firestone Boulevard
Norwalk, CA 90650
562-863-1417

Bel Marin Animal Hospital
25 Commercial Boulevard
Novato, CA 94949
415-883-0578

Center Veterinary Clinic
1553 South Novato
 Boulevard #B
Novato, CA 94947
415-892-0891

Novato Veterinary Hospital
7454 Redwood Boulevard
Novato, CA 94945
415-897-2173

Kirk Animal Clinic
370 Ventura Avenue
Oak View, CA 93022
805-649-4094

Country Veterinary Clinic
4901 River Road
Oakdale, CA 95361
209-847-1691

Oakdale Veterinary Group
20 South Stearns Road
Oakdale, CA 95361
209-847-2257

Sierra View Animal Health
114 Davitt Avenue
Oakdale, CA 95361
209-847-4146

Oakhurst Veterinary Hospital
40799 Highway 41
Oakhurst, CA 93644
559-683-2135

Animal Medical Center
8660 East 14th Street
Oakland, CA 94621
510-636-1535

Claremont Veterinary Hospital
5331 College Avenue
Oakland, CA 94618
510-652-5835

Foothill Pet Hospital
3561 Foothill Boulevard
Oakland, CA 94601
510-534-7387

Montclair Veterinary Clinic
1961 Mountain Boulevard
Oakland, CA 94611
510-339-8600

Telegragh Avenue Veterinary Hospital
5666 Telegraph Avenue
Oakland, CA 94609
510-652-1003

Cypress Veterinary Hospital
2037 Main Street
Oakley, CA 94561
925-625-5330

Oakley Veterinary Medical Center
3807 Main Street
Oakley, CA 94561
925-625-1878

Occidental Veterinary Clinic
3996 Bohemian Highway
Occidental, CA 95465
707-874-2417

College Pet Clinic
475 College Boulevard #8
Oceanside, CA 92057
760-631-2080

Lone Star Veterinary Hospital
3870 Mission Avenue #D6
Oceanside, CA 92054
760-722-4840

Mission Animal and Bird Hospital
3308 Mission Avenue
Oceanside, CA 92054
760-433-3763

Pacific Animal Hospital
2801 Oceanside Boulevard
Oceanside, CA 92054
760-757-2442

Matilija Veterinary Hospital
108 Bryant Street
Ojai, CA 93023
805-646-5539

City Pet Hospital
1511 West Holt Boulevard #H
Ontario, CA 91762
909-984-1233

Inland Animal Hospital
2409 South Vineyard
 Avenue #F
Ontario, CA 91761
909-947-4040

Mountain Avenue Animal Hospital
1155 North Mountain Avenue
Ontario, CA 91762
909-986-4548

Ontario Veterinary Hospital
121 East E Street
Ontario, CA 91764
909-984-2211

All-Cat Veterinary Clinic
600 East Chapman Avenue
Orange, CA 92866
714-538-2287

Chapman Animal Hospital
4750 East Chapman Avenue
Orange, CA 92869
714-639-0392

Orange Pet Care Center
811 East Katella Avenue
Orange, CA 92867
714-771-3870

Orange Veterinary Hospital
2006 West Chapman Avenue
Orange, CA 92868
714-978-6260

Tustin Avenue Veterinary Hospital
434 South Tustin Street
Orange, CA 92866
714-633-3323

Villa Animal Hospital
4250 East Chapman Avenue
Orange, CA 92869
714-633-9780

American River Animal Hospital
9391 Greenback Lane
Orangevale, CA 95662
916-988-1721

Orinda Veterinary Clinic
23 Orinda Way #M
Orinda, CA 94563
925-254-0211

Mid-Valley Vet Hospital
4422 County Road North
Orland, CA 95963
530-865-5634

Orland Veterinary Hospital
1137 8th Street
Orland, CA 95963
530-865-4478

Walker Street Veterinary Clinic
512 Walker Street
Orland, CA 95963
530-865-3630

Buck-Dent Animal Hospital
750 Oro Dam Boulevard West
Oroville, CA 95965
530-533-0521

Butte Oroville Veterinary Hospital
751 Oro Dam Boulevard East
Oroville, CA 95965
530-533-1194

Adobe Animal Hospital
1420 South Oxnard Boulevard
Oxnard, CA 93030
805-486-8333

Cottage Animal Hospital
906 East 5th Street
Oxnard, CA 93030
805-487-3985

Oxnard Veterinary Hospital
651 South Ventura Road
Oxnard, CA 93030
805-984-1850

P

Montecito Animal Clinic
5280 Pacheco Boulevard
Pacheco, CA 94553
925-686-0683

Ocean View Veterinary Hospital
109 Central Avenue
Pacific Grove, CA 93950
831-649-4111

Highlands Veterinary Hospital
526 Palisades Drive
Pacific Palisades, CA 90272
310-454-2917

Palisades Animal Clinic
16636 Marquez Avenue
Pacific Palisades, CA 90272
310-454-6503

Linda Mar Veterinary Hospital
985 Linda Mar Boulevard
Pacifica, CA 94044
650-359-6471

Pacifica Pet Hospital
4300 Coast Highway #1
Pacifica, CA 94044
650-359-3685

Country Club Animal Clinic
74998 Country Club Drive
Palm Desert, CA 92260
760-776-7555

Desert Dunes Animal Hospital
42065 Washington Street
Palm Desert, CA 92211
760-345-8227

Eldorado Animal Hospital
74320 US Highway 111
Palm Desert, CA 92260
760-340-4243

Animal Medical Hospital
606 South Oleander Road
Palm Springs, CA 92264
760-327-1355

Desert Animal Hospital
550 South Oleander Road
Palm Springs, CA 92264
760-323-1794

High Desert Animal Care Hospital
3243 East Palmdale Boulevard
Palmdale, CA 93550
661-272-1616

Palmdale Veterinary Hospital
38568 6th Street East
Palmdale, CA 93550
661-273-1555

El Camino Animal Hospital
2951 El Camino Real
Palo Alto, CA 94306
650-326-1211

Page Mill Pet Hospital
461 Page Mill Road
Palo Alto, CA 94306
650-327-6771

Stanford Pet Clinic
4111 El Camino Real
Palo Alto, CA 94306
650-493-4233

Cow Creek Veterinary Hospital
9182 Deschutes Road
Palo Cedro, CA 96073
530-547-4441

Paradise Veterinary Clinic
503 Pearson Road
Paradise, CA 95969
530-877-3468

Skyway Pet Hospital
7334 Skyway
Paradise, CA 95969
530-877-4153

Garfield Animal Hospital
16301 Garfield Avenue
Paramount, CA 90723
562-630-2082

Foothill Veterinary Hospital
2204 East Foothill Boulevard
Pasadena, CA 91107
626-792-1187

Hastings Animal Hospital
927 North Michillinda Avenue
Pasadena, CA 91107
626-351-8863

VCA-A Breed Apart Animal Hospital
777 South Arroyo Parkway #106
Pasadena, CA 91105
626-795-4444

Whiskers to Tails Cat Hospital
156 South Rosemead Boulevard
Pasadena, CA 91107
626-795-4134

Large Animal Clinic
2280 Meadowlark Road
Paso Robles, CA 93446
805-238-2150

North County Animal Hospital
825 24th Street
Paso Robles, CA 93446
805-238-5882

Paso Robles Vet Clinic
725 Walnut Drive
Paso Robles, CA 93446
805-238-4622

Patterson Veterinary Hospital
24 South 3rd Street
Patterson, CA 95363
209-892-8387

Perris Animal Hospital
257 East 4th Street
Perris, CA 92570
909-657-3139

Perris Valley Veterinary Clinic
802 Navajo Road #A
Perris, CA 92570
909-657-8389

Adobe Family Pet Clinic
700 East Washington Street
Petaluma, CA 94952
707-762-7387

Canyon Large Animal Clinic
5675 Roblar Road
Petaluma, CA 94952
707-792-4335

East Petaluma Animal Hospital
1420 South McDowell Boulevard #B
Petaluma, CA 94954
707-765-9098

Santa Rosa Equine Practice
200 Vlaardingen Lane
Petaluma, CA 94952
707-794-8090

Country Animal Care
4525 Phelan Road
Phelan, CA 92371
760-868-2188

Phelan Animal Hospital
4359 Phelan Road #67
Phelan, CA 92371
760-868-4646

Pico Rivera Animal Hospital
9221 Slauson Avenue
Pico Rivera, CA 90660
562-949-2494

Surrey Junction Veterinary
17285 Ridge Road
Pine Grove, CA 95665
209-296-7070

Pinole Pet Hospital
1400 San Pablo Avenue
Pinole, CA 94564
510-724-8766

Pioneer Veterinary Clinic
24796 State Highway 88
Pioneer, CA 95666
209-295-7222

Pismo Beach Veterinary Clinic
990 Price Street
Pismo Beach, CA 93449
805-773-0474

Animal Hospital of Pittsburg
216 Atlantic Avenue
Pittsburg, CA 94565
925-432-0818

Delta Animal Clinic
295 East Leland Road
Pittsburg, CA 94565
925-432-0181

Placentia Veterinary Clinic
234 East Yorba Linda Boulevard
Placentia, CA 92870
714-528-3145

Placerville Veterinary Clinic
6610 Mother Lode Drive
Placerville, CA 95667
530-622-3943

Pleasant Valley Pet Clinic
4570 Pleasant Valley Road #M
Placerville, CA 95667
530-644-2424

Sierra Animal Hospital
7476 Green Valley Road
Placerville, CA 95667
530-626-4838

Diablo View Veterinary Medical
2601 Pleasant Hill Road
Pleasant Hill, CA 94523
925-938-5555

Pleasant Hill Animal Hospital
31 West Hookston Road
Pleasant Hill, CA 94523
925-977-9000

Amador Pet Hospital
243 Main Street #C
Pleasanton, CA 94566
925-462-9590

Town and Country Veterinary Hospital
923 Main Street
Pleasanton, CA 94566
925-462-1666

Point Reyes Animal Hospital
11030 State Route 1
Point Reyes Station, CA 94956
415-663-1533

Apple Hill Animal Hospital
5730 Pony Express Trail
Pollock Pines, CA 95726
530-644-6069

Pollock Pines Veterinary Hospital
6223 Pony Express Trail #A
Pollock Pines, CA 95726
530-644-5421

Pomona Animal Hospital
1254 East Mission Boulevard
Pomona, CA 91766
909-623-2144

Pomona Valley Veterinary Hospital
158 West McKinley Avenue
Pomona, CA 91768
909-623-2602

Channel Islands Vet Hospital
741 West Channel Islands Boulevard
Port Hueneme, CA 93041
805-984-9868

All Creatures Pet Care Center
842 North Westwood Street
Porterville, CA 93257
209-784-1955

Henderson Veterinary Hospital
238 West Henderson Avenue
Porterville, CA 93257
559-781-2106

Portola Veterinary Hospital
74504 Highway 70
Portola, CA 96122
530-832-4771

Portola Valley Veterinary Clinic
808 Portola Road
Portola Valley, CA 94028
650-851-7578

Poway Valley Animal Clinic
13027 Poway Road
Poway, CA 92064
619-748-1447

Q

Quartz Hill Veterinary Clinic
42237 50th Street West
Quartz Hill, CA 93536
661-943-7896

American Valley Animal Hospital
77 Alta Avenue
Quincy, CA 95971
530-283-4500

Quincy Veterinary Center
2453 East Main Street
Quincy, CA 95971
530-283-1636

R

High Valley Veterinary Hospital
1029 D Street
Ramona, CA 92065
760-788-6250

Ramona Animal Hospital
1735 Main Street #E
Ramona, CA 92065
760-788-0960

Folsom Boulevard Animal Hospital
10131 Folsom Boulevard
Rancho Cordova, CA 95670
916-363-6561

Rancho Cordova Animal Medical Center
3342 Mather Field Road
Rancho Cordova, CA 95670
916-362-1863

Animal Hospital of Rancho
9488 Foothill Boulevard
Rancho Cucamonga, CA 91730
909-980-1788

Upland Animal Hospital
8763 Grove Avenue
Rancho Cucamonga, CA 91730
909-982-8854

Cat Clinic
42487 East Veldt Street
Rancho Mirage, CA 92270
760-346-1634

Desert View Animal Hospital
71075 US Highway 111
Rancho Mirage, CA 92270
760-346-6103

Murieta Animal Hospital
7238 Murieta Drive #A5
Rancho Murieta, CA 95683
916-354-1670

Rolling Hills Animal Clinic
28916 South Western Avenue
Rancho Palos Verdes, CA 90275
310-831-1209

VCA Golden Cove Animal Hospital
31236 Palos Verdes Drive West
Rancho Palos Verdes, CA 90275
310-377-7804

San Dieguito Equine Group
6525 Calle Del Nido #H
Rancho Santa Fe, CA 92091
619-759-9964

Veterinary Specialty Hospital
6525 Calle Del Nido
Rancho Santa Fe, CA 92091
619-759-1777

Antonio Animal Hospital
22461 Antonio Parkway #A120
Rancho Santa Margarita, CA 92688
949-858-0949

Rancho Santa Margarita Vet Hospital
29881 Aventura #A
Rancho Santa Margarita, CA 92688
949-858-3181

Valley Veterinary Clinic
420 Antelope Boulevard
Red Bluff, CA 96080
530-527-5259

All Cats Veterinary Hospital
455 Lake Boulevard
Redding, CA 96003
530-244-2287

Alpine Animal Hospital
1073 Hartnell Avenue
Redding, CA 96002
530-222-0195

Companion Animal Veterinary
2133 Eureka Way
Redding, CA 96001
530-225-8910

Redding Veterinary Clinic
4220 Westside Road
Redding, CA 96001
530-243-8335

Redlands Animal Hospital
1093 West Colton Avenue
Redlands, CA 92374
909-793-2181

Tri-City Pet Hospital
25837 Business Center Drive #C
Redlands, CA 92374
909-796-4277

Animal Medical Clinic
2006 Artesia Boulevard
Redondo Beach, CA 90278
310-376-0072

P V Pet Hospital
1020 South Pacific Coast
Highway
Redondo Beach, CA 90277
310-540-5656

Village Pet Clinic
201 Palos Verdes Boulevard
Redondo Beach, CA 90277
310-375-6811

**Sequoia Veterinary
Hospital**
1409 El Camino Real
Redwood City, CA 94063
650-369-7326

Valley Veterinary Clinic
6951 East Road #E
Redwood Valley, CA 95470
707-485-7641

**Kings River Veterinary
Hospital**
819 I Street
Reedley, CA 93654
559-638-8252

**Reedley Veterinary
Hospital**
21311 East Dinuba Avenue
Reedley, CA 93654
559-638-5466

**Community Animal
Hospital**
562 West Rialto Avenue
Rialto, CA 92376
909-874-4660

**Richmond Veterinary
Hospital**
4704 Macdonald Avenue
Richmond, CA 94805
510-232-3465

**VCA Lammers Animal
Hospital**
13128 San Pablo Avenue
Richmond, CA 94805
510-235-0471

**Bishop Veterinary
Hospital**
100 San Bernardino
Boulevard #100
Ridgecrest, CA 93555
760-375-8790

**High Sierra Veterinary
Clinic**
1425 South Holly Canyon
Street
Ridgecrest, CA 93555
760-384-2138

Alpine Animal Hospital
26375 Pine Avenue
Rimforest, CA 92378
909-336-6966

**Rim Forest Animal
Hospital**
1299 Bear Springs Road
Rimforest, CA 92378
909-337-8589

**Rio Linda Veterinary
Clinic**
432 M Street
Rio Linda, CA 95673
916-991-2068

**Ripon Veterinary
Hospital**
134 West Main Street
Ripon, CA 95366
209-599-6153

**River-Oak Veterinary
Hospital**
2369 Patterson Road
Riverbank, CA 95367
209-869-3692

**Animal Hospital-
Riverside**
11748 Magnolia Avenue #A
Riverside, CA 92503
909-689-5533

**Canyon Crest Animal
Hospital**
5225 Canyon Crest Drive #75
Riverside, CA 92507
909-684-2121

**Lincoln Plaza Veterinary
Clinic**
2955 Van Buren
Boulevard #H8
Riverside, CA 92503
909-359-0363

Riverside Cat Hospital
5222 Arlington Avenue #A
Riverside, CA 92504
909-785-5287

**Town & Country
Veterinary Clinic**
1845 University Avenue
Riverside, CA 92507
909-682-3803

**Van Buren Animal
Hospital**
5535 Van Buren Boulevard
Riverside, CA 92503
909-687-2630

**Stanford Ranch Village
Animal**
2311 Sunset Boulevard
Rocklin, CA 95765
916-624-5582

**Sunset Whitney Vet
Hospital**
5405 Pacific Street
Rocklin, CA 95677
916-624-3322

**Animal Care Center-
Sonoma County**
6620 Redwood Drive #1
Rohnert Park, CA 94928
707-584-4343

**North Park Veterinary
Clinic**
5700 State Farm Drive
Rohnert Park, CA 94928
707-585-2899

**Rohnert Park Veterinary
Clinic**
7300 Commerce Boulevard
Rohnert Park, CA 94928
707-795-6701

Center Animal Hospital
897 Silver Spur Road
Rolling Hills Estates, CA 90274
310-377-5548

**Peninsula Center Pet
Hospital**
728 Deep Valley Drive
Rolling Hills Estates, CA 90274
310-377-6761

**Community Animal
Hospital**
8338 Valley Boulevard
Rosemead, CA 91770
626-573-2650

**Rosemead Animal
Hospital**
9639 Valley Boulevard
Rosemead, CA 91770
626-444-0565

**All American City Vet
Hospital**
123 Washington Boulevard
Roseville, CA 95678
916-783-4646

**Granite Bay Veterinary
Clinic**
6500 Douglas Boulevard
Roseville, CA 95746
916-791-1143

**Roseville Veterinary
Hospital**
810 Riverside Avenue
Roseville, CA 95678
916-782-2123

**West Roseville
Veterinary Hospital**
1251 Baseline Road
Roseville, CA 95747
916-773-3451

**Animal Clinic of Rough
and Ready**
14715 Rough And Ready
Highway
Rough And Ready, CA 95975
530-272-1924

**Walnut Valley Animal
Hospital**
844 Nogales Street
Rowland Heights, CA 91748
626-965-4941

S

**Auburn Boulevard
Veterinary**
3132 Auburn Boulevard
Sacramento, CA 95821
916-484-6022

**Broadway Veterinary
Hospital**
1632 Broadway
Sacramento, CA 95818
916-446-6154

**Country Oaks Pet
Hospital**
4636 Fair Oaks Boulevard
Sacramento, CA 95864
916-485-2777

**El Camino Veterinary
Hospital**
4000 El Camino Avenue #100
Sacramento, CA 95821
916-488-6878

Franklin Animal Hospital
5021 Franklin Boulevard
Sacramento, CA 95820
916-452-5443

La Riviera Animal Medical Center
8726 La Riviera Drive
Sacramento, CA 95826
916-361-9274

Midtown Animal Hospital
1917 P Street
Sacramento, CA 95814
916-446-7788

Northgate Pet Hospital
3046 Northgate Boulevard
Sacramento, CA 95833
916-924-1329

Sacramento Animal Hospital
5701 H Street
Sacramento, CA 95819
916-451-6445

South Sacramento Pet Hospital
5651 Franklin Boulevard
Sacramento, CA 95824
916-421-0619

Salida Veterinary Hospital
4566 Salida Boulevard
Salida, CA 95368
209-545-9590

Canyon Veterinary Hospital
1018 El Camino Real North
Salinas, CA 93907
831-663-2836

Harden Ranch Veterinary Hospital
1770 North Main Street
Salinas, CA 93906
831-443-8387

Northridge Veterinary Hospital
1850 North Main Street
Salinas, CA 93906
831-449-2446

Calaveras Vet Hospital
1910 Gold Strike Road
San Andreas, CA 95249
209-754-5123

Animal Hospital
729 Sir Francis Drake Boulevard
San Anselmo, CA 94960
415-453-2080

Ross Valley Veterinary Hospital
190 Sir Francis Drake Boulevard
San Anselmo, CA 94960
415-453-7372

San Anselmo Veterinary Clinic
780 Sir Francis Drake Boulevard
San Anselmo, CA 94960
415-454-7700

Millbrae Veterinary Hospital
805 Masson Avenue
San Bruno, CA 94066
650-952-6454

San Bruno Veterinary Clinic
195 El Camino Real
San Bruno, CA 94066
650-583-9787

Camino Veterinary Clinic
620 Camino De Los Mares #D
San Clemente, CA 92673
949-661-1255

San Clemente Veterinary Hospital
1833 South El Camino Real
San Clemente, CA 92672
949-492-5777

All Care Cat Hospital
4680 Clairemont Mesa Boulevard
San Diego, CA 92117
619-274-2287

Animal Center of San Diego
246 West Washington Street
San Diego, CA 92103
619-299-7387

Balboa Veterinary Hospital
7931 Balboa Avenue
San Diego, CA 92111
619-279-0425

Bernardo Heights Veterinary
15721 Bernardo Heights Parkway #K
San Diego, CA 92128
619-485-9111

Boulevard Animal Clinic
7047 El Cajon Boulevard
San Diego, CA 92115
619-698-7250

Carmel Valley Pet Clinic
3890 Valley Centre Drive #101
San Diego, CA 92130
619-259-8881

Center Veterinary Clinic
8977 Mira Mesa Boulevard
San Diego, CA 92126
619-271-1152

Colina Veterinary Hospital
5530 University Avenue
San Diego, CA 92105
619-286-3360

Hillcrest Veterinary Hospital
3949 1st Avenue
San Diego, CA 92103
619-298-7714

Kearny Mesa Veterinary Hospital
7677 Ronson Road #100
San Diego, CA 92111
619-279-3000

Kensington Veterinary Hospital
3817 Adams Avenue
San Diego, CA 92116
619-584-8418

Mission Valley Pet Clinic
4329 Twain Avenue
San Diego, CA 92120
619-281-2934

North Park Veterinary Hospital
4054 Normal Street
San Diego, CA 92103
619-299-6020

Pacific Petcare Veterinary
12720 Carmel Country Road #100
San Diego, CA 92130
619-481-1101

Point Loma Veterinary Clinic
2158 Catalina Boulevard
San Diego, CA 92107
619-222-4482

Rancho Bernardo Vet Clinic
12540 Oaks North Drive #D
San Diego, CA 92128
619-487-4130

Rancho Mesa Animal Hospital
8710 Miramar Road
San Diego, CA 92126
619-566-0422

Rancho San Carlos Pet Clinic
7850 Golfcrest Drive
San Diego, CA 92119
619-462-6820

San Carlos Veterinary Hospital
8618 Lake Murray Boulevard
San Diego, CA 92119
619-460-3100

Scripps Ranch Veterinary Hospital
9990 Scripps Ranch Boulevard
San Diego, CA 92131
619-566-4912

South San Diego Vet Hospital
2910 Coronado Avenue
San Diego, CA 92154
619-423-7121

Tierrasanta Veterinary Hospital
10799 Tierrasanta Boulevard
San Diego, CA 92124
619-292-6116

Turquoise Animal Hospital
950 Turquoise Street
San Diego, CA 92109
619-488-0658

Westwood Bernardo Veterinary
11605 Duenda Road #D
San Diego, CA 92127
619-485-7570

Arrow Animal Hospital
334 West Arrow Highway
San Dimas, CA 91773
909-592-1931

Dill Veterinary Hospital
11207 San Fernando Road
San Fernando, CA 91340
818-899-5287

San Fernando Pet Hospital
1523 Truman Street
San Fernando, CA 91340
818-361-8636

All Pets Hospital
269 South Van Ness Avenue
San Francisco, CA 94103
415-861-5725

Animal Farm Pet Hospital
5601 Mission Street
San Francisco, CA 94112
415-333-0813

Balboa Pet Hospital
3329 Balboa Street
San Francisco, CA 94121
415-752-3300

Especially Cats Veterinary
1339 Taraval Street
San Francisco, CA 94116
415-681-5553

Lombard Pet Hospital
2308 Lombard Street
San Francisco, CA 94123
415-567-1550

Marina Pet Hospital
2024 Lombard Street
San Francisco, CA 94123
415-921-0410

Nob Hill Cat Clinic & Hospital
1540 California Street
San Francisco, CA 94109
415-776-6122

Ocean Beach Veterinary Clinic
1434 Irving Street
San Francisco, CA 94122
415-664-9801

Park Animal Hospital
1207 9th Avenue
San Francisco, CA 94122
415-753-8485

San Francisco Pet Hospital
1371 Fulton Street
San Francisco, CA 94117
415-931-8312

Valley Veterinary Hospital
1007 East Valley Boulevard
San Gabriel, CA 91776
626-288-0600

Animal Medical Center
1230 South State Street
San Jacinto, CA 92583
909-654-4444

San Jacinto Valley Vets
1330 North Ramona Boulevard
San Jacinto, CA 92582
909-654-3085

Akal Animal Clinic
1710 Berryessa Road #106
San Jose, CA 95133
408-254-2525

All Creatures Animal Clinic
6570 Felter Road
San Jose, CA 95132
408-926-3932

Almadale Animal Hospital
512 Giuffrida Avenue
San Jose, CA 95123
408-227-1661

Almaden Animal Clinic
6055 Meridian Avenue #A
San Jose, CA 95120
408-927-8387

Berryessa Animal Hospital
940 Berryessa Road
San Jose, CA 95133
408-453-3045

Boulevard Pet Hospital
1555 South Winchester Boulevard
San Jose, CA 95128
408-379-5554

Camden Pet Hospital
4960 Camden Avenue
San Jose, CA 95124
408-265-2200

East Valley Animal Clinic
1272 East Julian Street
San Jose, CA 95116
408-286-1757

Mayfair Veterinary Hospital
2810 Alum Rock Avenue
San Jose, CA 95127
408-258-2735

Princeton Veterinary Clinic
1378 Blossom Hill Road
San Jose, CA 95118
408-264-3550

Sara Creek Veterinary Clinic
375 Saratoga Avenue #D
San Jose, CA 95129
408-246-1470

West Valley Pet Clinic
1360 South De Anza Boulevard
San Jose, CA 95129
408-996-1155

San Juan Animal Hospital
32391 San Juan Creek Road
San Juan Capistrano, CA 92675
949-493-1147

Alameda County Emergency Pet
14790 Washington Avenue
San Leandro, CA 94578
510-352-6080

San Leandro Veterinary Clinic
13740 East 14th Street
San Leandro, CA 94578
510-357-6161

San Lorenzo Vet Hospital
17500 Hesperian Boulevard
San Lorenzo, CA 94580
510-276-7234

Animal Care Clinic
129 Granada Drive #D
San Luis Obispo, CA 93401
805-545-8212

Edna Valley Veterinary Clinic
4850 Davenport Creek Road
San Luis Obispo, CA 93401
805-541-8246

San Luis Obispo Veterinary
2963 South Higuera Street
San Luis Obispo, CA 93401
805-543-4912

Stenner Creek Animal Hospital
191 Santa Rosa Street
San Luis Obispo, CA 93405
805-543-2500

ABC Veterinary Hospitals
330 Rancheros Drive #A
San Marcos, CA 92069
760-598-2222

Levitt Animal Hospital
1155 Grand Avenue
San Marcos, CA 92069
760-744-5242

San Marcos Veterinary Clinic
145 South Rancho Santa Fe Road
San Marcos, CA 92069
760-744-5400

San Marino Veterinary Clinic
2463 Huntington Drive
San Marino, CA 91108
626-795-9637

St. Francis of Assisi Animal
12000 Murphy Avenue
San Martin, CA 95046
408-778-1095

Bayshore Animal Hospital
233 North Amphlett Boulevard
San Mateo, CA 94401
650-342-7022

Bayside Veterinary Clinic
300 North Bayshore Boulevard
San Mateo, CA 94401
650-347-6634

Peninsula Avenue Veterinary
440 Peninsula Avenue
San Mateo, CA 94401
650-348-8022

South Hillsdale Animal Hospital
15 37th Avenue
San Mateo, CA 94403
650-571-0377

Estrella Equine Clinic
8390 Estrella Road
San Miguel, CA 93451
805-239-0461

Animal Care Clinic
207 El Portal Drive
San Pablo, CA 94806
510-234-7800

Parks Veterinary Hospital
1615 23rd Street
San Pablo, CA 94806
510-236-0781

South Shores Pet Clinic
2318 South Western Avenue
San Pedro, CA 90732
310-832-5327

East San Rafael Veterinary
450 4th Street
San Rafael, CA 94901
415-456-4463

Marin Pet Hospital
840 Francisco Boulevard West
San Rafael, CA 94901
415-454-4414

Northbay Animal Hospitals
4140 Redwood Highway
San Rafael, CA 94903
415-499-8387

Alcosta Veterinary Clinic
12199 Alcosta Boulevard
San Ramon, CA 94583
925-828-9570

Crow Canyon Veterinary Clinic
2260 Camino Ramon
San Ramon, CA 94583
925-866-8387

Academy Veterinary Hospital
80 Academy Avenue
Sanger, CA 93657
559-875-9303

Sanger Veterinary Hospital
819 Academy Avenue
Sanger, CA 93657
559-875-2922

Grand Pet Care Center
1602 North Grand Avenue
Santa Ana, CA 92701
714-558-7622

Santa Ana Animal Clinic
2421 West Edinger Avenue
Santa Ana, CA 92704
714-546-7416

Santa Ana Veterinary Hospital
1933 South Main Street
Santa Ana, CA 92707
714-545-8281

Seventeenth Street Animal Hospital
1745 West 17th Street #C
Santa Ana, CA 92706
714-542-4107

South Main Animal Hospital
1614 South Main Street
Santa Ana, CA 92707
714-542-6151

ABC Veterinary Hospital
335 South Salinas Street
Santa Barbara, CA 93103
805-564-1464

Adobe Animal Hospital
3230 State Street
Santa Barbara, CA 93105
805-682-2555

Foothill Pet Hospital
675 Cieneguitas Road
Santa Barbara, CA 93110
805-967-0119

Montecito Animal Hospital
1252 Coast Village Circle
Santa Barbara, CA 93108
805-969-2213

Pacific Emergency Pet Hospital
2963 State Street
Santa Barbara, CA 93105
805-682-5120

Santa Barbara Equine Practice
15 Saint Ann Drive
Santa Barbara, CA 93109
805-962-4414

Southcoast Equine Practice
5335 University Drive
Santa Barbara, CA 93111
805-683-8191

Animal Clinic
45 Cronin Drive
Santa Clara, CA 95051
408-241-8200

Santa Clara Pet Hospital
830 Kiely Boulevard #107
Santa Clara, CA 95051
408-296-5857

Cat Doctor
23120 Lyons Avenue #13
Santa Clarita, CA 91321
661-259-5288

Sierra Veterinary Clinic
17755 Sierra Highway
Santa Clarita, CA 91351
661-252-3333

Adobe Animal Hospital
1600 Soquel Drive
Santa Cruz, CA 95065
831-475-6365

All Pets Veterinary Clinic
1226 Soquel Avenue #B
Santa Cruz, CA 95062
831-425-0945

Ocean Animal Clinic
404 Ocean Street
Santa Cruz, CA 95060
831-429-5100

Santa Cruz Veterinary Hospital
2585 Soquel Drive
Santa Cruz, CA 95065
831-475-5400

Rosecrans Pet Hospital
13451 Rosecrans Avenue
Santa Fe Springs, CA 90670
562-921-5551

Adobe Animal Clinic
2255 South Broadway #D
Santa Maria, CA 93454
805-925-1131

All Valley Pet Hospital
230 East Betteravia Road #A
Santa Maria, CA 93454
805-922-0305

Animal Clinic of Santa Maria
2650 South Miller Street
Santa Maria, CA 93455
805-937-7671

Evergreen Animal Clinic
3440 Orcutt Road
Santa Maria, CA 93455
805-937-6341

Santa Monica Dog & Cat Hospital
2010 Broadway
Santa Monica, CA 90404
310-453-5459

Santa Clara Valley Vet Clinic
811 West Telegraph Road
Santa Paula, CA 93060
805-525-5509

Santa Paula Animal Clinic
705 East Santa Barbara Street
Santa Paula, CA 93060
805-933-1341

Alderbrook Pet Hospital
1533 4th Street
Santa Rosa, CA 95404
707-542-7387

Cat Doctor
1037 West College Avenue
Santa Rosa, CA 95401
707-546-2287

Coddingtown Veterinary Clinic
2210 County Center Drive
Santa Rosa, CA 95403
707-546-4646

Guardian Pet Hospital
3501 Industrial Drive #C
Santa Rosa, CA 95403
707-524-2464

Laguna Veterinary Hospital
5341 Sebastopol Road
Santa Rosa, CA 95407
707-528-1448

Lakeside Pet Hospital
4331 Montgomery Drive
Santa Rosa, CA 95405
707-539-3393

Montecito Veterinary Center
4900 Sonoma Highway
Santa Rosa, CA 95409
707-539-2322

Northtown Animal Hospital
3881 Old Redwood Highway
Santa Rosa, CA 95403
707-546-6355

Redwood Equine Practice
1275 4th Street #133
Santa Rosa, CA 95404
707-545-0737

Rincon Valley Animal Hospital
4200 Sonoma Highway
Santa Rosa, CA 95409
707-539-1262

Santa Rosa Veterinary Hospital
2002 4th Street
Santa Rosa, CA 95404
707-544-1313

Westside Veterinary Clinic
900 Fresno Avenue
Santa Rosa, CA 95407
707-545-1622

Santa Ynez Pet Hospital
3523 Numancia Street
Santa Ynez, CA 93460
805-688-4944

Mission Carlton Vet Hospital
9302 Carlton Hills Boulevard
Santee, CA 92071
619-258-1150

Santee Pet Hospital
8936 Carlton Hills Boulevard
Santee, CA 92071
619-449-4100

Saugus Animal Hospital
27737 Bouquet Canyon Road #130
Saugus, CA 91350
661-297-8373

Sausalito Animal Hospital
1917 Bridgeway #A
Sausalito, CA 94965
415-332-2212

Mount Hermon Veterinary Clinic
266 Mount Hermon Road #P
Scotts Valley, CA 95066
831-438-0803

Scotts Valley Veterinary Clinic
4257 Scotts Valley Drive
Scotts Valley, CA 95066
831-438-2600

Rossmoor Center Animal Clinic
12231 Seal Beach Boulevard
Seal Beach, CA 90740
562-594-6676

Coast Veterinary Hospital
780 Elm Avenue
Seaside, CA 93955
831-899-2381

Analy Veterinary Hospital
900 Gravenstein Highway North
Sebastopol, CA 95472
707-823-7614

Animal Kingdom Veterinary Hospital
6742 Sebastopol Avenue
Sebastopol, CA 95472
707-823-5337

South County Veterinary Hospital
1811 Whitson Street
Selma, CA 93662
559-896-8616

Adler Veterinary Group Hospital
16911 Roscoe Boulevard
Sepulveda, CA 91343
818-893-6366

Sherman Oaks Veterinary Group
13624 Moorpark Street
Sherman Oaks, CA 91423
818-784-9977

Shingle Springs Veterinary
4211 Sunset Lane #101
Shingle Springs, CA 95682
530-677-0390

Alamo Veterinary Hospital
2780 Tapo Canyon Road
Simi Valley, CA 93063
805-583-8855

Rancho Sequoia Vet Hospital
3380 East Los Angeles Avenue
Simi Valley, CA 93063
805-522-7476

Tri-Valley Equine Clinic
255 East Easy Street #H
Simi Valley, CA 93065
805-583-3977

Four Paws Pet Hospital
261 North Haight Drive
Smith River, CA 95567
707-487-4475

Academy Animal Hospital
741 Academy Drive
Solana Beach, CA 92075
619-755-1511

Los Coches Animal Hospital
Nestles Road
Soledad, CA 93960
831-678-2658

Somis Veterinary Hospital
5375 Bell Street
Somis, CA 93066
805-386-4143

Altimira Animal Hospital
975 Boyes Boulevard
Sonoma, CA 95476
707-938-4546

Sonoma Animal Hospital
19275 Arnold Drive
Sonoma, CA 95476
707-996-4561

Sonoma Veterinary Clinic
21003 Broadway
Sonoma, CA 95476
707-938-4455

Sierra Veterinary Care
708 Mono Way
Sonora, CA 95370
209-532-7387

Tuolumne Veterinary Hospital
15107 Tuolumne Road
Sonora, CA 95370
209-532-0129

Creekside Veterinary Hospital
2505 South Main Street
Soquel, CA 95073
831-462-8989

Emerald Bay Veterinary Hospital
1022 Emerald Bay Road
South Lake Tahoe, CA 96150
530-544-2518

Sierra Veterinary Hospital
3095 US Highway 50
South Lake Tahoe, CA 96150
530-542-1952

South Tahoe Veterinary Hospital
964 Rubicon Trail
South Lake Tahoe, CA 96150
530-541-3551

Spruce Avenue Pet Hospital
135 South Spruce Avenue
South San Francisco, CA 94080
650-873-6880

Westborough Pet Hospital
2228 Westborough Boulevard
South San Francisco, CA 94080
650-761-6640

Animal Medical Hospital
704 Grand Avenue
Spring Valley, CA 91977
619-464-5125

Paradise Valley Road Pet Clinic
8360 Paradise Valley Road #B
Spring Valley, CA 91977
619-475-9770

St. Helena Veterinary Hospital
929 Main Street #C
St. Helena, CA 94574
707-963-3094

Upper Valley Animal Clinic
1163 Ehlers Lane
St. Helena, CA 94574
707-963-7161

California Dog and Cat Hospital
848 South California Street
Stockton, CA 95206
209-465-5726

Crosstown Animal Hospital
1122 West Fremont Street
Stockton, CA 95203
209-462-8331

Fremont Veterinary Clinic
2223 East Fremont Street
Stockton, CA 95205
209-465-7291

Sierra Veterinary Clinic
711 West Hammer Lane
Stockton, CA 95210
209-477-4841

Village Veterinary Hospital
3125 West Benjamin Holt Drive
Stockton, CA 95219
209-951-5180

Walker Veterinary Hospital
7600 West Lane
Stockton, CA 95210
209-478-8883

Animal Emergency Center
11740 Ventura Boulevard
Studio City, CA 91604
818-760-3882

Studio City Animal Hospital
11800 Ventura Boulevard
Studio City, CA 91604
818-769-1338

Sunset Animal Clinic
274 Sunset Avenue
Suisun City, CA 94585
707-425-4050

Canyon Lake Animal Clinic
31704 Railroad Canyon Road
Sun City, CA 92587
909-244-3401

Not Just 4 Paws Animal Hospital
31564 Railroad Canyon Road
Sun City, CA 92587
909-244-4199

East Valley Veterinary Clinic
8709 Sunland Boulevard
Sun Valley, CA 91352
818-767-7116

Shadow Hills Pet Clinic
11090 Sheldon Street
Sun Valley, CA 91352
818-767-3904

Verdugo Pet Hospital
8416 Foothill Boulevard
Sunland, CA 91040
818-353-8508

Arroyo Animal Clinic
1211 Sycamore Terrace
Sunnyvale, CA 94086
408-241-4450

Pet's Friend Animal Clinic
158 San Lazaro Avenue
Sunnyvale, CA 94086
408-739-2688

Sunnyvale Vet Clinic
1036 West El Camino Real
Sunnyvale, CA 94087
408-736-8296

Sun-Surf Animal Hospital
16571 Pacific Coast Highway
Sunset Beach, CA 90742
562-592-1391

Hemphill Animal Hospital
472 Sharp Lane
Susanville, CA 96130
530-257-2239

Lassen Veterinary Hospital
472 Theatre Road
Susanville, CA 96130
530-257-6311

Five Star Veterinary Center
13725 Foothill Boulevard
Sylmar, CA 91342
818-362-6599

Roxford Veterinary Clinic
13571 Glenoaks Boulevard
Sylmar, CA 91342
818-364-2394

T

Taft Veterinary Hospital
627 Harrison Street
Taft, CA 93268
661-763-1581

North Lake Veterinary Clinic
2933 Lake Forest Road
Tahoe City, CA 96145
530-583-8587

Capri Plaza Pet Clinic
19588 Ventura Boulevard
Tarzana, CA 91356
818-881-6344

Tarzana Pet Clinic
18452 Burbank Boulevard
Tarzana, CA 91356
818-342-3142

Canyon Equine Clinic
34174 De Portola Road
Temecula, CA 92592
909-676-3220

Del Rio Care Animal Hospital
29738 Rancho California Road #A
Temecula, CA 92591
909-676-4690

Rancho Equine Clinic
41065 1st Street
Temecula, CA 92590
909-676-8608

Main Street Small Animal Hospital
80 South Main Street
Templeton, CA 93465
805-434-2002

Templeton Veterinary Clinic
1485 Eureka Lane
Templeton, CA 93465
805-434-1115

Cat Doctor
760 East Thousand Oaks Boulevard
Thousand Oaks, CA 91360
805-495-1678

East West Veterinary Clinic
1625 East Thousand Oaks Boulevard #A
Thousand Oaks, CA 91362
805-496-2930

Animal Emergency Clinic
72374 Ramon Road
Thousand Palms, CA 92276
760-343-3438

Animal Clinic of Topanga
115 South Topanga Canyon Boulevard #B
Topanga, CA 90290
310-455-1330

Companion Animal Clinic
1555 Sepulveda Boulevard #J
Torrance, CA 90501
310-530-5633

Country Hills Animal Clinic
2919 Rolling Hills Road
Torrance, CA 90505
310-539-3851

Harbor Animal Hospital
2078 Torrance Boulevard
Torrance, CA 90501
310-328-3733

Jansen Animal Hospital
22231 South Vermont Avenue
Torrance, CA 90502
310-328-0380

Old River Veterinary Hospital
520 West 11th Street
Tracy, CA 95376
209-835-5166

Tracy Veterinary Clinic
20 West Grant Line Road
Tracy, CA 95376
209-835-0626

Donner-Truckee Veterinary Hospital
9701 State Highway 267
Truckee, CA 96161
530-587-4366

Sierra Pet Clinic of Truckee
10411 River Park Place
Truckee, CA 96161
530-587-4366

Cross Street Veterinary Clinic
400 East Cross Avenue
Tulare, CA 93274
559-688-0631

Tulare Veterinary Hospital
861 North Highway 99
Tulare, CA 93274
559-686-8544

First Street Veterinary Center
1342 South 1st Street
Turlock, CA 95380
209-634-4974

Lander Veterinary Clinic
2930 Lander Avenue
Turlock, CA 95380
209-634-5801

Taylor Veterinary Hospital
1231 West Taylor Road
Turlock, CA 95382
209-669-8600

Animal Clinic of Tustin Ranch
13115 Jamboree Road
Tustin, CA 92782
714-730-1442

North Tustin Veterinary Clinic
14081 Yorba Street #103
Tustin, CA 92780
714-838-7440

Saddleback Animal Hospital
1082 Bryan Avenue
Tustin, CA 92780
714-832-8686

Twain Harte Vet Hospital
22629 Twain Harte Drive #B
Twain Harte, CA 95383
209-586-3232

High Desert Animal Hospital
70513 Twenty-nine Palms Highway
Twenty-nine Palms, CA 92277
760-367-9511

U

Mendocino Animal Hospital
2251 South State Street
Ukiah, CA 95482
707-462-8833

North State Animal Hospital
2280 North State Street
Ukiah, CA 95482
707-468-5965

ABC Veterinary Clinic
4235 Horner Street
Union City, CA 94587
510-487-8344

Mountain View Vet Hospital
1655 North Mountain Avenue #110
Upland, CA 91784
909-982-3288

V

Animal Care Center
1100 East Monte Vista Avenue
Vacaville, CA 95688
707-448-6275

Family Pet Hospital
500 Elmira Road #F
Vacaville, CA 95687
707-448-1648

Oak Animal Hospital
2020 Peabody Road
Vacaville, CA 95687
707-447-5044

Solano Home Veterinary Care
3859 Joslin Lane
Vacaville, CA 95688
707-448-3118

Vaca Valley Vet Hospital
851 Alamo Drive
Vacaville, CA 95688
707-446-0466

All Creatures Veterinary Hospital
509 Benicia Road
Vallejo, CA 94590
707-642-4405

Broadway Pet Hospital
1000 Broadway Street
Vallejo, CA 94590
707-642-0633

Glen Cove Animal Hospital
1235 Warren Avenue
Vallejo, CA 94591
707-643-2571

Springs Veterinary Clinic
1912 Springs Road
Vallejo, CA 94591
707-552-4811

All Equine Health Care
13925 Charlan Road
Valley Center, CA 92082
760-751-0807

Valley Center Veterinary Clinic
14219 Cool Valley Road
Valley Center, CA 92082
760-749-0560

Valley Springs Vet Clinic
46 Laurel Street
Valley Springs, CA 95252
209-772-1283

Livingston Pet Hospital
5845 Sepulveda Boulevard
Van Nuys, CA 91411
818-786-9470

Valley Animal Hospital
7721 Sepulveda Boulevard
Van Nuys, CA 91405
818-785-5483

Animal Doctor
9308 Telephone Road #A
Ventura, CA 93004
805-647-8596

Buena Animal Hospital
3986 East Main Street
Ventura, CA 93003
805-642-2191

East Ventura Animal Hospital
10225 Telephone Road
Ventura, CA 93004
805-647-8430

Mission Animal Hospital
40 West Santa Clara Street
Ventura, CA 93001
805-643-5479

Ventura Veterinary Hospital
1784 East Thompson Boulevard
Ventura, CA 93001
805-648-2797

Mesa Animal Hospital
15028 7th Street #10
Victorville, CA 92392
760-245-0109

Victor Valley Veterinary
14904 7th Street
Victorville, CA 92392
760-245-5566

Diamond Veterinary Medical Hospital
120 North Akers Street
Visalia, CA 93291
559-732-8651

Redwood Veterinary Hospital
1727 East Mineral King Avenue
Visalia, CA 93292
559-733-2703

Visalia Veterinary Hospital
442 South Goddard Street
Visalia, CA 93292
559-732-4801

Alta Mira Animal Hospital
998 South Santa Fe Avenue
Vista, CA 92084
760-726-8918

East Vista Pet Clinic
2020 East Vista Way
Vista, CA 92084
760-724-8313

Melrose Veterinary Clinic
1680 South Melrose Drive #104
Vista, CA 92083
760-727-5151

Tri-City Veterinary Clinic
1929 West Vista Way #J
Vista, CA 92083
760-758-2091

W

Animal Hospital of Walnut
20670 Carrey Road
Walnut, CA 91789
909-594-1737

Encina Veterinary Hospital
2803 Ygnacio Valley Road
Walnut Creek, CA 94598
925-937-5000

Muller Veterinary Hospital
1411 Treat Boulevard
Walnut Creek, CA 94596
925-934-8042

Ygnacio Animal Hospital
941 Ygnacio Valley Road
Walnut Creek, CA 94596
925-935-4880

Wasco Veterinary Clinic
717 7th Street
Wasco, CA 93280
661-758-2977

Animal Hospital of Watsonville
150 Pennsylvania Drive
Watsonville, CA 95076
831-728-1439

East Lake Animal Clinic
740 East Lake Avenue
Watsonville, CA 95076
831-724-6391

South Hills Animal Hospital
1414 South Azusa Avenue #13
West Covina, CA 91791
626-919-7661

West Covina Pet Hospital
1823 West San Bernardino Road
West Covina, CA 91790
626-337-2023

West Hills Animal Hospital
6402 Platt Avenue
West Hills, CA 91307
818-888-8111

Westside Veterinary Hospital
1550 Jefferson Boulevard
West Sacramento, CA 95691
916-371-8900

Village Veterinary Clinic
822 Hampshire Road #G
Westlake Village, CA 91361
805-496-0883

Westlake Veterinary Clinic
7 Duesenberg Drive
Westlake Village, CA 91362
805-497-3777

Amigo Animal Hospital
13951 Milan Street
Westminster, CA 92683
714-894-5558

Westminster Dog and Cat Hospital
8201 Westminster Boulevard
Westminster, CA 92683
714-893-2451

Bear River Veterinary Clinic
6998 Eric Lane
Wheatland, CA 95692
530-633-2957

Washington Boulevard Animal Hospital
12116 Washington Boulevard
Whittier, CA 90606
562-693-8233

Clinton-Keith Veterinary Hospital
32395 Clinton Keith Road #1B
Wildomar, CA 92595
909-678-7800

Paradise Veterinary Clinic
39032 Highway 299
Willow Creek, CA 95573
530-629-2310

Burnham Veterinary Clinic
6543 County Road 48
Willows, CA 95988
530-934-3311

Willows Animal Hospital
915 North Tehama Street
Willows, CA 95988
530-934-3801

Lockeford Veterinary Group
10163 Badger Creek Lane
Wilton, CA 95693
916-687-6870

Conde Veterinary Hospital
8063 Conde Lane
Windsor, CA 95492
707-837-9745

Township Animal Hospital
8465 Old Redwood Highway 5#700
Windsor, CA 95492
707-838-4364

Windsor Oaks Veterinary Clinic
8888 Lakewood Drive
Windsor, CA 95492
707-837-8101

Winters Veterinary Clinic
27956 State Highway 128
Winters, CA 95694
530-795-4459

Oakwood Veterinary Hospital
18815 North Lower Sacramento #A
Woodbridge, CA 95258
209-333-7010

Animal Care Clinic of Woodland
214 5th Street
Woodland, CA 95695
530-666-1973

Woodland Veterinary Hospital
445 Matmor Road
Woodland, CA 95776
530-666-2461

Cat's Meow Veterinary Clinic
19909 Ventura Boulevard
Woodland Hills, CA 91364
818-346-7161

Fallbrook Pet Clinic
22720 Ventura Boulevard
Woodland Hills, CA 91364
818-225-7071

Warner Center Pet Clinic
20930 Victory Boulevard
Woodland Hills, CA 91367
818-710-8528

West Hills Pet Clinic
23333 Mulholland Drive
Woodland Hills, CA 91364
818-222-7390

Y

Canyon Hills Animal Clinic
23259 La Palma Avenue
Yorba Linda, CA 92887
714-692-8232

East Lake Animal Hospital
20429 Yorba Linda Boulevard
Yorba Linda, CA 92886
714-777-1661

Imperial Highway Animal Clinic
17455 Imperial Highway #A
Yorba Linda, CA 92886
714-996-7610

Yorba Linda Veterinary Hospital
4872 Olinda Street
Yorba Linda, CA 92886
714-777-2314

Napa Nook Veterinary Clinic
2556 Napa Nook Road
Yountville, CA 94599
707-944-2258

American Veterinary Hospital
201 Greenhorn Road
Yreka, CA 96097
530-842-5719

Yreka Veterinary Hospital
106 West Oberlin Road
Yreka, CA 96097
530-842-2231

Adobe Animal Hospital
480 North Palora Avenue
Yuba City, CA 95991
530-673-4744

Northpointe Veterinary Hospital
1463 Live Oak Boulevard
Yuba City, CA 95991
530-674-8670

Yuba-Sutter Veterinary Hospital
1368 Colusa Highway
Yuba City, CA 95993
530-673-8853

Adobe Veterinary Clinic
31535 Dunlap Boulevard
Yucaipa, CA 92399
909-794-6773

Green Valley Vet Clinic
35037 Avenue B
Yucaipa, CA 92399
909-790-2963

Animal Clinic of Yucca Valley
57053 Twenty-Nine Palms Highway
Yucca Valley, CA 92284
760-365-0641

Northridge Veterinary Clinic
56728 Twenty-Nine Palms Highway
Yucca Valley, CA 92284
760-365-7663

Index

About the Author...
From a Dog's Point of View

Dreamer Dawg, office manager and "cover girl" for Bon Vivant Press, is a twelve-year-young Labrador Retriever. When not exploring the food and lodging for each regional book, you can find Dreamer relaxing onboard her boat in the Monterey harbor or running with the horses in Pebble Beach.

Owners Kathleen & Robert Fish, authors of the popular "Secrets" series, have researched and written twenty-six award-winning cookbooks and travel books, and are always on the lookout for lodgings with style and character.

Other titles in the Pets Welcome™ series are *Pets Welcome™America's South, Pets Welcome™New England and New York, Pets Welcome™ Pacific Northwest, Pets Welcome™ Southwest, Pets Welcome™Mid-Atlantic and Chesapeake* and *Pets Welcome™ National Edition.*

Bon Vivant Press

A division of The Millennium Publishing Group
PO Box 1994
Monterey, CA 93942
800-524-6826 • 831-373-0592 • 831-373-3567 FAX • www.millpub.com

Send _____ copies of **Pets Welcome America's South** at $15.95 each.

Send _____ copies of **Pets Welcome California** at $15.95 each.

Send _____ copies of **Pets Welcome Mid-Atlantic and Chesapeake** at $15.95 each.

Send _____ copies of **Pets Welcome New England and New York** at $15.95 each.

Send _____ copies of **Pets Welcome Pacific Northwest** at $15.95 each.

Send _____ copies of **Pets Welcome Southwest** at $15.95 each.

Send _____ copies of **Pets Welcome National Edition** at $19.95 each.

Add $4.50 postage and handling for the first book ordered and $1.50 for each additional book. Please add 7.25% sales tax per book, for those books shipped to California addresses.

Please charge my ☐ Visa   # _____
                ☐ MasterCard

Expiration date _____ Signature _____

Enclosed is my check for _____

Name _____

Address _____

City _____ State _____ ZIP _____

☐ **This is a gift. Send directly to:**

    Name _____

    Address _____

    City _____ State _____ ZIP _____

☐ **Autographed by the author**
    Autographed to _____

Bon Vivant Press

A division of The Millennium Publishing Group

PO Box 1994 • Monterey, CA 93942

800-524-6826 • 831-373-0592 • 831-373-3567 FAX • www.millpub.com

Send _____ copies of **Cooking With the Masters of Food & Wine** at $34.95 each.

Send _____ copies of **The Elegant Martini** at $17.95 each.

Send _____ copies of **Cooking Secrets from Mid-Atlantic and Chesapeake** at $19.95 each.

Send _____ copies of **Vegetarian Pleasures** at $19.95 each.

Send _____ copies of **California Wine Country Cooking Secrets** at $14.95 each.

Send _____ copies of **Cape Cod's Cooking Secrets** at $14.95 each.

Send _____ copies of **Cooking Secrets for Healthy Living** at $15.95 each.

Send _____ copies of **Cooking Secrets From America's South** at $15.95 each.

Send _____ copies of **Cooking Secrets From Around the World** at $15.95 each.

Send _____ copies of **Florida's Cooking Secrets** at $15.95 each.

Send _____ copies of **Jewish Cooking Secrets From Here and Far** at $14.95 each.

Send _____ copies of **Louisiana's Cooking Secrets** at $15.95 each.

Send _____ copies of **Monterey's Cooking Secrets** at $13.95 each.

Send _____ copies of **New England's Cooking Secrets** at $14.95 each.

Send _____ copies of **Pacific Northwest Cooking Secrets** at $15.95 each.

Send _____ copies of **San Francisco's Cooking Secrets** at $13.95 each.

Send _____ copies of **The Gardener's Cookbook** at $15.95 each.

Send _____ copies of **The Great California Cookbook** at $14.95 each.

Send _____ copies of **The Great Vegetarian Cookbook** at $15.95 each.

Add $4.50 postage and handling for the first book ordered and $1.50 for each additional book.
Please add 7.25% sales tax per book, for those books shipped to California addresses.

Please charge my ☐ Visa   # _____
                ☐ MasterCard

Expiration date _____ Signature _____

Enclosed is my check for _____

Name _____

Address _____

City _____ State _____ ZIP _____

☐ **This is a gift. Send directly to:**

Name _____

Address _____

City _____ State _____ ZIP _____

☐ **Autographed by the author**

Autographed to _____

Reader's Response Card

Please return to:
  Bon Vivant Press
  P.O. Box 1994
  Monterey, CA 93942
  Fax your information to: (831) 373-3567

Please assist us in updating our next edition. If you have discovered an interesting or charming inn, hotel, guest ranch or spa in California that allows pets, or any special neighborhood parks in California that allow pets, with or without a leash, please let us hear from you and include the following information:

Type of lodging (check one):
  ☐ Bed and Breakfast   ☐ Hotel   ☐ Inn   ☐ Guest Ranch   ☐ Spa

Lodging Name _____

Lodging Address _____

City _____ State _____ ZIP _____

Phone (_____) _____

Comments _____

_____

_____

_____

_____

Park Name _____

Address or Cross Streets _____

City _____ State _____ ZIP _____

Phone: (if known) (_____) _____ Leashes required? Yes | No

Comments _____

_____